THE MEANING OF MEAT AND THE STRUCTURE OF THE *ODYSSEY*

This comprehensive study of the *Odyssey* sees in meat and meat consumption a central theme of the poem that is essential for its interpretation. It aims to place the cultural practices represented in the poem against the background of the (agricultural) lived reality of the poem's audiences in the archaic age, and to align the themes of the adventures in Odysseus' wanderings with the events that transpire at Ithaca in the hero's absence. The criminal meat consumption of the Suitors of Penelope in the civilized space of Ithaca is shown to resonate with the adventures of Odysseus and his Companions in the pre-cultural worlds they are forced to visit. The book draws on folklore studies, the anthropology of hunting cultures, the comparative study of oral traditions, and the agricultural history of archaic and classical Greece. It will also be of interest to narratologists and students of folklore and Homeric poetics.

EGBERT J. BAKKER is Professor of Classics at Yale University. Within the wider area of the interaction between linguistic analysis and literary interpretation he works mainly on the language, poetics, and interpretation of the Homeric poems. He has lectured and published widely on both linguistic and literary subjects. Among his publications are *Linguistics and Formulas in Homer* (1988); *Poetry in Speech: Orality and Homeric Discourse* (1997); and *Pointing at the Past: From Formula to Performance in Homeric Poetics* (2005). He has co-edited *Brill's Companion to Herodotus* (2002) and is the editor of *A Companion to the Ancient Greek Language* (2010).

THE MEANING OF MEAT AND THE STRUCTURE OF THE *ODYSSEY*

EGBERT J. BAKKER

CAMBRIDGE UNIVERSITY PRESS
Cambridge, New York, Melbourne, Madrid, Cape Town,
Singapore, São Paulo, Delhi, Mexico City

Cambridge University Press
The Edinburgh Building, Cambridge CB2 8RU, UK

Published in the United States of America by Cambridge University Press, New York

www.cambridge.org
Information on this title: www.cambridge.org/9780521111201

© Egbert J. Bakker 2013

This publication is in copyright. Subject to statutory exception
and to the provisions of relevant collective licensing agreements,
no reproduction of any part may take place without
the written permission of Cambridge University Press.

First published 2013

Printed and bound in the United Kingdom by the MPG Books Group

A catalogue record for this publication is available from the British Library

Library of Congress Cataloging in Publication data
Bakker, Egbert J., author.
The meaning of meat and the structure of the Odyssey / Egbert J. Bakker.
pages cm
ISBN 978-0-521-11120-1 (Hardback)
1. Homer. Odyssey. 2. Meat in literature. I. Title.
PA4167.B27 2013
883'.01–dc23
2012036030

ISBN 978-0-521-11120-1 Hardback

Cambridge University Press has no responsibility for the persistence or
accuracy of URLs for external or third-party internet websites referred to
in this publication, and does not guarantee that any content on such
websites is, or will remain, accurate or appropriate.

For Melissa

Contents

Preface		*page* ix
Prologue: food for song		x
1	*Epos* and *aoidē*	1
2	*Nostos* as quest	13
3	Meat in myth and life	36
4	Of hunters and herders	53
5	Feasting in the land of the dawn	74
6	The revenge of the Sun	96
7	The justice of Poseidon	114
8	Remembering the *gastēr*	135
Epilogue: on "interformularity"		157
Bibliography		170
Index locorum		182
Index		188

Preface

The seed for this book was planted when I browsed through the reader for a graduate seminar on "Environmental Anthropology" at McGill University, Montreal in the Summer of 2000. The emphasis on the symbolic value and religious importance of meat for traditional hunting cultures seemed immediately relevant to the *Odyssey*, the Circe episode in particular. When starting to work on this project, first in the form of preparation for lectures and seminars, it began to occur to me that the theme of meat eating could grow into something more than an "interesting insight from anthropology," that it could be formulated as one of the unifying forces in the poem, providing thematic coherence between the hero's tale of his Wanderings and the poet's tale of the hero's Homecoming.

The resulting argument was shaped in an extended process of lecturer–audience interaction. A long series of conferences and departmental gatherings in various countries and continents, beginning with the University of Georgia at Athens in September 2000 and ending with Boston University and the University of Konstanz, Germany in November 2011, witnessed points in an ongoing gestation process. Each new presentation yielded some progress, whether through a provocative question or the need to rephrase an argument in light of audience reaction. This very fruitful process includes students at various levels in various universities. I am thinking in particular of the participants of a graduate seminar on the *Odyssey* at Yale University in the Fall of 2005. I hope that all those who attended the earlier discussions and presentations, to the extent that they remember them at all, will agree upon reading the following pages that some progress has been made.

Prologue: food for song

Song and food, or more precisely, meat, are intimately connected in the Homeric world. Aristocratic banquets are the prime occasion for the performance of heroic song, as exemplified in the *Odyssey* by Demodokos' songs at the feast in the hall of Alkinoos, king of the Phaeacians (*Od.* 8.62–82, 471–520), the songs of the anonymous "divinely inspired singer" (*theîos aoidós*) in Menelaos' hall (*Od.* 4.17–19), or the compulsory performance of Phemios before the Suitors in Odysseus' *megaron* (*Od.* 1.150–5, 325–7; 17.261–3). But the connection holds for different, less illustrious settings as well. The humble meal in the hut of Eumaios, Odysseus' faithful swineherd, provides a natural setting for storytelling (15.398–402), and even though the tale of the traveler, whether mendacious or true, is in itself not song, the *Odyssey*, as we shall see, has many ways to act as if it is.

The unbreakable bond between song and its setting is the backdrop for the typically Odyssean interconnection between singer and hero. Demodokos is called "hero" (ἥρῳ Δημοδόκῳ, *Od.* 8.483), after Odysseus offers him a choice piece of meat: the singer becomes part of the aristocratic feasting group by being allowed to participate in the meat distribution that takes place among the members of his audience. Singing the songs of heroes well, as Demodokos does, is to become subsumed in the world of heroes. Conversely, Odysseus the hero comes to be cast in terms appropriate to singers throughout the poem, from his performance in Alkinoos' hall to the stringing of the bow in his own *megaron*. The bow will become the "accompaniment of the banquet" (ἀναθήματα δαιτός, *Od.* 21.430; cf. 1.152), the singer's habitual lyre turning into a lethal and destructive weapon in the hero's hands.

The Suitors' final banquet is the occasion at which the singing of the song breaks through its confines as self-contained art and becomes epic action in and of itself. The massacre of the Suitors, notionally carried out by the singer who performs at their feast, forms in this way (and in others as well) the climax of the *Odyssey*'s self-conscious and metapoetic tendencies. We can also say, and this is the subject of this book, that the poem comes to encompass its own setting, making the banquet itself one of its important themes.

The killing of the Suitors is the end of a banquet that started, strictly speaking, not on the day of the mass killing itself, the day of the festival of Apollo of the New Moon, but three years earlier, as a deliberate and concerted effort literally to eat Odysseus' house to ruin. The absent king's herds and flocks are systematically plundered with the intention of wiping them out completely, and thereby destroying the king's son's inheritance. The poem's central act is an extended feast, criminally perverted and magnified. The nature of this feast is highlighted in the contrast with good banquets in the poem, such as Nestor's sacrificial feasts at Pylos, the Phaeacians' banquet in honor of their mysterious guest, or the humble meal in Eumaios' hut.

Even more central to the poem's thematics and narrative structure is the relation between the Suitors' extended feast and other examples of problematic feasting carried out, far outside the confines of civilization, by another group of Ithacans. During their involuntary extended voyage, which takes them to the ends of the world and back in time from their own Bronze Age to both the barbaric and the paradisiacal realities of the Golden Age, Odysseus and his Companions encounter a variety of situations that resonate with the situation back home in Ithaca. The description of these situations, when aligned with the narrative of the events at Ithaca, lends a depth and intensity to the Suitors' depredations that a narrative using simple Bronze (or Iron) Age terms could not have achieved.

The book's three central chapters (Chapters 4, 5, and 6) explore the extensive paradigmatic relationships between the adventures in the Otherworld and the situation at Ithaca. The chapters focus, respectively, on the Cyclops episode, the Circe episode, and the episode of the Cattle of the Sun. Each of these three adventures confronts Odysseus with a different type of Master of Animals and revolves around meat eating and its many modalities. The Companions eat the meat of hunted animals and farmed animals; they enjoy extreme hospitality and serve as meal to their host themselves; they enjoy effortless and limitless plenty, and are faced with absolute taboo. The situations they encounter present meat and its consumption as the essential prerequisite of civilization, even humanity itself; yet, at the same time, these situations have the potential to bring down the human eater to the level of the beast he consumes. If eating meat is what ultimately constitutes civilized man and his relation to the divine, it also represents a danger zone in which transgression is a real and constant possibility. Ultimately, *nostos* – in the sense not only of return, but also of survival, of the individual and his community – is a matter of restraint and moderation, the ability to resist the temptation that meat presents.

Structural parallels with the Wanderings turn the killing of the Suitors into a many-layered event, providing Odysseus with roles in addition to that of the deadly singer. In particular, Polyphemos the Cyclops and Helios the Sun gain significance beyond the confines of their respective episodes, as Odysseus takes on features of both when he goes about his gruesome work of effecting the kind of mass killing of which he himself was once the sole survivor. The food perspective reveals that the Suitors and the Companions are, as unrestrained consumers of meat, paradigmatically linked to each other, whereas Odysseus himself provides the link to the previous episodes in taking on the role of returning and revenging Master of Animals.

The three first chapters provide in various ways the background for this reading of the Wanderings in light of the wider themes of the poem. Chapter 3 offers an account of meat consumption and its symbolic value in the *Iliad* as backdrop for a characterization of the Suitors' meat consumption as a systematic perversion of the heroic feast. The outrage of their actions acquires economic color and shape when set against the background of the realities of animal husbandry in the Iron Age, the time frame of the *Odyssey*'s historical audiences. The *Odyssey* in this way comes to be seen as a tale of the transgression of limits and of the depletion of finite resources.

The first two chapters provide the basis for a reading of the poem in which the Wanderings and the main story, the hero's tale and the poet's, are strongly and systematically interconnected. Chapter 1 makes a case for eliminating the narratological hierarchy inherent in making Odysseus an "embedded" narrator, arguing that the hero and the poet are on the same footing in the presentation of the tale. Chapter 2 detects a basic narrative pattern running through the *Odyssey* with numerous variations and transpositions, and linking the hero's tales of adventures in exotic lands with the poet's story of a social conflict in a remote corner of rural Greece.

The two final chapters take up problems and questions raised by the earlier parts of the book. Chapter 7 revisits some of the old theological problems in the interpretation of the *Odyssey*, questions revolving around theodicy and human responsibility. Of particular importance here is the question of the guilt of the Companions in eating the Cattle of the Sun. My conclusions focus on a conflict on the divine plane (Poseidon versus Zeus) that is deeper than sometimes supposed, reflecting tensions in the poem regarding the ambiguous poetic traditions of its central hero. Chapter 8 takes up the metapoetic aspects of Odysseus' disguise as wanderer and teller of liar tales, a disguise that crucially involves that part of the human anatomy that is most physically involved in the consumption of food: the belly. The shedding of the beggar's disguise will not only reveal the hero who was hiding behind it, but will also seal his successful return by aligning him with the ultimate epic hero, the Iliadic Achilles.

The argument of the book frequently relies on the interpretation of formulaic repetition as the means by which paradigmatic linkage between episodes is articulated. An Epilogue will address the poetic and semantic problems raised by this method. The central question to be addressed is whether the deliberate "quotation" of a formula can be reconciled with a conception of the *Odyssey* as oral poetry, as proposed in the work of Milman Parry and Albert Lord. Readers who are used to approaching Homeric problems from the oral-formulaic side may want to start with the Epilogue, although full appreciation of the case studies presented may require the detail provided in the preceding chapters.

CHAPTER 1

Epos *and* aoidē

> "Upon you is comeliness of *epea*, in <you> are noble *phrénes*;
> and the tale, as an *aoidos* you have most expertly told it in all
> its detail."
>
> (Alkinoos to Odysseus, *Od.* 11.367–8)

The *Odyssey* is a poem of paradoxes. Its central hero is both poet and liar, hero and trickster, emphatically famous and notoriously anonymous, endowed with a ravenous belly, yet capable of extreme fasting. The poem itself provides a narrative context entirely worthy of such ambiguity. Hailed by many for its self-reflexive narrative sophistication, it resorts nonetheless to primitive folktales featuring witches, ogres, and magical objects. And it does so precisely in what confirms the poem as a narratological *tour de force*, the extended tale of Odysseus' Wanderings told by the hero himself at the court of Alkinoos, king of the Phaeacians. The pull between ancient and modern seems to be reflected in the uncertain generic status of the poem as a whole: is this tale of the Homecoming Husband not some kind of elaborate folktale rather than an instance of heroic epic? Or is the poem, with marriage as its *telos*, a very early specimen of the novel, the genre of the future?

Part of the paradox is due to the fact that our idea of what constitutes "epic," and what not, has been too confident and too rigid. Epic has been seen as a transcendental norm, best exemplified by the *Iliad* and its unambiguous setting in a heroic age. The *Odyssey* can only fall short of such a norm, due not only to its fairytale and folktale elements, but also to its domestic scenes. The poem, with its social conflict playing out on a small rural island at the periphery of the Greek world, evokes no less Hesiod's troubled Iron Age and the agricultural world of the poem's historical audiences in the archaic age than a long-vanished Bronze Age of heroes.

Scholars frequently attribute the difference between the two poems to a difference in time – and hence in style and taste – between two poets

2 Epos *and* aoidē

(the aging of an individual poet has also been assumed), or to a more "modern" style of the younger epic. But we do not have to reach for such individual or biographical explanations. Today's reflection on "epic" as genre allows for more inherent heterogeneity, yielding a conception in which epic appears as much more diverse and fluid than before.[1] Instead of a retrojected primordial literary genre, preceding other literary genres and being sharply delimited from such rivaling verbal art as "folktale" or "myth," we may now think of an "umbrella" genre that loves to incorporate other genres, alluding to them in an intertextual play between competing performance traditions. Also incorporated can be a plethora of presumably non-sung, but still traditional speech genres, such as proverbs, praise, blame, prayer, supplication, etc.[2] The "umbrella" may also be a specific poem (or, better, poetic tradition), such as the *Odyssey*, alluding to other, competing traditions, such as the *Iliad*, as we will see in Chapter 8.

The widespread embedding of such minor genres within epic – if "epic" is still a meaningful term in this regard – does not compromise or dilute epic; it *is* epic, *aoidē*: the all-embracing matrix genre takes on the features of the genres it swallows and conversely transforms them: all ingested material turns into epic, metrically and thematically. A new diachronic perspective takes the place of a previous one that has long provided the backbone to the history of "early literature." Instead of an evolutionary progression from pre-literary genres to literary (and literate) epic (and then on to sub-epic or post-epic genres), we have a *dialogue* of genres over time.[3]

The very name "epic" as it comes to us out of the Greek language itself is an important element in this complex. In Homer, the matrix genre of "epic," the stage on which the heroes perform, is always referred to as ἀοιδή, an action noun designating the act of ἀείδειν, 'sing'.[4] The speech of characters, on the other hand, that is, the speech genres performed within the framework of the epic performance are often called ἔπος or ἔπεα,

---

[1] The recent spate of "companions" and "handbooks" on Homer and/or epic (as on so much else), each with its own chapter on "epic as genre," has produced useful statements to this effect. See Ford 1997; Foley 2004; and Martin 2005.
[2] Foley 2004: 172: "omnibus genre." On the incorporation or representation of "speech genres" in Homer, see Minchin 2007: 23–141.
[3] The idea of a dialogue between genres is indebted to the work of Bakhtin (e.g., 1981: 3–4; 1986: 60–102). Yet ironically, Bakhtin sees in epic a fundamentally un-dialogic genre, seeing dialogue at work mostly in the novel and in its "precursors" (such as the Socratic dialogue).
[4] The verb ἐν(ν)έπειν can also be used for epic song, though its subject is then always the Muse(s) in an invocation by the poet: *Od.* 1.1; *Il.* 2.484; 11.218; 14.508; 16.112); but in contrast to ἀείδειν the verb can also be used for speech or storytelling inside the tale: *Od.* 17.549, 556, 561; 23.301.

Epos and aoidē

"words," or rather "utterances."[5] But that term is also, from outside the epic tale, the term for "epic," or more generally, all poetic utterances in dactylic hexameter.[6] This includes epic in our sense of "epic" (Homeric or otherwise), of course, but also oracles and poetry that *we* would not easily qualify as "epic," such as Hesiodic wisdom poetry or Theognidean sympotic elegy. In other words, epic comes to be called by the generic term for all the speech activity to which it yields the floor. The focus on (metrical) *form* is important, for whereas epic admits a potentially unlimited number of diverse speech genres, shaping itself to their likeness and orientation, it does subject everything to one and the same meter, the dactylic rhythm of *epos*, thereby complementing a reciprocal process.[7]

In the *Odyssey* the reciprocity between the matrix narrative and the embedded utterance is particularly significant in that *epos*, which I will henceforth use as shorthand for Odysseus' tales, is at various moments likened to *aoidē*, epic song. The inset tale is not merely part of epic; it competes with its "container," shaping the narrative tension within the *Odyssey*. In this chapter, and book, I will speak of the opposition between *epos* and *aoidē* in terms of the interaction – and rivalry – between hero and poet, Odysseus and Homer.

Epos and *aoidē*

If epic is the shell that holds *epos*, then the *Odyssey* is the most "epic" poem imaginable. It turns itself inside out in the way in which it presents its hero in the proem (*Od.* 1.1–10):

Ἄνδρα μοι ἔννεπε, Μοῦσα, πολύτροπον, ὃς μάλα πολλὰ
πλάγχθη, ἐπεὶ Τροίης ἱερὸν πτολίεθρον ἔπερσε·
πολλῶν δ' ἀνθρώπων ἴδεν ἄστεα καὶ νόον ἔγνω,
πολλὰ δ' ὅ γ' ἐν πόντῳ πάθεν ἄλγεα ὃν κατὰ θυμόν,
ἀρνύμενος ἥν τε ψυχὴν καὶ νόστον ἑταίρων.

---

[5] The other major term for "spoken utterance" in Homer is μῦθος. For the use of μῦθος and ἔπος in Homer, see Martin 1989: 1–42. Martin redefines μῦθος in Homer as "a speech act indicating authority, performed at length, usually in public, with a focus on full attention to every detail" (p. 12), whereas ἔπος is glossed as "an utterance, ideally short, accompanying a physical act, and focusing on message, as perceived by the addressee, rather than on performance as enacted by the speaker." By these criteria much of what in the present study is called *epos* would be *mûthos*. But I will use *epos* as the unmarked term for "speech within epic" on account of this word being able to designate "epic" as a whole (see below). Note that *epos* can also apply (e.g., *Od.* 17.519) to song of the *aoidos*.
[6] Perhaps first in Pindar (*Nem.* 2.2 ῥαπτῶν ἐπέων . . . ἀοιδοί); cf. Hdt. 2.116.3; 4.29. On *epos*, see also Koller 1972.
[7] For ideas on epic meter, the dactylic hexameter, being derived diachronically from the (Aeolic) meters of sung poetry (even though epic is attested earlier than our extant specimens of song in Aeolic meters), see Nagy 1990: 11, 48–51, 439–64.

Epos *and* aoidē

ἀλλ' οὐδ' ὧς ἑτάρους ἐρρύσατο, ἱέμενός περ·
αὐτῶν γὰρ σφετέρῃσιν ἀτασθαλίῃσιν ὄλοντο,
νήπιοι, οἳ κατὰ βοῦς Ὑπερίονος Ἠελίοιο
ἤσθιον· αὐτὰρ ὁ τοῖσιν ἀφείλετο νόστιμον ἦμαρ.
τῶν ἁμόθεν γε, θεά, θύγατερ Διός, εἰπὲ καὶ ἡμῖν.

> Sing to me of the man, Muse, the one of many turns, who wandered
> far and wide, blown off course after he had sacked the sacred citadel
>   of Troy;
> of many men he saw the cities and learned their mind and ways;
> and many woes on the high seas he suffered in his spirit,
> striving for his life and the safe return of his Companions.
> But still he could not save his Companions, much as he tried:
> through their own culpable recklessness they perished,
> fools, who ate the cattle of Helios Hyperion.
> But he took away the day of their safe return.
> Of these events, from some point, goddess, daughter of Zeus, speak to
>   us too.

The proem's fame may obscure the remarkable fact that the hero is *not* introduced as, say, "the man who, disguised as beggar, completed his *nostos* after wandering for many years, and who punished the Suitors of his wife, who thus died because of their own criminal recklessness." The "woes" that the hero "suffered in his spirit" (πάθεν ἄλγεα ὃν κατὰ θυμόν, *Od.* 1.4) are his tribulations "on the high seas" (ἐν πόντῳ), not the insults at the hand of the Suitors in his own house, though the poem emphasizes that suffering too.[8] In other words, the poem in its programmatic self-presentation draws on Odysseus' own tale of his Wanderings rather than on the poet's tale of the hero's Homecoming, favoring inset tale over matrix story, and *epos* over *aoidē*.

The proem showcases just one out of the many adventures of the hero, the Cattle of the Sun episode, a choice that has puzzled some readers, who also feel that the condemnation of the Companions here – a verdict involving the term ἀτασθαλίη, to be understood as "criminal recklessness" – is too strong and not borne out by the narrative: many more companions will be killed in the adventure of the Laestrygonians than in the Cattle of the Sun episode, and, some readers have felt, the behavior of the Companions in that last episode does not deserve to be condemned in such a harsh way.[9] There will be opportunities later, in Chapters 6 and 7, for addressing these concerns in detail (the poem's strong verdict will be upheld); here

---

[8] For example, *Od.* 18.346–8; 20.18, 284–6. This does not mean, of course, that the matrix narrative does not recount tribulations on the high seas (as in the shipwreck of Odysseus' raft in Book Five).
[9] For example, Fenik 1974: 208–30; S. West 1988: 71–2. See also Nagler 1990 and Cook 1995: 15–18.

we may note that the very prominent role the Cattle of the Sun episode is allowed to play in the proem is related to the interplay between *epos* and *aoidē*, hero and poet. If the poet's story is one of criminal feasting on cattle that belongs to someone else, so is the hero's. Both stories revolve around instances of ἀτασθαλίη, of humans who in and through the act of eating meat meet with self-inflicted doom.

The *Odyssey* subverts the hierarchizing narratological distinction between primary and secondary (or internal, embedded) narrator, narrator *of* the tale, and narrator *in* the tale,[10] placing Odysseus as storyteller on the same level as Homer. This is reflected in the poem's various starts and restarts, which enter into an "intratextual" dialogue with each other. The beginning of the hero's story is preceded by a reactivation of the important themes of the poem's proem. Odysseus' narrative is requested by his host Alkinoos in language that brings back the themes of wandering (πλάγχθη, 'was blown off course') and travel (πολλῶν δ' ἀνθρώπων ἴδεν ἄστεα, 'and of many men saw the cities'), inviting the hero to elaborate on the proem's neutral καὶ νόον ἔγνω, 'and he learned their mind and ways' (*Od.* 8.572–6):[11]

ἀλλ' ἄγε μοι τόδε εἰπὲ καὶ ἀτρεκέως κατάλεξον,
ὅππῃ **ἀπεπλάγχθης** τε καὶ ἅς τινας ἵκεο χώρας
ἀνθρώπων, αὐτούς τε **πόλιάς** τ' ἐῢ ναιεταούσας,
ἠμὲν ὅσοι χαλεποί τε καὶ ἄγριοι οὐδὲ δίκαιοι,
οἵ τε φιλόξεινοι καί σφιν **νόος** ἐστὶ θεουδής.

But now tell me this and give me the report, unswerving, on
what ways you were blown off course, and what lands you reached,
of humans, they themselves and their cities well-built,
<on the one hand> all those who are hard to deal with, and savages,
  unjust,
and <on the other hand> those who are friendly to strangers, with a
  mind that fears the gods.

And when the hero can finally, after answering Alkinoos' earlier questions ("What is your name" "What land are you from?" *Od.* 8.548–63), start his story, the brief narrative of the first adventure in the Wanderings picks up the remaining themes of the primary proem (*Od.* 9.39–46):

Ἰλιόθεν με φέρων ἄνεμος Κικόνεσσι πέλασσεν,
Ἰσμάρῳ· ἔνθα δ' ἐγὼ **πόλιν ἔπραθον**, ὤλεσα δ' αὐτούς·
ἐκ πόλιος δ' ἀλόχους καὶ κτήματα πολλὰ λαβόντες
δασσάμεθ', ὡς μή τίς μοι ἀτεμβόμενος κίοι ἴσης.

---

[10] See de Jong 1987: 33.
[11] On the formulaic ironies of this passage, see the Epilogue as well as Chapter 2.

6   Epos *and* aoidē

> ἔνθ' ἦ τοι μὲν ἐγὼ διερῷ ποδὶ φευγέμεν ἡμέας
> ἠνώγεα, τοὶ δὲ μέγα **νήπιοι** οὐκ ἐπίθοντο.
> ἔνθα δὲ πολλὸν μὲν μέθυ πίνετο, πολλὰ δὲ μῆλα
> ἔσφαζον παρὰ θῖνα καὶ εἰλίποδας ἕλικας βοῦς.
>
> From Ilium the carrying wind took me to the Cicones,
> to Ismarus; there <u>I sacked the city</u>, and destroyed them all;
> taking their wives and many possessions from the city,
> we divided it all, so that no one was cheated of his fair share.
> There I urged that we be fleeing with swift foot;
> but they, <u>fools</u>, they would not listen.
> Then much wine was drunk and many sheep
> they slaughtered and many cattle with rolling gait and curvy horns.

Just like the poet, the hero takes the sack of a city as starting point (πόλιν ἔπραθον, 'I sacked the city', picking up the proem's Τροίης ἱερὸν πτολίεθρον ἔπερσε, 'after he had destroyed Troy's sacred citadel', *Od.* 1.2). And in both cases there is a contrast between the hero and his Companions, who ignore, as νήπιοι, 'fools', his advice and indulge in the undue consumption of meat, thus bringing doom upon themselves.[12] There is also interlocking: in the one case, told by the hero, the undue feast happens in a decidedly heroic and Iliadic setting; in the other case, the poet reports on events that occurred in an Otherworld, far from the battlefields on which epic glory is won. But regardless, each time the Companions perish in spite of all the efforts of their leader to save them.

We begin to see, then, that the hierarchical relation between the two narrators is coming under pressure. And so is the distinction of the hero's internal and the poet's external audience. "I will now first tell you my name, *so that you too know it*" (ὄφρα καὶ ὑμεῖς εἴδετ', *Od.* 9.16–17), says the hero before beginning his long story, using language that recalls the beginning of the poem in yet another way: the scalar particle καί, which includes the audience in the set formed by the speaker himself ("you too as well, in addition to me"), is reminiscent of the end of the proem, where the audience, and the narrator, are included by the same particle (εἰπὲ καὶ ἡμῖν, 'tell us as well', *Od.* 1.10). We may perhaps see in this inclusion a veiled reference to Odysseus himself, the narrator of the second proem, whose story is being referred to ("tell us, Muse, so that we too [in addition to Odysseus] know it"); after all, the poet invokes the Muse to tell about

---

[12] The contrast between Odysseus and the Companions is also highlighted at yet another significant starting point in the poem, *Hermes' speech to Calypso*, just before the actual first appearance of the hero (5.110–11; cf. 5.133–4).

events for which Odysseus, who has been there and seen it himself, is the sole source.[13] The hero is the only human who does not need the Muse to gain access to the monstrous and fabulous world of the Wanderings, and in addressing the Muse, the poet asks her to grant him access to what Odysseus already knows. Soon we will hear it from the man himself.

When the hero takes over the floor from the poet, his story is not merely "embedded"; the boundary between the internal and the external audience begins to fade, and we are listening to Odysseus himself. The impact of *epos*, Odysseus' narrative, is such that *aoidē* has to reassert itself by means of explicit references to its own proem after the hero has finished his tale and the poet can resume *his* (*Od.* 13.88–92):

ὡς ἡ ῥίμφα θέουσα θαλάσσης κύματ' ἔταμνεν,
ἄνδρα φέρουσα θεοῖς ἐναλίγκια μήδε' ἔχοντα,
ὃς πρὶν μὲν μάλα **πολλὰ πάθ' ἄλγεα ὃν κατὰ θυμὸν**
ἀνδρῶν τε πτολέμους ἀλεγεινά τε κύματα πείρων,
δὴ τότε γ' ἀτρέμας εὗδε, λελασμένος ὅσσ' ἐπεπόνθει.

Thus running lightly, it cut through the swellings of the sea,
carrying <u>a man</u> with thoughts similar to the gods,
<u>who</u> earlier had <u>suffered many woes in his spirit</u>,
living through wars of men and the painful waves;
but then he slept undisturbed, forgetful of all that he had suffered.

The placement of ἄνδρα at the beginning of the line and its combination with a digressive relative clause containing μάλα πολλὰ πάθ' ἄλγεα ὃν κατὰ θυμὸν are unmistakable echoes of the primary proem.[14] It is striking that the epic poet can retake the floor only when Odysseus is fast asleep. The hero's forgetting "all that he had suffered" becomes the reverse of his remembering, that is, telling, enacting his sufferings. In other words, the hero's forgetting becomes the necessary condition for the poet's remembering and the continuation of the tale.

Just like an *aoidos*

The relationship between Odysseus and the narrator takes on supplementary features when the hero in the course of his story reaches subjects that belong to the domain of recognizable contemporary genres of song and performance. During his account of his visit of the dead in Book Eleven,

---

[13] Bakker 2009: 134. On the semantics of inclusive scalar particles (*also, too, even*), see Bakker 1988a: 27–56).
[14] See also de Jong 2001: 317; Bakker 2009: 130. For the placement of ἄνδρα, see Kahane 1992.

8 Epos *and* aoidē

Odysseus tells of his encounters with the queens and heroines of the past, in a poetically charged and complex stretch of his narrative (11.225–327). The hero's performance is a clear allusion to the Hesiodic *Catalogue*, as numerous critics have noticed.[15] Odysseus the "amateur" competes with the poetic "professional," outdoing him in fact, in having the advantage of the eyewitness: he has been there and seen these mythical subjects – mythical for Odysseus no less than for us – with his own eyes. The rivalry involves the narrator of the matrix narrative in which Odysseus performs, if we assume that Homeric and Hesiodic poetry both belonged to the repertoire of the rhapsode, the performer of *aoidē*.[16] In rhapsodizing the *Catalogue*, Odysseus does what the performer does in rhapsodizing Homer. The *Odyssey* incorporates another genre in the way outlined earlier, but in having a character, not the narrator, perform the rivaling genre, it achieves effects specific to this poem. Poet and hero coalesce. The two roles, Odysseus and Homer, hero and poet, merge into each other in a passage that has been considered spurious and interpolated by Analysts,[17] but which is in fact one of the great moments in this poem that is driven by intertextual poetics.

Odysseus' performance of a *Catalogue* is the context for Alkinoos' famous compliment of his guest (*Od.* 11.367–8):

σοὶ δ' ἐπὶ μὲν **μορφὴ ἐπέων**, ἔνι δὲ φρένες ἐσθλαί,
μῦθον δ' **ὡς ὅτ' ἀοιδὸς** ἐπισταμένως κατέλεξας.

Upon you is <u>comeliness of *epea*</u>, in <you> are noble *phrénes*;
and the tale, <u>as an *aoidos*</u> you have most expertly told it in all its detail.

These words can be taken as applying to Odysseus' extended *epos* as a whole, but their utterance at this particular juncture, after Odysseus' performance of his *Catalogue*, is significant. It is as if Alcinoos is taking μορφὴ ἐπέων, 'shapely form of words/lines' in the external sense: not as words represented in epic, but as the hexametric lines that *are* epic. There are multiple coalescences and alignments here. The hero becomes a poet,

---

[15] Most recently Rutherford 2012: 161–7.
[16] See Martin 2001, in a discussion of the intertextual features of Odysseus' account in a socio-poetic perspective ("one performer responding to contemporary and *competing* repertoire traditions," p. 29), suggesting the possibility, furthermore, of a Homeric response to Orphic (rhapsodic) performance traditions centering on the autobiographical account of the poet's descent. On first-person narrative as a shamanistic feature, see Meuli 1935: 168 (cf. Thornton 1970: 16–37; Burkert 1996: 68).
[17] For example, Page 1955: 33–9, who considers both the *Catalogue* and the "Intermezzo" (i.e., the conversation between Odysseus and his hosts interrupting the narrative: *Od.* 11.333–84) interpolations into a *Necyia* that is in itself an interpolation. Some thoughts on the genetic status of the *Necyia* in Chapter 5 below.

epos is posing as *aoidē*, and the poem's external audience merges with the Phaeacians in Alkinoos' hall.

The link between Odysseus' narrative and the features of recognizable performance genres is formally, formulaically, encoded. Odysseus finishes his *Catalogue* with language that anyone in the audience familiar with a parallel (competing?) poetic tradition will have recognized (*Od.* 11.328–30):[18]

πάσας δ' οὐκ ἂν ἐγὼ μυθήσομαι οὐδ' ὀνομήνω
ὅσσας ἡρώων ἀλόχους ἴδον ἠδὲ θύγατρας
πρὶν γάρ κεν καὶ νὺξ φθῖτ' ἄμβροτος.

All of them, there is no way I could tell or name them,
all those women I saw who were consorts or daughters of heroes;
Before <I could do this>, the immortal night would have dwindled away.

These lines are built on the same formulaic pattern as the invocation of the Muses in the *Iliad* at the beginning of the *Catalogue of Ships* (*Il.* 2.488–92):

πληθὺν δ' οὐκ ἂν ἐγὼ μυθήσομαι οὐδ' ὀνομήνω,
οὐδ' εἴ μοι δέκα μὲν γλῶσσαι, δέκα δὲ στόματ' εἶεν,
φωνὴ δ' ἄρρηκτος, χάλκεον δέ μοι ἦτορ ἐνείη,
εἰ μὴ Ὀλυμπιάδες Μοῦσαι Διὸς αἰγιόχοιο
θυγατέρες μνησαίαθ' ὅσοι ὑπὸ Ἴλιον ἦλθον.

Their multitude, there is no way I could tell or name <them all>,
not if I had ten tongues, ten mouths,
a voice unbreakable and a heart of bronze,
if the Olympus-dwelling Muses, daughters of Zeus who holds the aegis
did not make present in my mind all those who came under Ilion.

There used to be a time when such repetitions were thought to be without poetic or even semantic significance: due to the work of Parry and Lord, the formulaic system was thought to have generated the phraseology appropriate to a particular kind of situation, which could then be used by poets throughout the tradition as a formulaic, ready-made way of expressing that situation.[19] In the present case, that situation would be a speaker being confronted with the magnitude of a given body of information. There would be no special relationship

---

[18] Note that *Od.* 11.328 occurs two more times in the *Odyssey*, once later in the *Necyia* (*Od.* 11.517), when Odysseus assumes the role of a chronicler of the Trojan War (and hence a poet of heroic epic material) in answering Achilles' question about his son Neoptolemos. The other occurrence happens at 4.240, again in connection with the Trojan saga, when Helen recounts (4.240–64) an episode in which Odysseus visits Troy in disguise. Book Four, with the story of Menelaos' Wanderings and Helen's storytelling, is a microcosmos of the Odyssean interaction of *epos* and *aoidē*. See also *Od.* 3.113–14 (Nestor about the Trojan War).
[19] Parry 1971.

between any two instantiations of a given formula, since each would be necessitated independently in its context.

The acknowledgment that Homeric language is formulaic, however, does not mean that the utterance of a formula is always done without the memory of other occurrences. Language (whether or not formulaic) is not autonomous, and utterances are never made in isolation, independently of a given context. In an oral tradition two contexts may be linked by the deliberate repetition of a significant formulaic utterance, which may be remembered for being performed in a particularly significant context. The argument of this book will rely at various points on such deliberate repetition. In the Epilogue there will be a more detailed discussion of this "interformularity." In the present instance, then, we may consider taking the formula as a deliberate evocation of the Muse invocation introducing the *Catalogue of Ships* in the *Iliad*. The formula links hero and poet in what has been called epic *recusatio*, a "refusal to give a full presentation of complex things."[20]

But the repetition does not mean that the two contexts are identical. Odysseus may not be a poet, but he is in a position to outdo one. Whereas the Iliadic narrator has to emphasize hearing and hearsay (in a word, *kleos*, *Il.* 2.486), Odysseus can claim personal memory and eyewitness status, in other words, the position not of the poet, but of the Muses themselves. Furthermore, the narrator of the *Iliad* begins his *Catalogue of Ships* with the *recusatio* formula, whereas Odysseus utters it to *conclude* his *Catalogue of Women*. And the second time he utters the formula precisely in order to *preclude* a catalogue: instead of the whole list of Neoptolemus' exploits the speaker will mention only one.[21] This difference in discourse function is matched by a difference in reason for making the *recusatio*. The narrator of the *Iliad* cites typically human, physical, limitations (lack of stamina, a voice that will wear out, *Il.* 2.489–90), but then goes on to present the catalogue all the same, with the indispensable help of the Muses (2.491–2). For Odysseus, on the other hand, the fundamental constraint is not a voice that will wear out, but time. It is lack of time that makes him cut short his *Catalogue of Women* and limit the catalogue of Neoptolemus' achievements to just one item.

Time, in fact, is what constrains Odysseus' tale in other ways as well. If *epos* is allowed to run its course unchecked, it will obstruct the progress of

---

[20] Ford 1992: 73–6.
[21] As in the case of Helen's *recusatio* formula. Note the ἀλλ' οἷον, '(not . . .) except such as' in both cases (*Od.* 4.242; 11.519).

aoidē: the night will run out and *nostos* might be jeopardized. Odysseus' skill as a narrator may pose a danger to the poem in which he is the principal hero. The same perspective on *epos* is opened a few days later in narrated time and three books later in narrative time, when Odysseus is once more facing an audience eager to hear his story, Eumaios the faithful swineherd whose hospitality the hero disguised as beggar is enjoying (*Od.* 14.196–8):[22]

ῥηϊδίως κεν ἔπειτα καὶ εἰς ἐνιαυτὸν ἅπαντα
οὔ τι διαπρήξαιμι λέγων ἐμὰ κήδεα θυμοῦ,
ὅσσα γε δὴ σύμπαντα θεῶν ἰότητι μόγησα.

Easily hereafter even for a full year
I would not be finished telling of the sorrows of my heart,
all, in their totality, that by the will of the gods I have toiled.

So close to the accomplishment of his *nostos*, the hero could easily lose a full year, the amount of time he had lost to Circe's excessive hospitality (the importance of this year will be discussed in Chapter 5). Once again the hero is compared with an *aoidos*, a singer, by his rapt audience, the same Eumaios speaking to Penelope (*Od.* 17.518–21):

ὡς ὅτ' ἀοιδὸν ἀνὴρ ποτιδέρκεται, ὅς τε θεῶν ἒξ
ἀείδῃ δεδαὼς ἔπε' ἱμερόεντα βροτοῖσι,
τοῦ δ' ἄμοτον μεμάασιν ἀκουέμεν, ὁππότ' ἀείδῃ·
ὣς ἐμὲ κεῖνος ἔθελγε παρήμενος ἐν μεγάροισι.

As when a man looks at an *aoidos*, who starting from the gods
sings having learned *epea* full of longing to mortals.
And they long insatiably to hear him whenever he sings:
This is how that man enchanted me sitting next to me in my hall.

Epos, then, tends to put on airs of *aoidē* and can be presented as posing a threat with its charms to the progress of the narrative. Conversely, *aoidē*, when represented by *epos*, can be downright lethal. The hero sails past the Sirens, whose song, explicitly called *aoidē* (12.183), is so enchanting that no sailor who is drawn to it will ever be able to leave, to the destruction of his *nostos*. The Sirens' song is the song of the Trojan War, the quintessence of *aoidē*.[23]

It is as if the poet and the hero are vying for the same space in the presentation of the poem. But they also head toward the same goal. The

---

[22] Typologically the *Apologoi* have the same function as the "liar stories" he tells on Ithaca, as is argued in Chapter 2.
[23] On the intertextual properties of the Song of the Sirens, see Pucci 1998: 1–9.

poem's fundamental themes, as this book will argue, will be visible in all their detail only when the two main acts of narration are studied closely together. In the *Odyssey*, *epos*, and *aoidē* are interdependent, and in interpreting the poem we have to listen to their dialogue. In Chapter 2 we will look in more detail into the ways in which these two fundamental Odyssean discourse modes are intertwined.

CHAPTER 2

Nostos *as quest*

"It is *nostos* that you seek, glorious Odysseus."
(Tiresias to Odysseus, *Od.* 11.100)

The complex interplay between the stories of Odysseus and the poet cuts across many of the narrative typologies that have been proposed for the *Odyssey*. The story of return as told in the *Odyssey* is often seen as an instance of the theme of the Homecoming Husband. We can call this a story type. The basic type, as formulated in Aarne's and Thompson's index of folktale types, is "Husband (lover) arrives home just as wife (mistress) is to marry another."[1] Many additional motifs are often present, such as the hero's magical return journey, his disguise, his recognition by an animal before his identity is discovered by his wife, all of which are, of course, present in the *Odyssey*. The Homecoming Husband motif may seem an adequate description of the events that transpire at Ithaca in the second half of the poem, but the *Odyssey* recounts not only the arrival of the husband, but also his adventures while absent from his wife. Since return in the *Odyssey*'s plot is not so much a given as the hero's principal intention and concern, not so much a point of departure as a goal, the motif of the returning husband alone does not penetrate deeply enough into the poem's structure.

The Returning Husband story type can be seen as a special case of a number of more general narrative sequences, which we could call story patterns. One such pattern comes from the study of the South-Slavic oral tradition, where the Homecoming Husband is particularly well represented. Albert Lord and John Miles Foley discuss it as the "Return Song." For Lord, the type of the returning husband is an instance of a more abstract pattern, in which the marriage to be concluded in the hero's absence is more generally a matter of something bad happening while the

---

[1] Aarne and Thompson 1981: 343; for the type and the *Odyssey*, Hansen 1997: 446–9 (types discussed: 442–3); Edmunds 2005: 35.

hero is away. Lord speaks of the "withdrawal, devastation, and return" pattern, which he succinctly formulates as: "The god or hero disappears for a relatively long period of time and is seemingly dead, but eventually he returns, or is sought after and brought back. During his absence there has been devastation, but upon his reestablishment, which is performed ceremonially, order is restored, prosperity returns, and frequently, he re-marries."[2] This pattern, which for Lord is associated with the death and resurrection inherent in myths of fertility and vegetation, would underlie not only the *Odyssey*, but also the *Iliad* with its returning hero, whose wrath and absence caused the Achaeans a myriad of grief.

This is not the place to discuss Achilles or the *Iliad* (Chapter 8 will be), though it is important for the present chapter to observe that "return" can mean different things in different stories, since Achilles' return to the battlefield, of course, eliminates all chances of his coming out of the Trojan War alive and hence his returning home; his return is not a *nostos*. As we will see later, the meaning of *nostos* is not limited to actual homecoming, but let us continue to think of "return" in this sense and of the hero, not as warrior, but as husband. Once again, the *Odyssey* conforms to the pattern very well: the hero's prolonged absence, his state of imprisonment at the moment when he enters the story line, the Suitors terrorizing his house in his absence, his revenge coinciding with the bridal contest, and his subsequent reunion with Penelope are all prime ingredients of the return pattern.

But there are also elements that fit the pattern less well. Usually, there is only one villain-suitor, as in the unhappy tale of Agamemnon, that other Homecoming Husband, with which the *Odyssey* loves to contrast its own successful return; but at Ithaca the villain has been multiplied into a crowd of over a hundred Suitors.[3] And usually the returning husband has been as chaste as his wife during his absence, but Odysseus' erotic encounters during his absence are so prominent and memorable that Penelope comes to be aligned with Circe, Calypso, and Nausicaa as multiforms of one and the same prototype.

A further relevant account of the story pattern in question is the sequence emerging from the structuralist analysis of Russian folktales by Vladimir Propp. In Propp's formal analysis, the bewildering diversity in the material of Russian fairytales disappears when actual story-events, or

---

[2] Lord 1972: 31; cf. Lord 1960: 186; 1991: 140–2. Foley 1990: 362 speaks of "Absence, Devastation, Return, Retribution, and Wedding."

[3] Exact numbers at *Od.* 16.247–53. See also Chapter 4, n. 33 and Chapter 8, n. 32.

the identity of the characters, are suppressed in favor of "functions," abstract units of plot action. Not all of the functions need be present in any given tale, but their number is limited (Propp distinguishes thirty-one functions) and their order is found, in the Russian material, to be fixed. The Homecoming (or Returning Husband) sequence (in which the hero does not have to be already married) corresponds with the final nine functions in Propp's extended series:[4]

23. The hero, unrecognized, arrives home or in another country.
24. A false hero presents unfounded claims.
25. A difficult task is proposed to the hero.
26. The task is resolved.
27. The hero is recognized.
28. The false hero or villain is exposed.
29. The hero is given a new appearance.
30. The villain is punished.
31. The hero is married and ascends to the throne.

Again, it is not difficult to recognize elements of the *Odyssey* when we think of Odysseus' disguise and delayed recognition, the Suitors with their unfounded claims to marriage, the bow contest as the difficult test, Odysseus' scar as recognition sign, among other elements.[5] But again, Odysseus' Homecoming, the subject of *aoidē*, cannot be isolated so easily from the story of the Wanderings (*epos*); moreover, the hero's "marriage" is not just a reward, as in many of the folktales, but the very purpose of the Return.

The three story types briefly discussed (Homecoming Husband folktale motif, Serbo-Croatian Return Song, and the final functions in Propp's series) are similar to one another in treating the hero's homecoming as the poem's typologically defining feature.[6] Much that happens at Ithaca,

---

[4] Propp 1968: 60–5. For a discussion of Propp's importance for the study of Greek myth, see Burkert 1979: 5–18; critique of Propp by Csapo 2005: 201–11 (and the discussion of "quest" below); comparison between Propp's syntagmatic approach and the paradigmatic orientation of the rival structuralist conception of Lévi-Strauss in Dundes 1997. For a discussion of the differences between Lord's notion of theme in oral composition and Propp's model, see Yen 1973.

[5] In his Introduction to the second edition of Propp's work in English (Propp 1968: xiv), Alan Dundes, wondering whether Propp's analysis can be extended to epic, notes the similarity of the last part of the *Odyssey* to functions 23–31. The applicability of Propp's analysis to narratives other than Russian "wondertales" calls into question the definition of "folktale" as well as of other traditional genres. Propp has by now been applied to a much wider range of literary and cultural expressions, e.g., Fell 1977; Wight 1986.

[6] Lord 1991: 129 does not find anything in the Serbo-Croatian Return Song material that resembles Odysseus' Wanderings.

however, is predicated on what happens earlier and elsewhere. We saw in Chapter 1 that at the level of the act of storytelling the hero's tale of the Wanderings is more than a mere inset story, and I will make the same point in the present chapter in the discussion of typology and story patterns. The pattern that typifies the *Odyssey* cannot be determined by leaving the tale of the Wanderings out of account. *Epos* is food for *aoidē* and a study of the latter cannot afford to deprive itself of the former's sustenance. So let us see whether a useful typology can be deduced from the tale of Odysseus' Wanderings.

Nostos and quest

From the standpoint of Lord's formulation of the return pattern, the Wanderings fill a gap that is opened up by the perspective evoked by phrases such as "the hero disappears" or "during his absence." Suddenly it appears that "return," whether as noun or as verb, conveys an ambiguous sense of perspective, since return(ing) is not the same thing for the hero as for those missing him (or not) at home. For those left behind, "return" can only be the hero's actual Homecoming, his arrival marking the end of his absence. For the hero himself, return may be in the first place an intention: a departure, or a desire the fulfillment of which is beyond his control. The Greek word νόστος, commonly translated as "return," conveys just this ambiguous perspective: as the idea of a *journey* it tends to emphasize beginning, departure, no less than ending or arrival at destination. And it deploys its full meaning precisely when the latter is not attained. Phemios, the epic bard in Odysseus' palace, sings, in the hero's absence, of the baneful *nostos* which Athena had imposed on the Achaeans,[7] clearly implying an unsuccessful *nostos*-journey that did not result in an actual return. Young Telemachos departs on a search for news about his father's *nostos*, which equally implies the opposite of return, since Telemachos has no illusions that his father is still alive.[8] And most importantly, Odysseus himself introduces the tale of his Wanderings, the poem's principal *epos*, as a *nostos*, at a moment when his homebound journey has not yet reached its completion (*Od.* 9.37):

εἰ δ' ἄγε τοι καὶ **νόστον** ἐμὸν πολυκηδέ' ἐνίσπω

So then, let me now tell you of my *nostos* of many sorrows.

---

[7] *Od.* 1.326–7: νόστον ... λυγρόν.   [8] For example, *Od.* 1.94, 287.

From the point of view of the Trojan War and its epic cycle, *nostos* denotes the return of the heroes to Greece after the war as well as the *songs* dealing with those homebound journeys. But this dominant perspective provided by a powerful epic tradition cannot completely hide the fact that the semantic range of νόστος, and of its cognate verb νέομαι, is wider. The return reported, or rather evoked, by νόστος/νέομαι is often not so much return or homecoming *tout court* as the escape from the dangers that stand in the way of return, which yields a meaning of "survival," as recently argued by Anna Bonifazi.[9] In the *Iliad*, "returns" of heroes typically do not presuppose the end of the Trojan War as a whole, and so come to mean the *survival* of the ordeal, with νόστος/νέομαι standing in pointed contrast to terms for death and destruction, such as ὀλέσθαι, 'perish'. So, for example, Achilles can speak of the "imperishable fame" that lies in store for him as compensation for the loss of his *nostos* (*Il.* 9.412–13):

> εἰ μέν κ' αὖθι μένων Τρώων πόλιν ἀμφιμάχωμαι,
> **ὤλετο** μέν μοι **νόστος**, ἀτὰρ κλέος ἄφθιτον ἔσται.
>
> If staying here I fight around the city of the Trojans,
> Then my *nostos* is lost, but my *kleos* will be everlasting.

It is, of course, implied by ὤλετο ... νόστος that Achilles will never see his fatherland again, but the phrase properly denotes that Achilles will not return from the battle. He will not be able to tell the story of his ordeal himself.

Such a privilege is, of course, granted to Odysseus, but not until he has braved the dangers of the high seas, where death is anonymous, and where there is no compensation in the form of *kleos* for loss of any *nostos*. He has to cling to life at all costs if he is to be able to tell the story of his ordeal – no poet will ever do it for him, at least not until he has told the story himself first. *Nostos*, which in the *Odyssey*'s proem is closely linked with "one's dear life,"[10] is for Odysseus the return to life and safety from mortal danger. See, for example, what the goddess Leucothea says to Odysseus in the hour of his last shipwreck (*Od.* 5.343–5):

> εἵματα ταῦτ' ἀποδὺς σχεδίην ἀνέμοισι φέρεσθαι
> κάλλιπ', ἀτὰρ χείρεσσι νέων ἐπιμαίεο **νόστου**
> γαίης Φαιήκων, ὅθι τοι μοῖρ' ἐστὶν ἀλύξαι.

---

[9] Bonifazi 2009. See also Frame 1978 on *nostos* as "return to life and light."
[10] *Od.* 1.5, ἣν ψυχὴν ... νόστον; also *Od.* 1.287, 2.218 (βίοτον καὶ νόστον).

> Take off those clothes and abandon your raft to be blown
> by the winds; swimming with your hands, strive for your *nostos*,
> in the land of the Phaeacians, where it is your destiny to escape.

In less desperate cases, to achieve *nostos* is to reach the final destination of one's journey safely. The Cretan sailors in the Homeric *Hymn to Apollo*, for example, mention Pylos as their *nostos* after they have landed unexpectedly and against their will at Delphi.[11] An actual homecoming, then, can strictly speaking be called a *nostos* only if the hero has escaped from life-threatening danger or has reached the goal for which he had set out in the beginning. A completed *nostos* can only be the successful completion of a quest.

The quest is an extremely versatile story pattern, perhaps the most universal template for storytelling, or for human experience, that exists. Walter Burkert reduces the quest pattern to the biological needs of the human organism: quests are "programs of action" revolving around the imperative "get" as the "deepest deep structure of a tale."[12] (We shall see in later chapters that the idea of quest for food or physical survival is remarkably appropriate for the *Odyssey*.) At a slightly less hardwired level, quests can provide the backbone for just about any traditional narrative genre: epics, folktales, myths, shaman's tales, and other reports on fantastic travel, such as tales of hunting and so on. In traditional narrative, the hero's quest is typically motivated by a "lack" of some sort: something is lost or has been stolen; someone has disappeared and is held captive; something is needed to ensure survival and continuity of the community or the hero's own life. He has to leave on a journey that typically takes him to the Otherworld, of which Underworld and Paradise are multiforms, and involves monstrous guardians, divine temptresses who may turn out to be donors or helpers, and seemingly insurmountable geographical boundaries.

Quest tales do not in themselves have to dwell on the hero's actual Homecoming: the real *nostos* is often the hero's surviving all the trials and his success in the liquidation of the lack. So in many quest myths or epics homecoming is simply taken for granted; the *Gilgamesh Epic* comes to mind, the story of the hero who had to overcome many obstacles in order to arrive at the ultimate object of his quest, but whose return was unproblematic and thematically unimportant. But return is in itself not incompatible with quest. After he has successfully completed the quest, the hero may have

---

[11] *H. App.* 469–72. See Verdenius 1969; Bonifazi 2009. Cf. Eur. *IA* 965–6, 1261.
[12] Burkert 1979: 14–16.

to face further adventures and challenges at home; nothing less than kingship may be at stake. Quest and return taken together, in fact, make up the entire series of "functions" in Propp's morphological analysis of the folktale. In addition to Propp's Homecoming sequence presented earlier, let us reproduce here his quest sequence, functions 9–20 in the extended series:[13]

9. Misfortune or lack is made known; the hero is approached with a request or command; he is allowed to go or he is dispatched.
10. The seeker agrees to or decides upon counteraction.
11. The hero leaves home.
12. The hero is tested, interrogated, attacked, etc., which prepares the way for his receiving either a magical agent or helper.
13. The hero reacts to the actions of the future donor.
14. The hero acquires the use of a magical agent.
15. The hero is transferred, delivered, or led to the whereabouts of an object of search.
16. The hero and the villain join in direct combat.
17. The hero is branded.
18. The villain is defeated.
19. The initial misfortune or lack is liquidated.
20. The hero returns.

Just as we can recognize Propp's return sequence in the narrative of Odysseus' Homecoming in the second half of the poem, the quest sequence is readily visible in some of the hero's adventures in the Otherworld. The Circe story in particular comes to mind, with Hermes as donor and the herb *moly* as magical agent. It would seem, then, that the *Odyssey* displays the same sequence that we see in Propp's extended series. What is specific to the *Odyssey*, however, is that the hero's *nostos* in the sense of voyage and survival of tribulations, and his *nostos* as actual homecoming are causally and thematically interrelated. The hero's quest, in the overall architecture of the plot, is not in search of some externally located object, in outbound, centrifugal travel; the primary lack and object of search is home(coming) itself and the quest is inbound, centripetal.

It would seem that on this basis we could say that in the *Odyssey* a quest sequence is directed toward becoming a return sequence. However, on the basis of the observation that *epos*, the hero's tale, and *aoidē*, the poet's tale, are interdependent, I will explore another possibility: *the return is part and*

---

[13] Propp 1968: 35–56.

ultimate object of the quest; it is subsumed in a pattern initiated during the Wanderings and continued all the way through to the poem's end – indeed, beyond – as hero and poet negotiate the accomplishment of a *nostos* that is their common goal.

Variations on a theme

Extended epics and short folktales do not differ in the themes or story patterns of which they are the expression – quests, returns, and other themes are common to both. What distinguishes them is precisely the basis for epic's considerably greater length. Epic can incorporate a narrative sequence of a given type and repeat it as a theme, modifying it and adjusting it to the narrative requirements of the overall story at any given point in the narrative progression. The *Odyssey* does exactly this. It has narratives in which we can clearly recognize Propp's functions; it has even imported wholesale folktales that are amply attested elsewhere, outside Homer and outside the Greek world.[14] And it fully digests the stories and story patterns it ingests, turning a recognizable narrative sequence into a basic pattern that not only recurs many times in the plot, but is also the engine for its progression.

Odysseus' adventures may seem diverse and varied at first sight, but on closer inspection they all conform to one and the same basic pattern, which extends beyond the Wanderings. The *Odyssey* thus provides *la leçon par l'exemple* of a structural approach to folktales and other traditional narratives in showing considerable unity in deep structure in spite of much surface diversity. Quests (which I now use as shorthand for instances of the quest pattern) can be: (i) following each other, concatenated in paratactic fashion; they may also be (ii) compressed and decompressed according to the story's needs and as the narrator wishes; and they may be (iii) recursively nested in other, higher-level quests (or, conversely, a given quest may be comprised of subquests). The quest, in other words, is an essential and versatile narrative building-block, a prime ingredient of the composition of the *Odyssey* which can be subjected to the three operations mentioned (concatenation, (de)compression, and recursion). Before Odysseus can enjoy the final *nostos* on his

---

[14] The prime example is the Cyclops story, which Page 1955: 5–6 (see also Hansen 1997: 451–2) analyzes as a blend of the two motifs of "the ogre blinded" and "noman." The tale is attested in Armenian, Russian, and Arabic folklore, among others, e.g., Grimm 1857; Glenn 1971. Some attestations of the Cyclops story outside of Homer, however, may be motivated by the *Odyssey*.

Variations on a theme 21

own island and regain his kingdom and his marriage, he needs to accomplish many *nostoi* in his quest for survival.[15]

The Circe episode is a good place to start. Not only does this tale contain the clearest and most detailed example of a folktale-grade quest sequence in the poem; it is also instructive in showing how a self-contained sequence can come to be incorporated in the continuing narrative.[16] We can discern various quest sequences here, the most recognizable one, and closest to Propp's folktale pattern, being the rescue mission that culminates in the "combat" between Odysseus and Circe. Almost all Propp's functions find articulation in Odysseus' adventure, with the exception of function, the branding of the hero.[17] Eurylochos' story about the mysterious disappearance of the Companions (*Od.* 10.251–60) is the lack that makes the hero decide to leave "home" (functions 9–11); Hermes' epiphany in the form of a young man addressing Odysseus is the appearance of the donor (functions 12–13), and the noble herb *moly* is a clear representation of folktale's magical agent (function 14), securing the hero's *nostos* (10.285). Finally, combat with the villain turns into lovemaking as the necessary condition for the release of the Companions, a feature that is not unknown in multiforms of this tale.[18]

This sequence is only a part of the entire episode, however. It leaves out events prior to Odysseus' rescue mission. These events, the reconnaissance expedition of the Companions, constitute a quest pattern in its own right, less conspicuously so than the rescue mission, but in a way more structurally

---

[15] The idea of repeated themes and narrative patterns in the *Odyssey* has been explored previously. Powell 1977 elaborates, from the viewpoint of oral composition, a narrative schema (given on pp. 2–3) that is repeated throughout the poem. Louden 1999 sees in the *Odyssey* the threefold repetition of an extended narrative pattern revolving around a "powerful female figure" and involving a "band of young men," i.e., Circe–Companions, Nausicaa/Arete–Phaeacian nobles, and Penelope–Suitors, an idea earlier proposed by Powell 1977: 33. Nagler 1990 stresses the "mirror" relation between the Suitors and the Companions, and in Nagler 1996 he concentrates on the role of the "axial" goddesses Circe and Calypso, on whom he argues that Penelope is predicated. Insights on the interaction between the Wanderings and the matrix narrative are also offered in Cook 1995.

[16] Hansen 1997: 458–9 notes differences between the Circe adventure and a pure folktale: in a folktale there are two opportunities for the donor (see below) to appear; for the Circe story to be a real folktale, the donor (Hermes) would have had to be rebuffed first by Eurylochos and subsequently accepted by Odysseus. But this is beside the point; we do not expect the import of a pristine, unmodified tale. By the principle laid down in Chapter 1, no genre imported into epic will remain unaffected or leave the matrix unaffected.

[17] Conversely, the element of the hero's recognition and the detail that his coming was prophesied earlier (*Od.* 10.330–2) are absent in Propp's series.

[18] Burkert 1979: 87, 182 n. 19 notes the similarity between the Circe adventure and the tale of Heracles getting back the horses of his chariot from the cave of Hylaie the Snake-Woman, with whom he has to make love (Hdt. 4.8–9).

important for the narrative progression and coherence of the *Odyssey*. Odysseus' reaching a new unknown island may not be the arrival at a deliberately chosen destination, but the encounter with its inhabitant(s) is intentional: a reconnaissance expedition typically takes place, usually at the sight of distant smoke. The expedition results in a first and unsuccessful encounter with the inhabitant(s): *nostos* is threatened, sometimes in the form of imminent mortal danger. This sequence is visible in all but one of the episodes that occur before the *Necyia*.

It typifies the brief Lotophagi episode in particular. Compared with the much more elaborate Circe episode this adventure exemplifies the first of the three operations on the quest sequence mentioned above, compression: the rescue mission that is the most salient part of the Circe episode, covering 126 lines (10.274–399), is here compressed to one single line: "and I led them, wailing, back to the ships, by force" (9.98). The episode is also otherwise condensed in lacking a donor in either the reconnaissance or the rescue quest. The donor is prominently present, by contrast, in the two remaining reconnaissance missions, in ways that evince the variability inherent in the system: the Laestrygonian episode has the daughter of King Antiphates, whom Odysseus' men encounter at the well Artakiē, and who leads them to the palace (10.111), and to death by cannibalism. In the *Odyssey*, donors can be anti-donors, offering "help" that leads to loss of *nostos*, or worse.

The Cyclops story presents a curious donor: Maron, Apollo's priest at Ismarus, whose life Odysseus saved when he and his men sacked the city of the Ciconians (9.199–200). The donor does not figure directly in the story, but the supernaturally strong wine he gave to Odysseus in gratitude appears in the Cyclops tale at the moment when the donor is called for in the sequence, and its function as magical agent is beyond dispute.[19] The Cyclops quest conforms to the reconnaissance pattern developed in the first part of the Wanderings, but Odysseus' desire for "guest gifts" (ξείνια, *Od.* 9.228–9) can qualify, at the surface level of the narrative, as the lack motivating the quest. When the story progresses, however, the real, underlying lack is liquidated in the theft of the Cyclops' sheep, which are more than a means of escape (more on this in Chapter 4).[20]

We can now refine Propp's quest sequence, adjusting it to the narrative of Odysseus' Wanderings and its specific features:

---

[19] Note that Propp 1968: 41–2 lists "request for mercy" as a stereotyped action of the future donor and the hero's sparing the suppliant's life as a possible reaction (functions 12 and 13); this, of course, matches Odysseus' treatment of Maron (*Od.* 9.197–201).
[20] Burkert 1979: 31–4.

1. Odysseus (alone or with his Companions) lands on an unknown island.
2. Distant smoke indicates the presence of inhabitants.
3. He explores the surroundings or sends out spies to do so.
4. He meets (or the spies meet) with someone who gives information or acts as guide, helper, or donor.
5. He tells him/her the/a story of his wanderings.
6. The guide/donor may provide a magical agent.
7. He reaches (or the spies reach) the abode of (an) inhabitant(s).
8. Three possible outcomes:
   8a. *Nostos* is achieved through flight, rescue, or victory in combat.
   8b. *Nostos* is not achieved, due to ignorance, carelessness, or recklessness.
   8c. Accomplishment of *nostos* creates a new goal/lack.

This pattern resembles Propp's quest sequence mostly in the donor function and the magical agent, if present (items 4–6). In addition to the donors already mentioned, there is Aiolos as a clear case, with the Bag of the Winds as magical agent, in a story that does not contain a reconnaissance mission, but instead has an item that is not always prominent in the series of Wanderings adventures as told by Odysseus, but highly characteristic of the *Odyssey* as a whole: the hero's interaction with the donor (Propp's function 13 at page 19, above) consists in language, in particular storytelling, the story of his Wanderings. In the Aiolos episode as told by Odysseus the storytelling is reported in just one line (*Od.* 10.14–16):

> μῆνα δὲ πάντα φίλει με καὶ ἐξερέεινεν ἕκαστα,
> Ἴλιον Ἀργείων τε νέας καὶ νόστον Ἀχαιῶν·
> **καὶ μὲν ἐγὼ τῷ πάντα κατὰ μοῖραν κατέλεξα.**
>
> And he entertained me kindly for a whole month and asked about everything,
> Ilion, the ships of the Argives, and the nostos of the Achaeans:
> <u>and I gave him a full and proper account of everything.</u>

But in later instantiations of this function, as we will see below in discussing the second half of the poem, the hero's verbal interaction with the donor turns into fully-fledged and detailed storytelling. The tale of the Wanderings itself as extended narrative speech act can be seen in this way, as can the Cretan Lies that Odysseus tells at various occasions on Ithaca – indeed, this function makes up the essence of *epos* as defined in Chapter 1.

The five adventures following the second departure from Circe's island (the Sirens, Charybdis, the Cattle of the Sun, Scylla, and Calypso) are rife with themes already encountered in the earlier stages of the Wanderings and central to the poem's central vision. They are not quests in themselves, however; no reconnaissance expeditions are launched and no unknown inhabitants are encountered until Odysseus is shipwrecked on Calypso's shore and adopted by the goddess. From being an inquisitive traveler distracted by proto-colonial explorations Odysseus has come to be steadfastly oriented toward the ultimate quest. *Nostos* has turned from coming out of it alive to coming home.

But there is a higher quest. Odysseus is able to survive the new ordeals due to indispensable advice and information from Circe. Her shift from dangerous adversary in the rescue quest to helpful guide leads us to a property of the quest pattern in the *Odyssey* that was mentioned above: quests can be nested recursively in higher quests, when erstwhile adversaries in the fulfillment of a quest come to play the role of donors in a further and higher quest. Circe does this twice. Her guidance is directed in the first instance to Odysseus reaching Tiresias in the Land of the Dead beyond Oceanus, a destination that is in many ways the ultimate object of the mythical quest. The blood of the victims she tells Odysseus to sacrifice to Hades and Persephone (10.524–37) can be seen as the magical agent with which Odysseus can attract and control the souls of the deceased. As donor in the Underworld quest, a theme that Michael Nagler calls the "consultation myth," Circe is equivalent to Siduri in the Babylonian *Gilgamesh Epic*, a comparison that casts Tiresias inevitably in the role of Uta-Napíshti in the Babylonian epic.[21]

But unlike Gilgamesh's ancestor, Tiresias is not the ultimate object of the hero's quest; the seer's consultation is relative to the quest, not the object of the quest itself. Tiresias puts the quest in perspective and tells Odysseus that the much-desired *nostos* and reunion with his wife will not be the end of the quest. And so the quest goes on, which puts Circe for a second time in the role of donor. Her guidance, after Odysseus' return to her island, helps Odysseus survive the deadly dangers of the second half of the Wanderings, and reach a *nostos* at Calypso's island Ogygia, situated at the "navel of the sea" (1.50). From here he will not be able to leave until after seven years, a departure due to the intervention of Hermes, the same god that enabled him to save his own life and that of his Companions at Circe's.

The Circe episode, then, is at the same time a folktale with shamanistic overtones and a cornerstone in the *Odyssey*'s architecture. In terms of

---

[21] Nagler 1996: 145–7. Nagler sees in Circe and Calypso hypostates of the divinity that resides at the *axis mundi*, the location of the ultimate source of wisdom and prophecy. See Chapter 5 below for more on Circe's relation with Death and the Underworld.

Table 2.1 *The basic story pattern in the Wanderings*

Function	*Lotophagoi*	Cyclops	Aiolos	Laestrygonians	Circe	Tiresias	Calypso
2. Smoke	–	9.167	–	10.99	10.149–50	–	–
3. Reconnaissance	X	X	–	X	X	–	–
4. Helper/donor	X	Maron	Aiolos	daughter	Hermes	Circe	Circe
5. Storytelling	–	–	10.16	–	–	–	12.35
6. Magical agent	–	wine	Bag of the Winds	–	*moly*	blood	guidance
7. Goal	rescue	sheep	Ithaca	flight	rescue	prophecy	*nostos*
8a. *Nostos*/rescue	X	X		X	X	X	X
8b. No *nostos*			X				
8c. New lack							

meaning, it conveys some of the poem's most central themes (about which more in Chapter 5), and in a structural sense it holds together a large part of the Wanderings. The hero meets with the insular Mistress of Animals when his fortunes are at their lowest point; he has experienced the wrath of the gods and lost the majority of his Companions. What starts out as a painful mission to undo the loss of even more Companions turns out to be a critical test; in passing it, Odysseus lays the basis for his eventually successful return.

The quest pattern in the Wanderings can now be set out in Table 2.1.

This account of the Wanderings as a series of instantiations of one and the same story pattern by way of concatenation, compression, or expansion, and recursion is an alternative to, but does not mean to replace, a more familiar vision in which the individual adventures are arranged according to a symmetrical pattern with the *Necyia* as the center of a ring-compositional structure.[22] On either side of this core are two further rings, with as center the Aiolos and Thrinacia episodes, respectively.[23] The groupings, furthermore, are arranged according to an alternation between opposite forces such as violence and temptation or lack versus excess of hospitality, resulting, respectively, in being eaten (i.e., incorporated physically) and being indefinitely entertained and detained (incorporated culturally).[24] The arrangement can be presented in Figure 2.1, based on Most (1989: 22).

---

[22] Going back ultimately to Whitman's desire to see geometrical structure in the Homeric compositions (1958: 288). See also Germain 1954: 333 and Nagler 1996: 144.
[23] Niles 1978, modified by Most 1989: 21–3, from whom Figure 2.1 has been taken.
[24] Redfield 1983: 237–8, who speaks of "hypo-entertainment" and "hyper-entertainment."

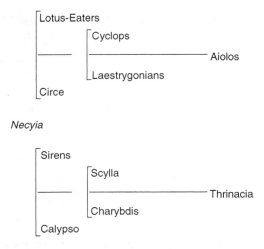

Figure 2.1 The symmetrical arrangement of the Wanderings

On either side of the two groupings around the *Necyia* are cases of excessive hospitality (Lotus-Eaters, Circe, Sirens, Calypso), causing forgetfulness in the traveler or other causes for extreme delay, or even annihilation of *nostos*. Within that outer circle is a circle (Cyclopes, Laestrygonians, Scylla, Charybdis) of total lack of hospitality, resulting in cannibalism or other forms of ingestion. In the middle are adventures (Aiolos, Thrinacia [Cattle of the Sun]) that have two important features in common: in both adventures Odysseus succumbs to a deep and prolonged sleep, during which, in both cases, the Companions destroy *nostos* by their ignorance or folly in the absence of their master's conscious attention.

The two ways of seeing the Wanderings are complementary. For example, the structural parallelism between the Lotus-Eaters and Circe in the symmetrical arrangement (both being cases of excessive, *nostos*-threatening hospitality) does not preclude the similarity between the Lotus-Eaters and Laestrygonians episodes as two instantiations of one and the same quest sequence. And the structural link between the Aiolos and Thrinacia episodes supplements the way in which Thrinacia, as one of the three adventures in the Otherworld that are told at length, relates to the two others, the Cyclops and Circe. Nor are the relational possibilities of these three episodes exhausted by the network of adventures in the Wanderings; each of them has complex ties with what happens at Ithaca, as Chapters 4, 5, and 6 will show in detail. As further preparation for that

From quest to return

We saw that Circe's guidance makes it possible for Odysseus to reach Calypso, and Calypso is where *epos*, Odysseus' narrative, comes to an end. But it is not where quest patterning comes to an end. Nor is the beginning of his tale the place where quest patterning starts. Odysseus' *epos* is a *mise en abîme*: in telling his tale, this sequence of quests and subquests, he is in the middle of a new quest sequence. His very tale, the hero's *epos*, uttered at the banquet of the Phaeacians, is wedged between narrative sequences, the poet's *aoidē*, displaying the same patterns that are at work in Odysseus' own tale. Indeed, this tale, taken as a whole as one act of narrative, is part of the pattern surrounding it: typologically, as we saw, Odysseus' act of narration, comprising four whole books of the poem, is the hero's interaction with the future donor (see Propp's function 13 at page 19, above), which in the *Odyssey* takes a metapoetic turn, as the hero begins to play the role of poet (function 5 in the adaptation of Propp's scheme to the *Odyssey* presented at page 23, above).

Odysseus' tale is an explicit response (ἀπαμειβόμενος, 'answering', *Od.* 9.1) to a series of requests by Alkinoos that puts the Phaeacians in the role of donors and their fabulous ships in the role of magical agent: (i) "tell us your name and stop hiding it with gainseeking thoughts" (*Od.* 8.548–54); (ii) "tell us what land, community, and city you are from, so that our ships that know the sailors' thoughts and need no rudder can bring you there" (*Od.* 8.555–63); (iii) "tell us about your wanderings, the lands and peoples that you reached, which of them are savage and unjust, and which ones hospitable and god-fearing" (*Od.* 8.572–6); (iv) "tell us about your grief, whom of those near and dear to you, a relative or a companion, you lost" (*Od.* 8.577–86).

Odysseus has reached this point in a narrative propelled forward by the quest pattern. Instead of the paratactic, catalogic succession of the tales of the Wanderings there is a progression in which the consecutive quests are interlocking: the liquidation of each lack is the creation of the conditions for the next lack (this is outcome 8c at page 23, above). The three initial quest sequences comprise Books Five, Six, and Seven, respectively. Book Five opens with the lack created by the hero's previous *nostos* and ends with the *nostos* at Scheria. Calypso's paradise at the navel of the sea embodies the lack resulting from surfeit, a timeless existence away from mortal needs that resembles the eternity of death. Once the hero is on his way toward the uncertainties of mortal life, Leucothea appears in the middle of Poseidon's storm as the donor of the sequence. Her veil fills the slot of the magical agent that helps Odysseus to reach the shore alive. This is pure *nostos*, as we saw earlier: physical survival as a return from certain death.[25] Survival, however, blurs the boundary between human and animal, for the description of the sheltered place where Odysseus falls into an exhausted sleep provides a link to the lair of the boar that young Odysseus hunted long ago on Mount Parnassus.[26] The stunning simile of the ember keeping the "seed of fire" alive far from the center of human civilization (5.488–90) underscores the precarious and liminal nature of Odysseus' condition. Life stripped to the state of pure nature is clinging to survival.

The next sequence, our Book Six, will be concerned with reintegration into humanity as goal. Its initial lack is general disorientation (see function 1 of the Odyssean sequence at page 23, above). Odysseus' first words are an example of how epic's formulaic language can be negotiated between the poet and the hero (*Od.* 6.119–21):

ὤ μοι ἐγώ, τέων αὖτε βροτῶν ἐς γαῖαν ἱκάνω;
ἦ ῥ' οἵ γ' ὑβρισταί τε καὶ ἄγριοι οὐδὲ δίκαιοι,
ἦε φιλόξεινοι, καί σφιν νόος ἐστὶ θεουδής;

Oh my, who are the mortals whose land I've reached?
Would they be brutes and savages, not righteous,
Or could they be hospitable, with fear of the gods in their minds?

These words, which will be repeated after the landing at Ithaca (13.200–2), resonate with Odysseus' speech to his Companions at the beginning of the Cyclops adventure (*Od.* 9.172–6):

ἄλλοι μὲν νῦν μίμνετ', ἐμοὶ ἐρίηρες ἑταῖροι·
αὐτὰρ ἐγὼ σὺν νηΐ τ' ἐμῇ καὶ ἐμοῖς ἑτάροισιν
ἐλθὼν **τῶνδ' ἀνδρῶν πειρήσομαι** οἵ τινές εἰσιν,
ἦ ῥ' οἵ γ' ὑβρισταί τε καὶ ἄγριοι οὐδὲ δίκαιοι,
ἦε φιλόξεινοι, καί σφιν νόος ἐστὶ θεουδής.

The rest of you stay here now, trusted Companions of mine,
but I myself, with my ship and my Companions,
I will go and <u>put these people to the test</u> <to see> who they are,
whether <they are> brutes and savages, not righteous,
or hospitable, with fear of the gods in their minds.

---

[25] See Frame 1978.   [26] *Od.* 5.478–80 = 19.440–2. On this repetition, see Russo 1993.

In Odysseus' narrative, the formulaic sequence functions as complement to πειρήσομαι, 'I will try out', a verb denoting active exploration and voluntary questing; in the narrative told by the poet, on the other hand, the formulaic lines function as anguished questions on the part of a stranded traveler who has no control over his situation and who can only wait for what the narrative, *aoidē*, has in store for him.[27]

The difference between the two scenes, the one from *epos*, the other from *aoidē*, is enhanced by the use of identical, formulaic phrases. The same is true for the sequence as a whole. Viewed in this perspective, the hero's first experiences at Scheria take on unmistakable features of the adventures of the first half of the Wanderings. Or rather, in terms of the poem's linear progression, the Wanderings – coming later in narrative time, though occurring earlier in narrated time – conform to a pattern that is set up at Scheria. Either way, the similarity of two or more episodes invites comparison between them, alerting us to possibilities not actually pursued by the narrative.

Nausicaa is the donor of the new sequence; she is led to Odysseus by Athena, the architect behind the scenes, so no reconnaissance expedition on the part of the hero is necessary. Nausicaa as unattended young female outside the protection of her city and her parents' house should remind the audience of the daughter of Antiphates, king of the Laestrygonians (10.105–8), assuming that this is not the first time they hear the tale. Linearly the Laestrygonian princess will remind them, conversely, of her Phaeacian counterpart. The comparison adds an alternative to the sexual potential of the scene at Scheria; the traveler, as Odysseus' own experience has shown, can get stranded not only to become someone's husband, but also to become someone's food, two opposite perversions of normal hospitality, as brought out by the symmetrical arrangement of the Wanderings adventures discussed earlier.[28] The latter possibility, unused and shaded over in the present instance, is nevertheless real due to the *Odyssey*'s constant play with the basic structure of the quest.

The sequence ends, like the previous one, with a solution that generates the new lack, now that starvation has been averted. Nausicaa's parting words, before she leaves the hero outside the city gates (6.255–315), announce her mother Arete as his next goal (6.303–15) and mention the

---

[27] See, however, πειρήσομαι at 6.126. Note that 9.175–6 is a response to Alkinoos' question at 8.575–6, implying a detached "anthropological" attitude. For the formulaic repetition involved, see also the Epilogue at the end of this book.

[28] Redfield 1983: 237–8.

city's young men, her suitors, as a potential problem for the visitor (6.273–85). As the hero is getting closer to home, the details of the quests begin to resemble the situation at Ithaca, where Penelope's Suitors will be his principal challenge.[29] In the sequence that follows we can recognize Athena in the shape of a young girl as the next donor (7.19–20). She appears when the magical agent she provides has already taken effect: Odysseus is covered in a mist that will hide him from view in his movement through the city to the object of his search, Arete and the hospitality she may, or may not, offer him (7.14–17). Odysseus' answer to Arete's question ("Who gave you those clothes?" 7.238), a narrative recapitulation of the two quest sequences he has just completed (7.241–97), introduces the power of *epos* as means to the hero's goals.

Arete, just like Circe, is both object of search and donor. But whereas Circe performs both functions at the same time (the first quest being nested within the larger one, as we saw), Arete is first Odysseus' goal and donor thereafter; the two sequences are linked through linear temporal progression. By the time we reach the scenes of Book Eight, the hero's goal is neither survival nor hospitality anymore, as in the two previous sequences of Books Six and Seven, but an escort and a return home.

As indicated earlier, we may see Odysseus' tale of his Wanderings and its narrative setting as part of a quest sequence, with Odysseus' being taunted by Euryalos (8.158–64) corresponding to Propp's function 12 (page 19, above: "The hero is tested, interrogated, attacked, etc., which prepares the way for his receiving either a magical agent or helper") and the telling of the tale of the Wanderings (Books Nine–Twelve) to function 13 ("the hero reacts to the actions of the future donor"). The conclusion of the episode must then be in Book Thirteen, where we witness the hero's transferral, by magical ship (function 14), to the object of his search (function 15). On the poem's reading as the coalescence of a quest and a return pattern (Propp's extended sequence), this is where we would expect the quest pattern, many times repeated and negotiated between hero and poet, to change into the return sequence with its stereotyped vicissitudes. Now that the hero has accomplished his *nostos*, the perspective, it seems, can shift and *nostos* can begin to mean what it means for those to whom the hero returns.

---

[29] This aspect of the poem has been illuminated by Louden 1999, who also draws attention (p. 15) to the importance of the Companions as possible rivals for Odysseus in his relation with Circe.

However, this is not a transition that is signaled or coded by the narrative. Nothing changes, in fact.[30] Odysseus lands on an unknown island, as he has done many times before. Disoriented and uncertain of his surroundings (and repeating the anguished words he had also uttered at Scheria: 13.200–2), he encounters a youthful character, Athena in disguise and in the role of donor (13.221–5), resembling Hermes in the Circe episode and Nausicaa at Scheria. The story Odysseus tells her, the first of his Cretan Lies (13.256–86), is another instance of his use of language as self-presentation to his donor (function 5 at page 23, above). The magical device Athena has to offer is the hero's metamorphosis into the disguise of an old beggar (13.429–38); she directs him to the whereabouts of his first object of search, Eumaios, whose function it will soon be to direct the hero, at *his* turn (being a donor now) to the ultimate quest object. The similarity of Athena to Hermes and Nausicaa in the earlier adventures points up similarities not only between Eumaios and Circe (another swineherd), but also between Eumaios and Alkinoos.[31] The Phaeacian king and Eumaios are paradigmatically linked as recipients of the hero's tale (Eumaios gets to hear the second Cretan Lie, 14.192–359), which aligns them, in the narrative pattern we are exploring here, as donors in the hero's quests.

After Eumaios has turned from goal into donor who guides Odysseus to his own palace (a moment reminiscent of his entry into the city of the Phaeacians),[32] the pattern becomes less pronounced, but it persists. Penelope, the key element in the hero's ultimate *nostos*, is helper first; she is the audience of the third Cretan Lie (19.165–202), which aligns her with a host of earlier audiences, donors from Eumaios all the way back to Aiolos. We can see in the bow and the axes the magical agent she provides for the hero, who will be able to overcome his adversaries in the bow contest. There are, of course, characters who help Odysseus more than does Penelope in his fight against the Suitors, but structurally the bow and its contest is the essential step toward the hero's completion of his quest. As he comes very close to the completion of the final *nostos*, the hero's own domestic possessions come to fill the slot of the pattern's magical agent.

---

[30] This is not the place to engage in a critique of Propp's model, but note that the *Odyssey* provides evidence for the suspicion that Propp's functions 25–29 (arrival, difficult task, new appearance for the hero) are, in fact, no more than a variant of the earlier functions 11–17 (arrival at abode of villain, combat, branding of the hero); see Csapo 2005: 210. Propp himself (1968: 102) notes that the two rarely occur as pairs in one and the same folktale.
[31] See Louden 1999: 50–68.
[32] The entrance into the palace has paradigmatic connections with Circe as well: see Chapter 5.

The climax of this development can be seen in the final sequence, in which recognition and acceptance by Penelope is the goal; the helper is, as earlier, Athena, who magically restores Odysseus' former youth and charm. But a more intriguing item, arguably playing the role of the magical agent, is the marriage bed immovably built by Odysseus himself on the taproot of an olive tree which serves as major recognition token.[33] Through the bed Odysseus and Penelope are donors to themselves, enabling the accomplishment of the quest that is their reunion, the one by building the bed as *sēma*, the other by using it as *sēma* against its encoder.

We can set out the story pattern across the successive scenes of the Return in Table 2.2.

Compared with the series of quests in the Wanderings the reconnaissance mission pattern has receded, due to the fact, of course, that Odysseus is now alone and that toward the end of the series the territory in which he has to operate is known. Instead, storytelling as interaction with the donor (function 5) is now very prominent, allowing yet another kind of "nesting," as the hero's *epos*, with all its quests and subquests, becomes part of a quest sequence told in the poet's *aoidē*. And instead of a mere repetition of the pattern across a series of separate adventures there is causal concatenation: each liquidation of a lack and attainment of a goal creates a new lack and goal. Accordingly, outcome 8c (see pages 23 and 33) is the preferred final function.

There is, however, an unexpected earlier donor, if that is the right term for him, whose "gift" encompasses not only Circe, but also the remainder of the Wanderings as well as the actual *nostos* story all the way to the end of the poem. Polyphemos' prayer to his father Poseidon, made after the successful if painful escape from the Cyclops' cave, calls for Odysseus' late and miserable return, the loss of his Companions, his arrival on a foreign ship, and the evil he will find in his house (*Od.* 9.534–5). We will discuss this prayer in detail in Chapter 7, along with Poseidon's vindictive wrath, which constitutes the plot of the entire poem. Here we note that Polyphemus' speech action, performed in reaction to Odysseus' verbal taunts, corresponds typologically with the action of the donor of the quest sequence. As in other cases in the *Odyssey*, the donor's action follows upon speech performed by Odysseus, and we may perhaps see Odysseus' fateful

---

[33] See Nagler 1996: 157 on the symbolism of the olive tree, characterizing it (n. 35) as "the axis-symbol informing the physico-political concept of the *oikos*." Note that a similarly axial tree, the pine "reaching into heaven" on Calypso's island (οὐρανομήκης, *Od.* 5.239), serves as magical agent in a previous sequence, equally due to Odysseus' skill as a craftsman (*Od.* 5.243–61; 23.192–201).

Table 2.2 *The basic story pattern in the Return*

Function	Episodes								
	Scheria	Nausicaa	Arete	Ithaca	Eumaios	Telemachos	Palace	Suitors	Penelope
4. Helper/donor	Leucothea	Athena 6.149–85?	Athena 7.241–97	Alkinoos	Athena	Athena	Eumaios	Penelope	Pen/Od 23.310–41
5. Storytelling	–			*Apologoi* (9–12)	1st Liar story	X	2nd Liar story	3rd Liar story	
6. Magical agent	κρήδεμνον (5.346)	rejuvenation (6.229–35)	mist (7.15)	ships	beggar disguise	rejuvenation	–	bow	bed
7. Goal	survival	Nausicaa	*xeinia*	transportation	Eumaios	recognition	escort	killing Suitors	marriage
8a. *Nostos*/rescue									
8b. No *nostos*									
8c. New *nostos*	X	X	X	X	X	X	X	X	X

self-disclosure as paradigmatically related to the various stories he tells about himself in order to secure the help of a future donor (*Od.* 9.502–5):

Κύκλωψ, αἴ κέν τίς σε καταθνητῶν ἀνθρώπων
ὀφθαλμοῦ εἴρηται ἀεικελίην ἀλαωτύν,
φάσθαι Ὀδυσσῆα πτολιπόρθιον ἐξαλαῶσαι,
υἱὸν Λαέρτεω, Ἰθάκῃ ἔνι οἰκί' ἔχοντα.

Cyclops! Should any of the mortal humans
ask you about the unseemly blinding of your eye,
tell that <it was> Odysseus the City-Sacker <who> blinded you,
the son of Laertes, who has his home on Ithaca.

Not that Odysseus acquires the use of any magical agent or that Polyphemos is a "donor" in any direct sense. But in creating the problems that the hero has to solve, the Cyclops can as "anti-donor" be said to enable the eventual completion of the hero's quest. And as in the other cases Odysseus gets what he wants: he asks for *kleos* and will eventually get it, in the form of the poem for which the Cyclops lays the foundation.

We can observe, then, that the oppositions between *epos* and *aoidē* and between the quest and the return sequence are bridged by the recurrence of a single narrative pattern. The observation of this pattern has possible consequences for the conception of the *Odyssey* as oral poetry. The considerable surface variety in the narrative shows that this repetition is not formulaic necessity or a requirement for oral composition in the way envisaged by Parry and Lord.[34] But the recurrence does not seem to be straightforwardly intentional or "untraditional" either. Both from the point of view of the composition of the story and from the point of view of its reception and comprehension the pattern's workings can be noticed and appreciated (and emphasized by a performer) only through multiple performances, allowing both performers and audiences to see connections between the narrative present and episodes yet to come in narrative time. The numerous narrative sequences function as transparent sheets placed on top of each other in a diaphanous layering that allows us not only to see the considerable overlap between the various tales, but also the ways in which each multiform can highlight or shade over a given feature or theme. In addition, formulaic language can be put to new uses here – over and beyond its usefulness for oral composition and comprehension – as a means of highlighting the links between scenes that occur at considerable

---

[34] See also Powell 1977 for an understanding of a repeated pattern as conducive to oral composition.

distance from each other. The Epilogue at the end of the book will collect and discuss some of the more striking cases we will encounter, and suggest a cognitive framework for their understanding.

The recurrence is especially important for the relation between the Wanderings and the Return. With its divine donors and magical agents the quest pattern seems particularly suited to the Wanderings with their unquestioned folktale quality. But this essential feature of *epos* spills over into *aoidē*, creating a basis for viewing the events of the Return through the lens of the quest. Immediate results of such a vision include the paradigmatic relationship between all recipients of Odysseus' tales, from Aiolos to Penelope or the alignment of Penelope with her divine homologues in the Otherworld. In the chapters that follow we will pursue this vision by shifting the perspective from the hero alone in his quest to those around him. In looking at the hero's Companions and the Suitors in his house as multiforms of each another, we will see that the Wanderings provide essential exemplars for the crimes committed in Odysseus' house in his absence. Those crimes revolve in no small measure around food, in particular meat, and the contexts and modalities of its consumption. Chapter 3 will provide some background to this paradigmatic function of meat as a catalyst of crime and transgression.

CHAPTER 3

Meat in myth and life

"Fish? Where does Homer say that one eats that?
Who of the Achaeans did? It's meat they ate, and only roasted.
He never had anyone of them boil it."
(Euboulos, *Fr.* 120)

"You know that during the Trojan War
Homer at the heroes' feasts does not entertain them with fish
– even though they are on the seashore in the Hellespont –
nor on boiled meat, but on grilled meat only."
(Plato, *Republic* 404b–c)

In his famous reflection on the heroic predicament, Sarpedon, important ally of the Trojans in the *Iliad*, speaks about the privileges of the *basileus* in his native Lycia, where heroes enjoy the seats of honor at the feast along with choice meats and numerous goblets of wine (*Il.* 12.310–21):

Γλαῦκε τί ἤ δή νῶϊ τετιμήμεσθα μάλιστα
ἕδρῃ τε κρέασίν τε ἰδὲ πλείοις δεπάεσσιν
ἐν Λυκίῃ, πάντες δὲ θεοὺς ὣς εἰσορόωσι,
καὶ τέμενος νεμόμεσθα μέγα Ξάνθοιο παρ' ὄχθας
καλὸν φυταλιῆς καὶ ἀρούρης πυροφόροιο;
τώ νῦν χρὴ Λυκίοισι μέτα πρώτοισιν ἐόντας
ἑστάμεν ἠδὲ μάχης καυστείρης ἀντιβολῆσαι,
ὄφρά τις ὧδ' εἴπῃ Λυκίων πύκα θωρηκτάων·
οὐ μὰν ἀκλεέες Λυκίην κάτα κοιρανέουσιν
ἡμέτεροι βασιλῆες, ἔδουσί τε πίονα μῆλα
οἶνόν τ' ἔξαιτον μελιηδέα· ἀλλ' ἄρα καὶ ἲς
ἐσθλή, ἐπεὶ Λυκίοισι μέτα πρώτοισι μάχονται.

Glaucos, why do we stand in so much honor,
with preferred seating <at the feast> and meats and full wine goblets,
<back> in Lycia? – all are looking up to us as gods
and we command a large precinct on the banks of the Xanthus,
with vineyards and wheat-bearing land.
That is why among the foremost Lycian fighters

we must stand and brave the caustic battle,
so that he may speak as follows, one of the densely armored Lycians:
'They are most certainly not without *kleos* as they rule Lycia,
our kings, and they eat our fattened sheep
and drink exquisite wine, sweet as honey; but their might
is valorous, since they fight among the foremost of the Lycians'.

The justification of the extensive privileges enjoyed by the Lycian chieftains is their prowess in battle, and it is a common rebuke on the Iliadic battlefield to say to a hero that his prowess and contribution to the battle do not match his participation in the feasts.[1] Conversely, the enjoyment of wine and fattened sheep is compensation for the hardships and high risks of heroic life. As Sarpedon continues to say, the "spirits of death" (κῆρες ... θανάτοιο, 12.326) surround the heroes everywhere in battle; whoever does not kill first will be killed himself. The compensation for such heroic death in battle is *kleos*, the hero's epic glory. The two types of compensation, meat and glory, are in fact interrelated: the privilege to enjoy choice meats is for the hero while he is alive what *kleos* is for him after his death.[2]

Sarpedon's account points up the importance of meat in heroic society as symbolic capital. The Homeric hero stands at the center of his community in what has been called a "chiefdom" economy, in which power, unstable and informal, depends on the wealth and military prowess of the individual *basileus*.[3] The hero in Sarpedon's Lycia enjoys a disproportionately large share of the community's goods, but as other Homeric cases show, from his position at the top of the food chain the chieftain can act as redistributor, sending goods back into the community. This happens in the Pylos of the stories of Nestor's youthful exploits, where Neleus first takes out his share of raided cattle and then distributes the rest among the people. The distribution and its wording are instructive (*Il.* 11.704–5):

> ἐξέλετ᾽ ἄσπετα πολλά· τὰ δ᾽ ἄλλ᾽ ἐς δῆμον ἔδωκε
> **δαιτρεύειν**, μή τίς οἱ ἀτεμβόμενος κίοι **ἴσης**.
>
> He took out innumerable head of cattle and the remainder he gave to the people
> <u>to divide among themselves</u>, so that no one would be cheated of his <u>equal share</u>.

---

[1] For example, *Il.* 4.338–48 (Agamemnon to Odysseus); 8.161–6 (Hector to Diomedes); 8.228–44 (Agamemnon to the Achaeans).
[2] On the symbolic significance of food, see also Griffin 1980: 14–17; on food and feasting in Homer, Rundin 1996.
[3] Seaford 1994: 22; cf. Rundin 1996: 182–3.

The same formula is used for the distribution of the sheep raided from the cave of the Cyclops (*Od.* 9.549–51):[4]

δάσσαμεθ', ὡς μή τις μοι ἀτεμβόμενος κίοι **ἴσης**.
ἀρνειὸν δ' ἐμοὶ οἴῳ ἐϋκνήμιδες ἑταῖροι
μήλων **δαιομένων** δόσαν ἔξοχα.

We divided <it all>, so that no one would go cheated of his fair <share>,
but the ram, to me alone my well-greaved Companions
as the sheep were being divided, they gave it as a special share.

Odysseus as chieftain receives an honorary portion of the goods to be distributed, which can be called *geras* in Homeric parlance. The division is "equal" (ἴσης, presumably modifying a suppressed μοίρης, 'portion, share'), but also "equitable" insofar as it is considered just that one or more members of the group receive more than others. The surplus value apportioned to the chieftain may enter into a prestige economy in which reciprocal bonds between aristocrats are created and maintained by means of gift exchange.[5]

Heroic feasting

An important subcategory of such prestige goods is meat, in particular, beef. The central terms in the distributional scheme for the division of spoils or raided herds or flocks, δαίειν, δαιτρεύειν, 'divide', 'partition', δάσσασθαι, δατέομαι, 'divide (among themselves)', as well as the adjective ἴσος are equally used for the actual consumption of the animal. The central term here is δαίς, commonly translated as "feast" or "banquet." But its transparent connection with the verb δαίειν highlights the feast as a moment of distribution in which aristocratic bonds and balances are created or confirmed by means of the division of the slaughtered animal. The idea of division and distribution is abundantly present in the following lines, describing the feast enjoyed by Telemachos after arriving at Nestor's palace in Pylos (*Od.* 3.65–6):

οἱ δ' ἐπεὶ ὤπτησαν κρέ' ὑπέρτατα καὶ ἐρύσαντο
μοίρας δασσάμενοι δαίνυντ' ἐρικυδέα δαῖτα.

And they, when they had roasted the outer meat and pulled it <from the fire>, after dividing the portions among themselves they dined on a *dais* rich in *kudos*.

---

[4] See also *Od.* 9.42, the division of the spoils of Ismaros, city of the Cicones, between Odysseus and his men.
[5] Rundin 1996.

Heroic feasting

The idea of distribution is present in no less than four of the five words in the second line, from μοίρας, the portion allotted to each participant, through the two related verbs for dining and dividing, to the feast-division, δαῖτα, itself. The meal as *dais*, then, highlights the symbolic value of food, in particular meat, in opposition to such terms as *deipnon* or *dorpon*, which denote the meal as a mere act of food consumption.[6]

The *dais*, consisting of the consumption of surplus economic products, is typically an event for aristocratic males, but its organization is modeled on the distribution events in which the chieftain and the community at large participate. Both are "equal" and "equitable" as signaled by the adjective ἴσος, and in the case of the feast of distribution it is not the shares that are characterized in this way, but the *dais* itself. The typical formula comes at the end of the following (in itself formulaic) description:[7]

> αὐτὰρ ἐπεὶ κατὰ μῆρε κάη καὶ σπλάγχνα πάσαντο,
> μίστυλλόν τ' ἄρα τἄλλα καὶ ἀμφ' ὀβελοῖσιν ἔπειραν,
> ὤπτησάν τε περιφραδέως, ἐρύσαντό τε πάντα.
> αὐτὰρ ἐπεὶ παύσαντο πόνου τετύκοντό τε δαῖτα
> δαίνυντ', οὐδέ τι θυμὸς ἐδεύετο **δαιτὸς ἐΐσης**.

> But when the thigh-bones had been burnt and they had tasted the organs,
> cut up the remaining parts and put it on skewers,
> they roasted it carefully and took everything <from the fire>.
> When they were done with the effort and had prepared the *dais*,
> they dined; nor was <anyone's> *thumos* left wanting <u>in the fair distribution</u>.

Again the "equal" distribution does not prevent some portions from being more equal than others.[8] One or more of the banqueters can receive a special share, as when Agamemnon "honors" (γέραιρεν, a verb related to γέρας) Ajax with the back of the sacrificial animal, a particularly honorific share (*Il.* 7.321–2). The guest at a *dais* typically receives this share: Menelaos offers his guest Telemachos the back of the slaughtered bull as γέρας, 'portion of honor' (*Od.* 4.65–6). The equivalent part of the slaughtered

---

[6] Saïd 1979: 14. Note that when meals are referred to primarily from the point of view of food intake in heroic contexts, δόρπον or δεῖπνον rather than δαίς is used, e.g., *Il.* 19.171, 208. Saïd 1979: 14–23 offers a detailed account of the δαίς in all its aspects; on the politics of food and feasting in Homer, see Rundin 1996; on Homeric feasting in general, see Sherratt 2004. For Mycenaean feasting, see Bendall 2004 and Palaima 2004 as well as the other articles in Wright 2004. The social and symbolic importance of meat division in the Greek world does not stop with Homer; see Grottanelli 1989. For meat division in other cultures, see, e.g., Stevenson 1937; Baudy 1983; Hayden 2001.

[7] *Il.* 1.464–8; cf. *Il.* 1.602; 2.431; 7.320; 23.56; *Od.* 16.479; 19.425. On sacrifice as a type-scene, see Kitts 2011.

[8] A point made in detail by Saïd 1979: 19–21; see also Schmitt-Pantel 1992: 49–50.

pig is what Odysseus offers the singer Demodokos (*Od.* 8.474–83) and what the faithful swineherd Eumaios offers the beggar Odysseus at the humble *dais* in his hut (*Od.* 14.432–8):

> ἂν δὲ συβώτης
> ἵστατο **δαιτρεύσων**· περὶ γὰρ φρεσὶν αἴσιμα ᾔδη.
> καὶ τὰ μὲν ἕπταχα πάντα **διεμμοιρᾶτο** δαΐζων·
> τὴν μὲν ἴαν Νύμφῃσι καὶ Ἑρμῇ, Μαιάδος υἷι,
> θῆκεν ἐπευξάμενος, τὰς δ' ἄλλας **νεῖμεν** ἑκάστῳ·
> νώτοισιν δ' Ὀδυσῆα διηνεκέεσσι **γέραιρεν**
> ἀργιόδοντος ὑός, κύδαινε δὲ θυμὸν ἄνακτος.

And the swineherd,
he stood up in order to divide <the meat>; he knew in his spirit
   what was fitting and decent:
and he cut up the meat, portioning it out in seven shares.
One share to the Nymphs and to Hermes the son of Maia
he put invoking them with prayer; the other shares he apportioned to
   each,
and he honored Odysseus with slices cut from the length of the chine
of the white-tusked boar, and this token of honor delighted the spirit of
   his master.

Eumaios' *dais* stands in stark contrast to feasts held elsewhere on the island. Not only does the swineherd respect the fundamental rules of hospitality in treating the stranger as the group's principal member; he also includes the gods in the division. The immortals "dine" (δαίνυνθ', *Il.* 9.535) on the hecatombs and in fact the *dais*'s "equality" and "fairness" explicitly includes the gods, as appears from the divine version of the formula mentioned above in Zeus' declaration of appreciation for Hector and the Trojans (*Il.* 4.48–9; 24.69–70):[9]

> οὐ γάρ μοί ποτε βωμὸς ἐδεύετο δαιτὸς ἐΐσης,
> λοιβῆς τε κνίσης τε· τὸ γὰρ λάχομεν **γέρας** ἡμεῖς.

My altar was never left wanting in the fair distribution,
of libation and the smell of burnt sacrifice; for that is what *we* receive
   as share of honor.

The *dais* is thus always a sacrifice. The gods are always participants in the *dais*, but their share in the distribution is qualitatively different from that of the humans. This underscores the fundamental divide between the

---

[9] At *Od.* 1.26 Poseidon is actually present at the *dais* of the Aethiopians, as is Zeus at *Il.* 1.424. The gods frequently have a *dais* among themselves, e.g., *Il.* 1.601–2; 15.95.

Heroic feasting

human and the divine, but at the same time establishes the feast-division as an essential channel of communication between the two realms.[10]

In spite of this essential religious component many Homeric feasts are motivated by human occasions, such as the arrival of a stranger, the reconciliation between two parties (*Il.* 1.457–74), a wedding (*Od.* 4.3–4), or a funeral (*Il.* 24.802). In the *Iliad* the *dais* is frequently the ritual prelude to important and much-needed moments of decision-making among the Achaean chieftains. "Dine (δαίνυ[11]) a *dais* for the elders," says Nestor to Agamemnon (*Il.* 9.70–5); "it is fitting for you to do so; ... you receive all the goods (πᾶσά τοι ἐσθ᾽ ὑποδεξίη) and rule over many. When many have gathered, you will be persuaded by the one who puts forward the best advice." Agamemnon as overlord and military commander is also the principal distributor among the Achaeans.[12]

The feasts he gives are "equal," but not reciprocal; Agamemnon dines more often than he is dined. His feasts serve as ritual preliminaries to important deliberations.[13] The feast to which Nestor exhorts him will result in the sending of the Embassy to Achilles, in whose tent the arrival of the guests is the occasion for a new feast, this time with Achilles in the role of distributor (ἀτὰρ κρέα νεῖμεν Ἀχιλλεύς, 'but the meats Achilles distributed', *Il.* 9.217). The rapid succession of two feasts lends extra meaning to Odysseus' first-person version of the epic equal-division formula (δαιτὸς ἐΐσης οὐκ ἐπιδευεῖς, '<We are> not left wanting in the equal feast-division', *Il.* 9.225), but presumably the ability to consume large quantities of beef is a test of heroic manhood.

The *dais*, then, is an important occasion on which a community reaffirms its cohesion and maintains its relations with the gods. Successful *daites* are the typical manifestation of a healthy community. If a traveler's arrival is not itself the occasion for a *dais*, he will typically find the community he reaches in the act of sacrificing bulls and dividing their meat. This happens to Tydeus at Thebes (*Il.* 4.385–6) and to Telemachos at Pylos (*Od.* 3.4–9). And anywhere in the Homeric world, from Lycia to Ithaca, it is the *basileus*, owner of the *temenos* and beneficiary of its agricultural yield, who is expected to participate in the *dais*, if not actually to initiate it. "Telemachos commands the <royal> precincts (*temenea*) and dines the equal *daites*" is what Odysseus' mother Anticleia tells her son (*Od.* 11.185–6) in the

---

[10] Burkert 1983; Vernant 1991.
[11] A unique use of the verb in the active voice; the middle is the standard use for participation in the *dais*.
[12] See Hitch 2009: 141–203, noting the connection between Agamemnon's sacrificial authority and Achilles' absence.
[13] Agamemnon's equal feasts: *Il.* 2.402–32; 7.313–23.

Underworld in answer to his question whether in his long absence some "best of the Achaeans" has married his wife, thus disinheriting her son.

The dangers of the *dais*

> "Unjust is the mind of the leaders of the community, for whom on account of their great hubris suffering of many pains lies ahead. They cannot control their greed, nor do they know how to arrange the festivity present in the civilized feast (*dais*)."
>
> (Solon, *Fr.* 4.7–10W)

Little does Anticleia know that in the meantime since her death the *dais* at Ithaca has been appropriated by the Suitors, who deplete the resources of the royal *temenos*. Their prolonged act of extreme transgression stands naturally at the thematic center of the poem, but we can appreciate it better if we approach dining in the *Odyssey* in general from the perspective just developed, which draws mostly on the *Iliad*. The feast that in the *Iliad* functions as a self-evident heroic habit whose function or occurrence is never questioned, becomes thematically important in the *Odyssey* in various ways. Feasts in the *Odyssey* tend to attract attention to themselves, in the limiting case simply by being good or bad and thus as a foil for their opposite. The elaborate detail, for example, in which the sacrificial meal in honor of Athena in Nestor's palace is described (*Od.* 3.418–74) may well reflect the perspective of Telemachos and his Ithacan companions, who presumably have not seen a proper sacrifice in many years, if ever. The sacrifice, including the gilding of the bull's horns, highlights the contrast between the flourishing society of Nestor's kingdom, where human and divine relations are maintained and respected, and the diseased situation at Ithaca, where the *dais* is perverted in all its aspects.

Even feasts that are in themselves beyond reproach can be problematic in the *Odyssey*. For the guest in whose honor the feasting takes place there is the risk of delay and being detained: his *nostos* may come to be jeopardized, the obverse of the hospitality that both Odysseus and his son enjoy. The traveler may also pose this risk himself, when his tale is too long to be told without significant loss of time. The prime occasion on which, as we saw in Chapter 2, *epos* threatens to take on a life of its own and eclipse *aoidē*, the progress of the matrix narrative itself, is the *dais*.

But feasts are frequently dangerous in a more direct way. The *dais* can become an occasion for *neîkos*, 'strife', 'quarrel', as in the first song of Demodokos, which tells of the *neîkos* of Achilles and Odysseus that occurred θεῶν ἐν δαιτὶ θαλείῃ, 'at the flourishing feast of the gods'

(8.76). And there is the constant possibility that the Suitors' feasting will devolve into a brawl so that the *dais* is "shamed" (16.292–4; 19.11–13; cf. 18.402–4). Feasts in the *Odyssey* are often in themselves inappropriate, dangerous, or even deadly. Odysseus' Companions are surprised by the returning Cicones while enjoying an undue *dais* (9.45–51) and in the ensuing fighting many of them are killed. Agamemnon and *his* companions were murdered while dining, the hero himself butchered like the beef on which he was feasting, and his Companions slaughtered "like white-tusked boars, for the feast of a wealthy man." In the end their corpses "were scattered among the tables laden with food," and "the floor of the dining hall was seething all over with blood" (δάπεδον δ' ἅπαν αἵματι θῦεν, 11.420).[14]

Dining to destroy

The reports on Agamemnon's disastrous return foreshadow the paradigmatically linked but opposite homecoming of Odysseus, which also finds its climax in the *dais*. The phrase just quoted recurs at 22.309 (cf. 24.185), at the height of the massacre in Odysseus' *megaron*, the Suitors' last feast. Why do the Suitors do what they do? Their collective name, μνηστῆρες, indicates that they woo Penelope, but their prolonged and destructive presence in Odysseus' house seems motivated more by an intention to force Penelope to confirm her status as a widow and acknowledge that she is available for marriage. The chief Suitor Antinoos says as much, putting the blame for the depletion of the resources of Odysseus' house on Penelope herself: she has been postponing her remarriage, which apparently is socially mandatory, for three years (2.85–92). His words are spoken in the embarrassed silence following Telemachos' passionate plea in the Ithacan assembly; there may be personal sympathy for his situation, but no one stands up to assist him in defending his case.

Does the *dēmos* refuse to intervene because the conflict is considered to be a private matter? Or could the Suitors' presence in Odysseus' house even be justified from a communal point of view? Telemachos tries, without success, to frame the conflict as a dispute between Odysseus and the "Achaeans," with the Suitors being used to force Odysseus to "pay back" for some wrong committed (2.71–4). Bringing the conflict from the private into the public sphere would make it easier to recover the losses incurred by Odysseus' household (2.74–8). But in a second speech, he has to admit that his mother is the problem. He cannot resolve the issue

---

[14] *Od.* 11.409–20 (Agamemnon's ghost to Odysseus); cf. 4.534–5 (Menelaos to Telemachos).

simply by sending her back to the house of her father, he says in much-disputed lines (2.130–7), since he, or his father's estate, would have to "pay back much" (πόλλ' ἀποτίνειν, 2.132) to Penelope's father, presumably referring to the dowry paid for her by Icarius to Odysseus.[15]

There is also the possibility that the Ithacan community refrains from intervening because the Suitors' actions are in themselves sanctioned by the community. In that case the Suitors would technically not be suitors. Winfried Schmitz has argued that the behavior of the Suitors goes back to a social reprimand system (*Rügebrauch*) that is attested for societies of lesser complexity with weakly developed juridical systems: the house of someone who violates a norm for socially acceptable behavior is invaded by a group of local youths (or other "unemployed" or marginal members of the community), who consume all its resources (*ausfressen*), thus forcing the owner to change his behavior or be ruined.[16] The reprehensible act to be censured in this case would be Penelope's: her refusal as a widow to be available for a new marriage.

If this is indeed the social reality behind the conflict at Ithaca, then its epic rendition has changed much of the original mechanism. The intruders are not local unemployed youths, but young aristocrats, most of whom are not even local. And they seem genuinely interested, as social equals and in spite of the considerable difference in age, in marrying Penelope. But more sinister motives are likely involved: according to Eurymachos, pleading for their lives when the beggar has revealed himself as the returning Odysseus, the real culprit was Antinoos, who was not so much interested in the marriage as in supplanting Odysseus as king of Ithaca (22.49–53). The alleged target of this Suitor's action would then not be Odysseus (who is assumed dead), nor even Penelope (who is no more than an excuse), but Telemachos, whose wealth has to be so diminished that his claims to being the "best" among the Ithacans as basis for taking his father's place in the island hierarchy will be rendered futile. In trying to ambush him on his way home from the Peloponnese the Suitors make a direct attempt on Telemachos' life (*Od.* 4.669–72).

We may say, then, that a local marriage dispute has been raised to the level of a conflict on an epic – even cosmic – scale. It has come to function within the framework of the quest and return story pattern, and its

---

[15] The question of the financial aspects of Penelope's (re)marriage remains problematic even after Perysinakis' attempt (1991) to show that the passages that seem to mention dowry are in reality referring to a bride-price paid by the successful suitor to the bride's father (1.277; 2.197). The present passage seems to refer to something more formal than a gift if goods have to be "paid back," and the value of the transaction must be considerable if it is comparable with the property destroyed by the Suitors.

[16] Schmitz 2004: 324–7.

principal elements, the insular queen, the group of young men, and the excessive consumption of meat, come to resonate with the paradigmatically related stories in the poem. Whatever the original or proper justification of the home invasion was, the consumption of the absent master's animals has been magnified into an act of almost grotesque transgression. The destruction of the king's property is accomplished by literally eating his wealth. We find expressions such as τρύχειν, 'wear out, deplete' (1.248; 16.125), or terms from the animal world, such as κατακείρειν, 'shave off', for the destructive grazing of ruminants,[17] or δαρδάπτειν, 'devour', putting the Suitors in the role of hungry predators (14.92; 16.315). Perhaps the most extreme characterization of the Suitors' crimes comes in the formulaic phrase οἵ τοι βίοτον κατέδουσι, 'who are eating up your βίοτος',[18] a term applying to the absent master's livelihood, his means of subsistence, but hinting at the idea of his (and his son's) physical life.[19] The Suitors' transgression, then, is a major property crime verging notionally on murder or even cannibalism. This gruesome and seemingly exaggerated understanding of their crime resonates with actions carried out elsewhere in the poem, as we will see in later chapters.

The Suitors' continuous feasting in Odysseus' *megaron* is cast, furthermore, in terms pertaining to warfare and meat consumption in a heroic context. It is framed in verbs built on the δαι-root that, as we saw, are typically used for the division of the booty of a plundered city.[20] But whereas in the heroic world the division of booty and the distribution of animals in the *dais* is the natural sequel to, and reward for, the sack of a city, the Suitors are intent on sacking Odysseus' house in and through the distribution and consumption of his animals.

The reversed order is, as Suzanne Saïd has systematically shown,[21] an outright perversion of the heroic feast. No risk is involved for the Suitors, and no military achievement justifies the feasting, which in the heroic code, as we saw, is strictly related to honor and martial excellence. The Suitors reduce heroic warfare to the innocent and harmless boys' games of discus and javelin throwing (*Od.* 4.626; 17.168). The asymmetry resulting from one *basileus* dining others more often than he is dined himself (in the *Iliad* the consequence of Agamemnon's power and resources) is at Ithaca

---

[17] 1.378; 4.686; 18.144; 22.36, 369; 23.356; 24.459; cf. *Il.* 11.560.
[18] *Od.* 11.116; 13.396, 428; 15.32; cf. βίοτον νήποινον ἔδουσι (*Od.* 1.160; 14.377; 18.280).
[19] For example, *Od.* 1.287; 2.218 (βίοτον καὶ νόστον); cf. *Il.* 16.787 (βιότοιο τελευτήν).
[20] For example, 3.316 = 15.13 κτήματα δασσάμενοι; 20.216 κτήματα δάσσασθαι 'to divide his possessions among themselves'.
[21] Saïd 1979: 23–41; see also Saïd 2011: 64–9.

directed at annihilating the resources of the most powerful house. And in the master's absence there is no principal distributor, who divides the meat and ensures the "equal *dais*" and its portions of honor. Instead, the meat is cut and divided by an anonymous δαιτρός, 'divider' (1.141; 17.331).

The disastrous lack of reciprocity at Ithaca is denounced by Telemachos at the beginning of the tale (*Od.* 1.374–80 = 2.139–45):

> ἄλλας δ' ἀλεγύνετε δαῖτας,
> ὑμὰ κτήματ' ἔδοντες, ἀμειβόμενοι κατὰ οἴκους.
> εἰ δ' ὕμιν δοκέει τόδε λωΐτερον καὶ ἄμεινον
> ἔμμεναι, ἀνδρὸς ἑνὸς βίοτον **νήποινον** ὀλέσθαι,
> κείρετ'· ἐγὼ δὲ θεοὺς ἐπιβώσομαι αἰὲν ἐόντας,
> αἴ κέ ποθι Ζεὺς δῷσι παλίντιτα ἔργα γενέσθαι·
> **νήποινοί** κεν ἔπειτα δόμων ἔντοσθεν ὄλοισθε.

> Prepare feasts other than these,
> eating your own possessions, distributing the burden equally among houses.
> And if this seems to you preferable and better,
> that the substance of one single man is destroyed <u>without compensation</u>,
> then shear off <this house>; but I will call on the gods who live forever,
> and if ever Zeus grants for acts of requital to happen,
> you may then perish <u>without compensation</u>, in this very house.

The adjective νήποινος denotes the absence of ποινή, 'retribution', and so signals a lack of negative reciprocity, or compensation through revenge. It is true that at the last moment, when Odysseus has shot his arrow through the throat of Antinoos, Eurymachos offers substantial compensation; he promises that each Suitor will "give back" twenty oxen as well as bronze and gold to make up for all that has been eaten (22.55–8: an ironic flashback to 2.203–4, where the same Eurymachos says that compensation or restitution is out of the question).

In terms of a distinction developed for the *Iliad* by Donna Wilson (2002), he offers "ransom" (ἄποινα) for himself and his companions, without using the term, presenting the restitution instead, implicitly, as ποινή. This is reminiscent of Agamemnon's offer of much wealth to Achilles, relayed by Odysseus at the *dais*.[22] Both Achilles and Odysseus

---

[22] Wilson herself (2002: 77) distinguishes Eurymachos' offer from that of Agamemnon, calling it a "culturally acceptable offer of *poinē*." It is true that Eurymachos does offer an admission of guilt, calling Odysseus' accusation αἴσιμα, 'reasonable', and acknowledging that ἀτάσθαλα, 'wanton, criminal', things have been done. But the singling out of Antinoos as the only one who is responsible for the crimes is a grossly inadequate characterization of what was a collective

forcefully reject the offer, in remarkably similar words (on which, see Chapter 8).[23] The compensation they desire is entirely different from material restitution. For Odysseus, ποινή requires nothing less than blood, for which no further compensation will be given: if the Suitors committed their crimes νήποινοι, then Odysseus will be νήποινος in destroying them.

The association of the terms ποινή and νήποινος with the sphere of murder in connection with the Suitors' meals leads to another reciprocity. As Saïd notes (1979: 25), just as the criminal meals of the Suitors are referred to in terms of murder, so their own murder, as νήποινος as their own transgression, is framed as a meal. Their *dais* of death is introduced by the lyre, called by Odysseus in grim humor the "delight" (ἀνάθημα) of the feast (21.430),[24] turning into a bow, and the singer turning into a hero. The song (μολπή), the companion of the *dais*, is the bow's twanging. The Suitors indulge and perish in the perversion of the *dais*.

Besides being a moral outrage and a social and political crime of the first magnitude, the Suitors' acts are also a major violation of religious custom. In flagrant disregard of the laws of hospitality strangers and guests are not welcomed at their meals; the *dais*, as we saw, is the typical, and welcoming, scene encountered by the arriving traveler. Worse still, the gods themselves are excluded from the feasting. Even without the element of theft and property destruction their eating and drinking are acts of mere consumption devoid of any sharing with the divine in the form of libations and sacrifices.[25]

The Suitors' godlessness also shows in the way in which they ignore all divine warning signs, beginning with the eagles sent by Zeus during the assembly (2.146–56). Their behavior, deliberate wanton evil in the face of increasing evidence that their actions will have severe consequences, is an extreme case of a type for which the poem reserves the term ἀτασθαλίαι.

---

undertaking, and the material compensation does not address the moral and religious outrage, not to mention the idea of murder implied by βίοτος, as mentioned above. In any case, Odysseus rejects the offer, not because he thinks it is insufficient as *apoina* (in fact, it would have yielded him considerable wealth, more than compensating for what he had lost – see Chapter 8, n. 32), but because he considers the Suitors' lives the only acceptable "exchange" for what had been done in his house.

[23] On the similarities between *Il.* 9.379–80 and *Od.* 22.61–2, see Schein 1999: 352–4; also Bakker 2006: 26–7; 2010: 48–9.

[24] Also the "companion" (ἑταίρη, 17.271), or the "spouse" (συνήορος, 8.99) of the *dais*.

[25] See Saïd 1979: 36–40, who also notes (p. 36) that the use of the verb ἱερεύειν does not in itself imply that actual sacrifices were performed: in a culture in which meat consumption is indissolubly connected with sacrifice there will be no separate vocabulary for butchery. Note, further, that the Suitor Leodes was the θυοσκόος, 'sacrificial priest, inspector of sacrificed animals' of the group (*Od.* 21.145; 22.318), a position that is apparently vacuous, and ironic in light of the Suitors' total lack of interest in divinatory signs.

This term will be discussed in Chapter 6 in connection with the acts of a parallel group of meat eaters.

Meat in the real world

"First get yourself a house, a wife, and an ox for plowing."
(Hesiod, *Works and Days*, 405)

The idea of abundantly available meat may lead us into a further perspective on the Suitors' crimes, in addition to their perverting the heroic *dais* and committing sacrilege against the gods. It may be useful, in addition to watching the events from inside the epic world, to adopt a more external perspective on the Suitors' crimes of consumption. We do not know directly how the historical audiences of the Homeric poems reacted to the epic representation of meat consumption, but we have some evidence for animal farming in the archaic and classical periods. And once we are aware of the external perspective, we can observe that the *Iliad* and the *Odyssey* differ in their representation of meat animals and their consumption.

Starting with the *Iliad*, we may note that the emphasis here on the importance of meat as symbolic capital is so strong, the role of the *dais* in heroic life so self-evident and unproblematic, and the place of meat in the heroic diet so obvious, that there is little interest in where all these animals come from, or in how such a steady consumption can be sustained.[26] It is true that the warrior community of the Achaeans on the Trojan plain constitutes a war economy, in which cattle and sheep are booty, to be redistributed by chieftains along with durable prestige goods; as we saw, the conception of proportionally "equal shares" applies to both.[27] But Sarpedon's Lycia presumably is a more structured and permanent economic system. Assuming that the fattened sheep that are the heroes' privilege are not obtained by plunder, but raised for food, we may wonder about the cost for Lycia and other Mediterranean regions of feeding its local heroes.

Meat is not only expensive as a luxury substance in a prestige economy, but also highly inefficient as a use of agricultural resources. The conversion rate of feed into meat is no more than 6.5 percent for cattle and 13 percent for sheep over the lifetime of the animal. That is, cows can convert only 6.5 percent of the energy in their feed to meat, and sheep 13 percent.[28] In order to gain a given increase in weight, an animal needs

---

[26] See also Rose 1992: 58–61 on the wider economy of the world depicted in the *Iliad*.
[27] Note, however, that at *Il.* 9.71–2 there is mention of daily deliveries to Agamemnon of wine from Thrace.
[28] Harris 1985: 67, who cites Bondi 1982: 209 as source.

Meat in the real world

to eat many times that weight. The animals' feed may not be suitable for human consumption, but it grows in places where humans may want to cultivate their own crops – bovines especially need grassy, humid meadows – and so husbandry of meat animals is often in direct competition with arable farming. The wastefulness of raising sheep and especially cattle for meat increases when the production accrues to the benefits of only a tiny subset of the population. Domestic animals are good to kill on a regular basis only when their masters have been killed before and their new masters are too busy waging war to be able to concentrate on the domains in which sheep and cattle are of greatest use: wool, dairy, and traction.

The epigraphic record of the historical period confirms the picture of a culture of animal husbandry shaped and constrained by the properties and limitations of the terrain in the Aegean basin.[29] With some exceptions, most of the land available to farmers was unsuitable for cattle,[30] and such frequent designations as βοῦς ἐργάται, 'working oxen', or βοῦς ἀροῦντες, 'plowing oxen', reflect an agricultural reality far removed from the image of entire herds of cattle (βοῦς ἀγελαῖαι) conveyed by the Homeric similes.[31] Only very infrequently do we find evidence for the raising of cattle on a scale that could enable the intensive meat consumption that the *Iliad* takes for granted. Even in Classical Athens there is no evidence for wealthy citizens possessing large herds of cattle. In the records of the auctioning of the property of the Athenians convicted of mutilating the Hermes statues in 415 BCE on the eve of the launching of the Sicilian expedition, the only cattle owner is Panaetios, who is said to possess no more than two plowing oxen, two more cattle, and four cows with calves (*IG* I³ 426.58–60).[32]

Nor were the small ruminants, sheep and goats, in spite of their much larger numbers, raised primarily for their meat.[33] Cheese and wool production enabled owners to live off their flocks in ways that were impossible

---

[29] On animal husbandry in general in the Greek world, see, e.g., Brendel 1934; Zeissig 1934; Georgoudi 1990; Isager and Skydsgaard 1992: 83–107; Chandezon 2003; Howe 2008; and most recently McInerney 2010 (on cattle). Semple 1922 discusses the geographical constraints on animal production.

[30] Chandezon 2003: 19, 100, 280, 411. Among the exceptions are Epirus, famous for its cattle (e.g., Arist. *Hist. An.* 522b; cf. Chandezon 2003: 281), the Boeotian plain at Orchomenos, for which herds of cattle are attested (*IG* VII.3171; cf. Chandezon 2003: 41–2), and Messenia (cf. [Plat.] *Alc.* 122d; Hom. *Od.* 4.602–4). See also Georgoudi 1990.

[31] Βοῦς ἀροῦντες: *SEG* 26: 1305.4; βόε ἐργάτα: *IG* I³ 426.58; βοῦς ἀγελαῖαι: *Il.* 23.845–6; *Od.* 10.410. For the inscriptional use of the phrase, see Chandezon 2003: 99–100.

[32] Chandezon 2003: 17–21; for more evidence for the relative lack of cattle ownership in Athens, see Howe 2008: 63–5; also McInerney 2010: 169.

[33] Chandezon 2003: 283–4.

with cattle, but personal subsistence relying exclusively on pastoral products was riskier than living off the land, and probably more infrequent.[34]

Meat, then, cannot have been a common item in the diet of the population at large.[35] Instead, it was consumed primarily in the context of religious festivals.[36] Most cattle available for sacrifice and consumption were raised on land belonging to sanctuaries and we have evidence for sanctuary lands being set aside for cattle grazing, instead of being used for crops, especially at Delphi. In the archaic and classical periods cattle are a linchpin of a sanctuary economy, rather than a matter of private ownership and consumption. But sanctuary cattle were not always destined for sacrifice and consumption; they could also be part of a sacred herd, as property of the god, and kept on sanctuary grounds for the divinity's pleasure and enjoyment. The sacred nature of cattle for historical audiences of the Homeric poems is of relevance for the interpretation of the *Odyssey*, as we will see in Chapter 6.[37]

The unproblematic and unembarrassed consumption of meat in the *Iliad*, then, may well be an idealized conception of life in the age of heroes, rather than a faithful reflection of Bronze Age agricultural conditions that were more favorable to intensive beef and mutton farming.[38] In any case, we can discern a markedly different perspective in the *Odyssey*. Whether Odysseus' poem wants to distance itself from the representations of heroic life in the *Iliad* or adopt a perspective that is more in line with Iron Age conditions of subsistence and the economy of the archaic Greek *polis*, meat consumption is not the same as in the *Iliad*. There is a fascination with the wealth in livestock of fabulous, faraway regions. Menelaos' description of Libya, which probably reflects a protocolonial interest in Cyrenaica, is characteristically cast in idealizing pastoral terms (*Od.* 4.84–9):[39]

---

[34] Halstead 1981: 314 (cited by Hodkinson 1988: 59) estimates that a minimum of twenty-five sheep were needed for the subsistence of a single individual, whereas he might support himself off approximately 1 ha of arable land.

[35] Trace-element analysis of skeletal remains from Classical Athens points to a diet low in meat. See McInerney 2010: 171.

[36] Schmitt-Pantel 1992: 334; McInerney 2010: 170–1.

[37] On cattle and sanctuary economy, see McInerney 1999: 101–8; 2010: 146–72; Chandezon 2003: 54–5. For the economy of sacrifice and festival, see Isager 1992; Rosivach 1994. For sacrificial cattle versus sacred herds, see Chandezon 2003: 286, 291–3.

[38] One could argue that deforestation and consequent erosion (the connection between the two was realized as early as Plato, *Critias* 111c) had not yet progressed in the Bronze Age to the point where pastures become sparse. But vegetation may have looked similar to the present as early as in Mycenaean times (Kroll 1984; Zangger 1992: 16). On environmental degradation (deforestation and soil erosion) in antiquity, see Hughes 1994: 73–90.

[39] Note the epithet μηλοτρόφος, 'sheep-nourishing', in the Delphic oracles concerning Cyrene as reported by Herodotus (4.155.3, 157.2); cf. the description at Pind. *Pyth.* 9.56–58: εὐλείμων, 'rich in pasture'.

Αἰθίοπάς θ' ἱκόμην καὶ Σιδονίους καὶ Ἐρεμβοὺς
καὶ Λιβύην, ἵνα τ' ἄρνες ἄφαρ κεραοὶ τελέθουσι.
τρὶς γὰρ τίκτει μῆλα τελεσφόρον εἰς ἐνιαυτόν·
ἔνθα μὲν οὔτε ἄναξ ἐπιδευὴς οὔτε τι ποιμὴν
τυροῦ καὶ κρειῶν οὐδὲ γλυκεροῖο γάλακτος,
ἀλλ' αἰεὶ παρέχουσιν ἐπηετανὸν γάλα θῆσθαι.

I reached the Aithiopes and Sidonians and the Eremboi
as well as Libye, where the rams grow horns right after birth;
thrice the ewes have lambs in the completion of the year.
There neither master nor shepherd is in need in any way
of cheese or meat, nor of sweet milk;
no, the flocks continuously provide year-round milk for suckling.

And Eumaios describes the fabulous island of his birth, which lies at the "turning points of the Sun" and where Golden Age living conditions obtain (there is neither famine nor disease), as "rich in cattle (or pastures), rich in sheep" (εὔβοτος εὔμηλος, *Od.* 15.406).

Such faraway places (and more will be discussed in the following chapters) stand in stark contrast to the realities of the Greek homeland, the vantage point from which such distant paradises are perceived. There is an attention to detail where meat animals are concerned that is alien to the *Iliad*. In what is probably the best and most elaborately described sacrifice in the poem, the victim, the ox with the gilded horns, has to come "from the plain" (3.421, 431); in other words, there apparently was no way to feed it closer to the palace. Ithaca itself, the epicenter of the poem, is described as rugged and rocky, without grassy plains; not a good place for horse-breeding, as Telemachos explains to Menelaos (4.601–8).[40] Its king Odysseus is certainly a wealthy man, but his herds have to be kept on the mainland, as Eumaios informs the stranger in his hut in a seminal conversation to which we will return (*Od.* 14.100).[41] As a natural pastoral environment, Ithaca is good only for sheep and goats.

The limited resources of the king of Ithaca are not only a recognizable reality for the poem's audiences from the archaic to the Hellenistic age; they are also at the center of the poem's thematic structure. The juxtaposition of near economic reality and far paradisiacal abundance – neither extreme being envisaged by the *Iliad* – releases much narrative energy for the *Odyssey*. On the one hand, in *aoidē*, the matrix narrative (i.e., the

---

[40] See also *Od.* 4.634–5. The same characterization of Ithaca is found in the disguised Athena's presentation of the island to Odysseus at 13.242.
[41] See also *Od.* 20.209–12. But note that Athena in describing Ithaca to Odysseus calls the island βούβοτος (*Od.* 13.246).

events transpiring in Odysseus' palace at Ithaca), we see a world depicted that is much closer to the lived experience of historical Greek audiences of the archaic age, a world in which livestock is valuable as property in itself and in which animal husbandry and meat consumption, in particular beef, are constrained by the realities of Mediterranean farming. On the other hand, there is *epos*, the story of Odysseus' Wanderings, which features a world, or worlds, much more exotic than the normative heroic world depicted in the *Iliad*.

Many of the adventures of Odysseus and his Companions in this Otherworld revolve around meat consumption and its concomitant associations and fantasies. Contrasted with the unproblematic availability of meat animals in the world of the *Iliad* or the realistically limited supply (and, hence, value) of such animals in Ithaca are two mythically enhanced types of experience: Odysseus is faced either with unreal, paradisiacal abundance and availability of meat animals, or with an equally unreal taboo on eating meat. Through the adventures that are concerned with meat runs an opposition between "one/counted/bounded" and "many/innumerable/unbounded," each term of the opposition intensifying the illicit consumption of meat animals by the Suitors in the "real world," in which abundance is artificially created out of a vast but limited number of meat animals owned by the absent master.

With their destructive intentions the Suitors not only create the illusion of an epic world in the rural and provincial space of Ithaca, a perversion of the *dais*; they also create the illusion of a paradise, a misguided fantasy of plenitude and unlimited abundance. The extensive interconnectedness between the Wanderings and the Return, which the previous chapters discussed in terms of the dialogue between *epos* and *aoidē*, invites us to extend these findings to the Otherworlds in which Odysseus must travel. The paradigmatic relations that these episodes from *epos* entertain with the scenes of reckless feasting in Odysseus' palace are not in the first place built on Odysseus being present in both; rather, what foreshadows the consumption of meat in Odysseus' *megaron* is the behavior of the hero's Companions.

Let us now review these two contrasted situations, unbounded abundance and bounded wealth, that become interrelated when seen in conjunction with the Suitors' feasting in an unstable and immoral paradise. First comes the Cyclops (Chapter 4), whose episode juxtaposes countless and counted, abundance and taboo. The subsequent major episodes in Odysseus' tale, Circe (Chapter 5) and the Cattle of the Sun (Chapter 6), are concerned with limitless abundance and strict taboo, respectively.

CHAPTER 4

Of hunters and herders

"Obliging our enemies with baneful guest gifts."
(Archilochus, *Fr.* 6)

The Cyclops episode, which occupies the greater part of Book Nine, is in many ways, both structural and thematic, the centerpiece of the *Odyssey*. Here is where the *Odyssey* finds its thematic anchor. Insofar as the episode revolves around meat and its consumption – and it does to a large extent – it sets the scene for the theme of limited and unlimited abundance, contracting paradigmatic relationships with both the other episodes of the Wanderings that are told at length (Circe and the Cattle of the Sun) as well as with the hero's return in Ithaca. But there is also the way in which the episode contributes to the linear progression of the narrative. The monster's prayer to his father Poseidon cements the poem's plot as it sets the hero on his extended quest for *nostos*. The episode itself is one of the many subparts of that quest, and so it partakes in the multiple paradigmatic relationships we can discern between the various episodes. In addition to systematic similarities of the episode with other adventures in the Wanderings (see pages 23 and 25), both Odysseus and Polyphemos provide models for the various structural components of the events at Ithaca after Odysseus' return. Both tales revolve around a home invasion, the encounter of the intruders with the returning master, and the uninvited guests being trapped in the house they entered. Odysseus plays a role in each episode, changing from intruder into returning master, a shift that makes possible multiple ironies and reversals, as we will see. But let us start with the most obvious link between the Cyclops episode and the situation at Ithaca.

The Suitors and the Cyclops

When Odysseus lies awake as beggar in the portal of his own *megaron*, witnessing the maidservants leaving the house to sleep with the Suitors, he recalls the Cyclops in the outrage of his heart (*Od.* 20.18–21):

> τέτλαθι δή, κραδίη· καὶ κύντερον ἄλλο ποτ' **ἔτλης**,
> ἤματι τῷ ὅτε μοι μένος ἄσχετος ἤσθιε Κύκλωψ
> ἰφθίμους ἑτάρους· σὺ δ' ἐτόλμας, ὄφρα σε **μῆτις**
> ἐξάγαγ' ἐξ ἄντροιο ὀϊόμενον θανέεσθαι.
>
> <u>Endure</u> this, my heart: you have once <u>endured</u> something even more outrageous,
> on that day when irresistible in his might the Cyclops ate them,
> my stout Companions, but you were daring, until my <u>*mētis*</u>
> led you out of the cave, when you expected to die.

Lying under sheep fleeces (20.2–3), just as he once clung for life under the fleece of the ram that carried him out of the cave, he aligns the ordeal he underwent there with the present ordeal in his own house, presenting both as prime occasions for displaying the qualities inherent in his two essential epithets πολύτλας, 'much enduring', and πολύμητις, 'many-minded'. The mental faculties denoted by these epithets come together in the typically Odyssean phrase κακὰ βυσσοδομεύων, 'building evil in the depth <of his heart>', which typifies Odysseus' mindset both in the cave and in his house at Ithaca (*Od.* 9.316; 17.465, 495; 20.184). The hero's own house, in other words, is like Polyphemos' cave.

The narrative confirms this link between the adventure in the cave and the hero's present predicament, when it endows the Suitors with clear Cyclopean qualities. Just like the Cyclops they throw objects at Odysseus' head. Antinoos hurls a footstool when "he was enraged even more in his heart" (ἐχολώσατο κηρόθι μᾶλλον, *Od.* 17.458) by Odysseus' taunting words, both gesture and formula recalling the throw of the Cyclops' first rock (9.480) when he is equally provoked by Odysseus. The two throws are linked: in both cases Odysseus strongly provokes his opponent by commenting on his behavior with respect to strangers and his violation of the rules of hospitality.

Similarly, another Suitor, Ctesippus, shares with the Cyclops the essential qualification ἀθεμίστια εἰδώς, 'well-versed in lawlessness' (20.287; cf. 9.189, 428), an epithet he receives at the moment when, just like the Cyclops, he perverts hospitality by using the language of guest friendship in order to commit a flagrant violation of all norms of behavior at the *dais* (*Od.* 20.292–8):[1]

> κέκλυτέ μευ, μνηστῆρες ἀγήνορες, ὄφρα τι εἴπω·
> μοῖραν μὲν δὴ ξεῖνος ἔχει πάλαι, ὡς ἐπέοικεν,
> ἴσην· οὐ γὰρ καλὸν ἀτέμβειν οὐδὲ δίκαιον
> ξείνους Τηλεμάχου, ὅς κεν τάδε δώμαθ' ἵκηται.
> ἀλλ' ἄγε οἱ καὶ ἐγὼ δῶ **ξείνιον**, ὄφρα καὶ αὐτὸς

---

[1] See also Saïd 1979: 31–2; Segal 1994: 160.

ἠὲ λοετροχόῳ δώῃ γέρας ἠέ τῳ ἄλλῳ
δμώων, οἳ κατὰ δώματ' Ὀδυσσῆος θείοιο.

Listen to me, you valiant Suitors, so that I tell you something:
the share which the stranger has had for a while now, it seems,
is equitable. For it is not nice, nor just, that they are cheated of it,
the guests of Telemachos, whoever might reach this house.
But come on, let *me* give him a hospitality gift *too*, so that he himself
can give it to the wine-pourer as a *geras*, or to anyone else
of the servants who live around the house of Odysseus the godlike.

The Cyclops used the word for "hospitality gift" (ξεινήϊον, 9.370) to designate Odysseus' "right" to be eaten last as compensation for the gift of the wine; Ctesippus uses the equivalent ξείνιον for the ox foot he throws at Odysseus' head in another gesture reminiscent of the rocks which the Cyclops hurls at Odysseus' ship.

The Suitors seem in fact to be an excellent match for the Cyclops in the way they treat strangers and make a mockery of hospitality. The thematic link is made explicit when Odysseus makes a final evaluation of the conduct of the Suitors, casting himself as the instrument of the justice of Zeus when he has killed them all in his *megaron* (*Od.* 22.413–15):

τούσδε δὲ μοῖρ' ἐδάμασσε θεῶν καὶ σχέτλια ἔργα·
οὔ τινα γὰρ τίεσκον ἐπιχθονίων ἀνθρώπων,
οὐ κακὸν οὐδὲ μὲν ἐσθλόν, ὅτίς σφεας εἰσαφίκοιτο.

These men, the doom of the gods subdued them as well as their own
    awful deeds,
for they did not honor anyone of the earth-dwelling humans,
neither base nor noble, whoever would come in contact with them.

These words, addressed to the nurse Eurycleia after the massacre of the Suitors, recall the way in which Odysseus first addresses the Cyclops from the relative safety of his boat (*Od.* 9.477–9):

καὶ λίην σέ γ' ἔμελλε κιχήσεσθαι κακὰ ἔργα,
σχέτλι', ἐπεὶ ξείνους οὐχ ἅζεο σῷ ἐνὶ οἴκῳ
ἐσθέμεναι· τῶ σε Ζεὺς τείσατο καὶ θεοὶ ἄλλοι.

Bad things were going to hit you,
you terrible brute, since you did not stand back in awe from eating
the strangers in your house. That is why Zeus has taken revenge on
    you and also the other gods.

The similarity between the Cyclops and the Suitors is further enhanced by the use of one of the quintessential epithets of the Suitors, ὑπερφίαλος, 'overweening', in the programmatic description that Odysseus gives of the Cyclopes, which he means to be the frame for the entire episode that follows (*Od.* 9.105–15):

Κυκλώπων δ' ἐς γαῖαν **ὑπερφιάλων ἀθεμίστων**
ἱκόμεθ', οἵ ῥα θεοῖσι πεποιθότες ἀθανάτοισιν
οὔτε φυτεύουσιν χερσὶν φυτὸν οὔτ' ἀρόωσιν,
ἀλλὰ τά γ' ἄσπαρτα καὶ ἀνήροτα πάντα φύονται,
πυροὶ καὶ κριθαὶ ἠδ' ἄμπελοι, αἵ τε φέρουσιν
οἶνον ἐριστάφυλον, καί σφιν Διὸς ὄμβρος ἀέξει.
τοῖσιν δ' οὔτ' ἀγοραὶ βουληφόροι οὔτε θέμιστες,
ἀλλ' οἵ γ' ὑψηλῶν ὀρέων ναίουσι κάρηνα
ἐν σπέεσι γλαφυροῖσι, θεμιστεύει δὲ ἕκαστος
παίδων ἠδ' ἀλόχων, οὐδ' ἀλλήλων ἀλέγουσι.

<It was> the land of the Cyclopes, <u>overweening and lawless</u>
<that> we now reached; these, trusting the gods immortal,
do not plant crops with their hands, nor do they plow the earth;
no, unsown and unplowed everything grows for them:
wheat, barley, and vines that carry
wine from rich grapes, and the rain from Zeus makes everything
 thrive.
For these <u>no assemblies where council is made, nor custom of law</u>;
instead, they inhabit the peaks of tall mountains,
living in hollow caves, and each of them lays down the law
for their wives and children, nor do they care about each other.

Not only is ὑπερφίαλος one of the standard characterizations of the Suitors and their behavior; the Ithaca dominated by the Suitors also is unaccustomed to assemblies or councils: the communal gathering convoked by Telemachos is the first one since Odysseus left for Troy (*Od.* 2.26–7).

The Cyclopes' lawlessness is in the first place, in a synchronic cultural perspective, a matter of non-Greek barbaric savagery, a definition of the standard conception of Greek culture as seen through the description of its opposite. But in a diachronic perspective it becomes a matter of a pre-civilization lack of societal constraints. The agricultural conditions of the Cyclopes (no sowing, plowing, or other agricultural labor) unmistakably recall the Golden Age, the αὐτόματος ἄρουρα, the earth that sends up fruit and harvest without prompting.[2]

Both perspectives can be said to apply to the Ithaca of the Suitors. There is the breakdown of the rituals and constraints on which a healthy society is based, but there is also the cultural regression to an artificial and

---

[2] For example, Kirk 1970: 164–5; Mondi 1983: 23–4; Vidal-Naquet 1986: 21–2; Nieto Hernández 2000: 348–9.

perverted Golden Age, based on the pretense and illusion that everything, in particular meat, is effortlessly and limitlessly available.

The subject of meat in connection with the Suitors and the Cyclops brings up a less obvious point of comparison between the two. Odysseus' description of the Cyclopes makes mention of the Cyclopes "putting their trust in the immortal gods" (θεοῖσι πεποιθότες ἀθανάτοισιν, 9.106). But in the actual story Polyphemos emphatically asserts that the Cyclopes do not care about Zeus or the other gods, claiming to be "much stronger" (9.275–8). Polyphemos' own godlessness is indirectly apparent in the way he lives with his animals. As a good pastoralist, he milks his goats and sheep (9.238, 244, 308), makes cheese (9.219, 246), and takes good care of his flocks. In fact, he humanizes his animals, addressing his favorite ram as a person and endowing him, in what probably can be called mock epic style, with heroic qualities (μακρὰ βιβάς, 'making big strides', 9.450; cf. *Il.* 7.213; see also 9.308, κλυτὰ μῆλα, 'renowned sheep'). There is no indication in the text that he ever eats any of his animals. In fact, everything suggests that his diet is dairy-based and strictly vegetarian.[3]

Sacrificial logic dictates that vegetarianism is an expression of a godless way of life, for someone who does not eat meat does not sacrifice, and one who does not sacrifice does not have, or does not want to have, a channel of communication with the gods. The absence of sacrifice in Polyphemos' life aligns him once more with the Suitors, the most reckless and indulgent meat-eaters in the poem. The Suitors, as already mentioned in Chapter 3, reduce the *dais* to an act of mere meat consumption entirely devoid of the essential division that constitutes the act of sacrifice.

The Cyclops, then, can be seen as a foil for the actions of the Suitors in a binary contrast – to use structuralist terms – between deficiency and excess.[4] The two parties, the poem seems to be saying, are aligned in being equidistant from a mean, the measured and balanced consumption of meat in the act of sacrifice. Such practice, which keeps gods and human consumers in the right balance, is what Telemachos witnesses in Nestor's Pylos.

The Master of Animals

But the Cyclops' vegetarian lifestyle does not prevent him, of course, from indulging in extreme carnivorous behavior in the form of cannibalism.[5] Walter Burkert connects the Cyclops' savage consumption of Odysseus'

---
[3] See also Cook 1995: 102.
[4] Best known from Lévi-Strauss' analysis of the Oedipus myth (1955: 433–4).
[5] On Golden Age, vegetarianism, and cannibalism, see also Vidal-Naquet 1986: 17, 21–2.

Companions (raw, just as a lion devours his prey) with what is for him a pre-Greek theme of extreme, possibly even Paleolithic, antiquity: the Master of Animals.[6] This divine creature is often thought of as part of Bronze Age (or earlier) religion and it is a frequent theme in the iconography of Cretan, Mycenaean, and early archaic Greek art.[7] To think of the Master of Animals as an archaic concept makes sense for the Greek world, but it is good to be aware of the fact that many contemporary hunting cultures around the world know a master or guardian of game animals of some sort, in a variety of shapes, and that the confrontation of humans with this supernatural being is not necessarily always as violent as in Odysseus' encounter with Polyphemos. The ethnographic and anthropological literature on "Masters of Animals" outside the Greek world up to the present day can provide, as we shall see in the present and following chapters, comparative insights in the worlds in which Odysseus is forced to travel.[8]

For Burkert, the deepest layer of the story, far more essential than the famous naming trick or the Cyclops being on the negative side of a series of Greek cultural binary oppositions, is the importance of the Cyclops' sheep as goal of the entire quest into the cave. Obtaining the sheep, owned by a savage protector who has to be overcome, is the successful end of the primordial quest for food and the survival of humanity.[9] One can get eaten oneself in the process, and the final escape, tied under the bellies of the sheep that will soon be consumed, is the ritual assimilation of the eater to the desirable meat animal to be obtained:

To gain the edible animals, man has to assimilate himself to them. To be eaten, or not to be eaten but to eat, these are the two sides of the basic process of life. Man eats animals, and consumes them, disturbing the balance of life; to make up for this, myth introduces an agent who preserves the flocks and eats man. The ogre, Master of Animals, is a term necessitated by structural logic, as it were, not childlike fantasy. (Burkert 1979: 33)

---

[6] Burkert 1979: 30–4; the primordial status of the Master of Animals concept is assumed also by Bremmer 2002: 143.
[7] For example, Marinatos 2000.
[8] For example, Röhrig 1959, 1961; Reichel-Dolmatoff 1971; Valeri 2000; Tuite 2006.
[9] Burkert 1979: 33–4. Note that Herodotus (9.92–5) has a story that is a clear allomorph of the Odyssean Cyclops episode, in which the Polyphemos slot is filled by a villager, Euenios, whose task it is to protect sheep sacred to Apollo that are penned in a cave. He fails in his duties when his flock is decimated by a pack of marauding wolves (note that Odysseus is the grandson of Autolykos). Both Polyphemos and Euenios get blinded and both are associated with prophecy (Polyphemos in and through his curse, see below, and Chapter 7). On Herodotus' story, see Griffiths 1999.

Burkert proposes to see the Cyclops tale as a Paleolithic quest myth. The analysis of this "folktale" he offers is very suggestive, not only in bringing out the "quest" element as delineated in Chapter 2 as an "underlying logic" of the tale, below and beyond the themes that appear to be prominent at the surface. Odysseus himself gives the desire to obtain "hospitality gifts" as his reason for undertaking the quest into the cave, or at least for not leaving it at his Companions' urgent bidding (*Od.* 9.224–30). Important also is the insistence on the importance of the theme of food and on the Cyclops being the owner of valuable meat animals. That same theme, however, raises questions not addressed in Burkert's brief analysis. The Master of Animals is typically an owner or guardian of wild animals that have to be acquired by hunting; the Cyclops' herd, however, is as domesticated as any sheep or goats known to Greek shepherds.

The Cyclops is a shepherd, not a guardian of game animals. This does not preclude the role that Burkert assigns to him, since beliefs about masters of animals have been known to persist even when a hunting culture has made the transition from hunting to animal husbandry.[10] We could read the quest into Cyclops' cave in this light as a mythicized memory of the rise of animal farming. But such an interpretation does not exhaust the episode's significance and will in fact give rise to new layers of meaning. Pursuing these will reveal that the episode is far more integrated into the texture of the poem than when we see it as a relic that has come to be incorporated, somehow, into the monumental *Odyssey*. Burkert himself admits that the Cyclops tale can hardly be a wholesale import of a tale that has survived intact from Paleolithic times. The incorporation of this ancient tale into the body of the poem, if incorporation is the right word, has not taken place without extensive interaction with the body in which it was received.

To begin, the explicit depiction of the Cyclops as a pastoralist creates an ironic context for Odysseus' initial characterization of the Cyclopean community as lawless and uncivilized (*Od.* 9.105–15, quoted above).[11] It is true that from a contemporary synchronic perspective the opposition between arable farming and animal husbandry can be aligned with a binary contrast between "culture" and "nature," the terms in which the Cyclops episode has been frequently discussed.[12] The shepherd is the typical rustic, opposed to the city-dweller and unaccustomed to the culture and laws of

---

[10] For example, Paulson and Auer 1964: 208 (Finland); Asatrian 2002 (Caucasus).
[11] Burkert himself considers this passage as not belonging to the Cyclops tale proper (1979: 31).
[12] For example, Kirk 1970: 162–71; O'Sullivan 1990.

the *polis*; in the Greek cultural imagination he can be easily associated with nomadism, hunting, even brigandage. Arable farming was routinely associated with civilization, the source and sustenance of the *polis*, whereas the abandoned *polis* becomes a sheep-walk.[13]

But the confident binary terms in which Odysseus casts the Cyclops community become less comfortable when we take into account the position from which Odysseus comes into contact with Polyphemos. For the adventure does not start in the land of the Cyclopes. Before Odysseus decides to embark upon his quest and enter the cave, he and his Companions find themselves on an island just off the land of the Cyclopes, where they have beached their ships when they arrive in the dark. If the Cyclops tale is, below the narrative surface, a quest for domesticated edible animals, then the lack motivating the quest must be felt on this island. Odysseus may be using solidly Greek categories at the time of the performance of his *epos* at the *dais* of Alkinoos, but at the moment when Odysseus actually encounters the Cyclops the roles are all but reversed. He and his men find themselves in the position of migratory hunters, whereas the Cyclopes are advanced and dedicated pastoralists. They have something that Odysseus has not.

Unlimited meats, innumerable goats

The island from which Odysseus launches his fateful expedition is a truly Otherworldly paradise, certainly from the point of view of the Ithacans and their barren, rocky island. The island, just like the mainland of the Cyclopes, is a paradisiacal αὐτόματος ἄρουρα, 'pristine and miraculously fertile land'.[14] Completely untouched by man (9.119–30), it has "soft, wet meadows" (λειμῶνες ... ὑδρηλοὶ μαλακοί, 9.132–3), which would not only provide excellent vineyards (9.133) and rich land for plowing (9.134–5) to prospective settlers, but would also, presumably, permit extensive cattle-grazing at a scale unlikely to be sustainable in the mother-city. In short, as has often been remarked, this place is the ultimate colonist's dream.[15]

---

[13] At Theogn. 53–6 there is talk of rustics dressed in goatskins as outsiders to the *polis*; nomadism and brigandage: Ar. *Pol.* 1256b29–40; abandoned *polis*: Isocr. 14.31. On Greek cultural concepts of the pastoral nomad, see Shaw 1982/3, whose discussion of the Odyssean Cyclops in this light does not take into account the ironies and complexities of the text.

[14] Note that the phrase ἄσπαρτος καὶ ἀνήροτος, 'unsown and unplowed' (9.123) picks up ἄσπαρτα καὶ ἀνήροτα (9.109) from Odysseus' programmatic description of Cyclopeia cited earlier.

[15] For example, Kirk 1970: 165; Vidal-Naquet 1986: 21; Doughtery 1993: 21; Malkin 1998: 160.

Wildlife is also abundant in this primordial paradise. In the absence of any hunters who "suffer hardship roaming over the peaks of the mountains" (9.121), the island teems with wild goats. This game is "innumerable" (ἀπειρέσιαι, 9.118), the first detail that Odysseus gives in his description of the island. Number and limit, or lack thereof, will from now on be an increasingly important theme in the story.

The next day the travelers "gaze in wonder" (θαυμάζοντες, 9.153) at their surroundings and wander around the island, which now turns into a hunter's paradise. No toil and hardship for these hunters, for not only are the game animals innumerable; they are also very easy to hunt (*Od.* 9.154–5):

ὦρσαν δὲ Νύμφαι, κοῦραι Διὸς αἰγιόχοιο
αἶγας ὀρεσκώους, ἵνα δειπνήσειαν ἑταῖροι

the nymphs, daughters of Zeus who holds the Aigis, stirred them up,
the goats born in the mountains, so that my Companions could have
a meal.

Odysseus tellingly presents the nymphs as intending to satisfy the Companions' needs, not his own, a detail that will be further developed as the narrative (and this book) proceeds.

Readers of Greek literature know the nymphs as local rural divinities, recipients of cult by shepherds and other rustic folk, or as subjects in Hellenistic poetry stylizing and idealizing life in the countryside. But nymphs are not in and of themselves shepherds' divinities. They are primeval beings, indissolubly connected with the natural environment and they have been around ever since Gaia "engendered the tall mountains, lovely haunts of goddesses, the nymphs, who dwell in the wooded mountain valleys" (Hes. *Theog.* 129–30). Nymphs have been appropriated by the Olympic pantheon (most prominently visible in the formulaic phrase κοῦραι Διὸς αἰγιόχοιο, 'daughters of aegis-bearing Zeus') and are frequently embedded in mythical genealogies; nor are they always easy to distinguish from human heroines.[16] But they are first and foremost a force of untamed nature, frequently associated with rivers and springs and often in the company of satyrs, the wild, sexually hyperactive hybrid forms between man and beast.[17] Odysseus speaks of a spring in a cave at the mouth of which poplars grow (9.140–1), exactly the kind of place where nymphs live (also on Ithaca itself: 17.205–11), and we may safely infer that this is the dwelling-place of the nymphs on Goat Island.

---

[16] See Larson 2001: 3–8.   [17] Larson 2001: 91–5.

Nymphs are easily seen as guardians of the animals in their habitat. The association of nymphs with hunting and herding is widespread in the Greek material, but perhaps we can go a step further and see in the nymphs on Goat Island a version of the supernatural being that is present, in some way or another, in most of the world's traditional hunting cultures. The Master of Animals, as noted above, is not limited to pre-Olympian divinity in the pre-history of Greek religion; many hunting traditions have supernatural beings that function as the lords of the forest and spiritual guardians of its animals, whose cooperation has to be secured in order for the hunt to be successful.[18]

Perhaps we can see in the nymphs on Goat Island a reflex of the kind of spiritual phenomena with which hunting cultures are concerned. But these animal guardians are far more generous than guardians in the real world, who typically grant the hunter the game much less abundantly, not without hardship, and often for a price. In addition, we hear that "a god gave a most pleasant hunt" (9.158). This hunt is not merely necessary for subsistence outside the confines of the cultural world as the hunters know it; the movement into the unknown is also a regression to a pre-cultural condition, in a typically Greek move of mapping the geographically unknown onto mythical space. Odysseus has drifted off course into the Otherworld, where he enjoys primeval abundance.

In spite of the unusual circumstances the consumption of the animals takes place in the form of a heroic *dais*, complete with proportionate division: each of the twelve ships' crews are allotted nine animals (9.160); only Odysseus' ship gets ten; presumably the hero gets a goat all to himself. What is conspicuously absent is sacrifice. More than 100 large mammals, a gift of the nymphs and of "a god," are being slaughtered and consumed, but no sharing with the divine takes place. This may very well be in line with the rigid distinction between wild and domestic animals that is frequently assumed for Greek religious practice – game animals caught in the wild are not owned by the hunter and consequently cannot be given to the gods;[19] moreover, what is wild and untamed cannot be of significance in the oppositions "men–gods" and "men–animals" around which Greek sacrificial thinking revolves.[20]

If we press the Golden Age motif, we can also follow the reasoning that in an era that predates the Olympian gods sacrifice to them is irrelevant

---

[18] For example, Reichel-Dolmatoff 1971; Valeri 2000.
[19] Sacrificing wild animals also means that they have to be captured alive first – not always easy.
[20] For example, Vernant 1979; 1990: 143–82.

Unlimited meats, innumerable goats 63

and superfluous; this seems to be the reasoning of Polyphemos himself across the strait. On the other hand, sacrifice of wild, hunted animals, though infrequent, is not unattested,[21] and the work of Walter Burkert and his teacher Karl Meuli stresses the continuity, historical and notional, between sacrifice and ritualized killing in the hunt.[22] At any rate, the lack of sacrifice, whether or not intentionally meant to signal religiously offensive neglect, resonates with the equally substantial and equally sacrificeless feasts of the Suitors for which Odysseus' paradisiacal *dais* serves as a foil. The *dais* proper is described in the following pair of formulaic lines (*Od.* 9.161–2):

ὣς τότε μὲν πρόπαν ἦμαρ ἐς ἠέλιον καταδύντα
ἥμεθα δαινύμενοι **κρέα τ' ἄσπετα** καὶ **μέθυ ἡδύ**.

So then all day long until the sun went down
we sat there feasting on unlimited meat and sweet wine.

These lines occur six times in the *Odyssey* and are confined to the Cyclops and Circe episodes.[23] They are the essential formulaic description in the poem of primordial paradisiacal plenty. There are parallels with the biblical notion of the "land flowing with milk and honey." The word μέθυ, cognate with English *mead*, must originally have referred to a drink made from fermented honey. In the context, μέθυ ἡδύ must be wine in view of the two lines immediately following (9.163–4), which mention the wine of the Cicones that was still left in the ships, but in the formula itself the phrase may well originally have had the older meaning.[24]

But the most striking element in the formula is the epic adjective ἄσπετος modifying "meats" (κρέα). Derived from the verb ἐννέπω, 'sing' (cf. forms like ἔσπετε), the word means properly "unsingable," "unspeakably much," "countless" or "boundless." Hermes uses the epithet (*Od.* 5.101) for the expanse of sea separating Calypso's island from the inhabited world, which is vast, even from the perspective of the gods; and in the description of Achilles' shield (*Il.* 18.403) it is used for nothing less than Oceanus itself. In an Iliadic simile the full depth of αἰθήρ as it is revealed to the gaze of the delighted shepherd when the cloud cover gives way is called ἄσπετος (*Il.* 8.558; 11.300), and the Presocratic philosopher Empedocles uses the adjective to denote the totality of all time: ἄσπετος αἰών, 'unmeasurable span of time' (Emp. B16 DK).

---

[21] See Stengel 1910: 197–202.   [22] Meuli 1946; Burkert 1979, 1983. See also Valeri 1994.
[23] *Od.* 9.161–2, 556–7; 10.183–4, 467–8 (slightly modified, see Chapter 5), 476–7; 12.29–30.
[24] See also Sherratt 2004: 202–3.

64   *Of hunters and herders*

The epithet aligns the meats on Goat Island with such awe-inspiring cosmic phenomena and gives fresh, retroactive force to the adjective used for the animals when they were still alive: ἀπειρέσιαι, 'without bounds', 'numberless'. The application of the idea of endless abundance to meat is striking. Meat is rarely boundless and edible animals are almost never available in unlimited numbers. Their owners, whether they are protective pastoralists, proud owners of livestock, or supernatural Masters of Animals, very much cherish them and count them, as does Proteus the Master of Seals in Menelaos' experience in the Otherworld (*Od.* 4.411, 451). Even hunting cultures whose living conditions are blessed with seemingly inexhaustible natural resources will typically conceive of their prey as granted to them piecemeal by the animal's supernatural owner or guardian. For example, the Amazonian Tukano, whom we will meet in more detail in Chapter 5, have a world view based on the principle that energy in the cosmos is limited and has to replenished; animals in this world view are created, by the Sun God, in limited numbers, and every kill will somehow have to be counterbalanced.[25] The Cyclops, who straddles the categories of owner of domesticated cattle and Master of Animals, treats his animals as persons and is naturally aware of their number.

The limits of wealth

The Homeric tradition can use ἄσπετος for numbers of livestock. The Thracian hero Iphidamas, a Trojan ally killed by Agamemnon, is said to have offered 100 heads of cattle and 1,000 ovicaprids, the latter being referred to as ἄσπετα (*Il.* 11.245); the adjective is also used to describe the share of animals that Pylian Neleus takes for himself out of the massive booty of a cattle raid on the Elians (*Il.* 11.704). But the most striking use of ἄσπετος in this regard occurs in Eumaios' description of the wealth of his absent master in the real world of Ithaca and surrounding territory. The swineherd talks to the stranger about all that is wrong on the island and indicates the extent of the Suitors' predatory transgression by emphasizing Odysseus' possessions (*Od.* 14.96–8):

> ἦ γάρ οἱ ζωή γ' **ἦν ἄσπετος**· οὔ τινι τόσση
> ἀνδρῶν ἡρώων, οὔτ' ἠπείροιο μελαίνης
> οὔτ' αὐτῆς Ἰθάκης.

[25] Reichel-Dolmatoff 1971; 1976: 309.

The limits of wealth

I am telling you, his wealth <u>was unlimited</u>; no one had so much
    <livestock>
of the heroes around, neither on the black mainland
nor here on Ithaca itself.

The cowherd Philoitios uses an equally strong word for the extent of Odysseus' wealth when he describes his master's herds, which he tends on the mainland (*Od.* 20.211–12):

νῦν δ' αἱ μὲν γίγνονται **ἀθέσφατοι**, οὐδέ κεν ἄλλως
ἀνδρί γ' ὑποσταχύοιτο βοῶν γένος εὐρυμετώπων

Now these <cows> are becoming <u>unutterably numerous</u>; not in an other way
could, at least under a man (i.e., a human cowherd), the race of broad-headed oxen increase like ears of wheat.

But, as Philoitios goes on to say, Odysseus' miraculously growing herd is being diminished by the voracious appetite of the Suitors.

This means that the Suitors enjoy κρέα ἄσπετα too, but only from the perspective of their own destructive and unstable paradise. In Eumaios' presentation, the qualification *aspetos* is not an epithet, but a predicative expression in the past tense. And Philoitios states that the explicit intention of the Suitors is to "divide up" Odysseus' possessions (μεμάασι γὰρ ἤδη | κτήματα δάσσασθαι, 'for they are now eager to divide <his> possessions among themselves', *Od.* 20.215–16). This does not mean the distribution of Odysseus' livestock as booty to a number of victorious enemies (the proper use of the verb δάσσασθαι, see Chapter 3), but its consumption till nothing is left. The depredations in the present erode the wealth that once was there. Odysseus' wealth in livestock, unlimited as it may once have seemed, becomes quite bounded as Eumaios goes on to specify the number of herds, flocks, and other pastoral units his master owned when he left for Troy: twelve herds of cattle on the mainland, twelve flocks of sheep, twelve herds of pigs, and twelve herds of goats (14.99–104). This is less than the numbers involved in the Pylian cattle-raid narrated by Nestor (fifty units of each species: *Il.* 11.677–9), but still very considerable. We will discuss the actual number of animals that these catalogues may imply in Chapter 6.

It is an integral whole that is being damaged and diminished by the Suitors in their deliberate effort to annihilate the house of Odysseus. The use of *aspetos* for such vast but bounded and counted wealth, at least in relation to the Companions' consumption of κρέα ἄσπετα or ἀθέσφατοι cows, marks Odysseus' livestock as combining the two features of abundance and boundedness that remain distinct in the adventures of the Companions.

Distinct, but not separate or unrelated. Perhaps the most remarkable thing about the feast on Goat Island is that while the consumption of the limitlessly plentiful meat of the game animals is still underway and before Odysseus and the Companions go to sleep on the beach, they look at the land across the strait and listen to the bleating of the sheep and goats of the Cyclopes (9.166–7). Apparently, the domesticated animals of the Cyclopean shepherds are more desirable than the easily available natural riches of their immediate environment. The proximity of edible domestic animals that are apparently more desirable than the hunted game animals they are consuming lends a transient quality to the company's present paradise. The Golden Age has to yield to the constraints and limitations of the Iron Age, of civilization, and even though the Cyclopes are depicted as being low on technology (9.125), at this moment in the progression of the narrative they represent, as sedentary pastoralists, a higher level of development than Odysseus and the Companions.

The fruits of Polyphemos' labors do not disappoint and are clearly very appealing to Odysseus and his men when they first enter the cave (*Od.* 9.218–23):

ἐλθόντες δ' εἰς ἄντρον **ἐθηεύμεσθα** ἕκαστα·
ταρσοὶ μὲν τυρῶν βρῖθον στείνοντο δὲ σηκοὶ
ἀρνῶν ἠδ' ἐρίφων· διακεκριμέναι δὲ ἕκασται
ἔρχατο, χωρὶς μὲν πρόγονοι, χωρὶς δὲ μέτασσαι,
χωρὶς δ' αὖθ' ἕρσαι· ναῖον δ' ὀρῷ ἄγγεα πάντα,
γαυλοί τε σκαφίδες τε, τετυγμένα, τοῖσ' ἐνάμελγεν.

Entering the cave we gazed in wonder at each of the things inside:
there were wicker baskets full of cheeses and there were pens crowded
with lambs and kids. The two groups were being kept apart,
and separate were the early-born lambs, separate the later-born ones,
and separate the "dew drops." All the vessels were overflowing with
    wey,
the pails and bowls, well made, in which he milked the animals.

The terminology is precise and affectionate, and apparently addressed to an audience familiar with shepherds' jargon (ἕρσαι, 'dew drops', as designating the youngest animals does not read as a poetic metaphor). But the verb used for the contemplation of the scene, ἐθηεύμεσθα, 'we gazed in wonder', suggests more than an everyday scene of ovicaprid farming. This is the verb, etymologically related to θαῦμα, 'wonder', that is also used for Hermes' amazement at the sight of Calypso's island (5.75), and Odysseus' admiration for Alkinoos' palace (7.133) and for the Phaeacian dancers (8.265). The Cyclops' animals are apparently something special, which should not surprise us given the Golden Age conditions obtaining in his land.

The Companions, not at ease with the situation, want to make off with the lambs and the kids and sail back to their island (9.224–7), urging the unlawful consumption of someone else's livestock, the central crime of the poem. Odysseus resists and prefers to wait for the inhabitant to return, citing an eagerness to receive gifts of hospitality (9.229). But at the end of the adventure the seven sheep under whose bellies the survivors were able to leave the cave (and presumably many more: πολλά, 9.465) are driven to the ship and taken on board, contrary to all common sense if Odysseus wants total silence in order not to betray their whereabouts to the Cyclops.

The theft of these sheep, not highlighted in Odysseus' narrative, but for Walter Burkert the goal of the entire expedition, is in the present quest sequence the liquidation of a lack only when we read the episode as a mythical representation of the rise of civilization from hunting to herding, with game animals being less desirable than domestic animals. There are clear features of the tale that point in this direction. The tale that stresses the Cyclopes' ignorance of ships and navigation (9.125) uses images from shipbuilding (9.384–6) and metallurgy (9.391–3) to celebrate Odysseus' victory over the monster, the latter perhaps in an ironical reference to the Cyclopes' role as smiths in the mainstream tradition.[26] In this perspective Odysseus emerges as a trickster hero whose double-edged achievements define culture as a complex compromise. Odysseus and his Companions win the sheep, but the hero will be laboring for many years under the curse of Poseidon, unleashed on him by the prayer of his blinded son.[27]

Unlimited meats, numbered sheep

The Cyclops episode concludes with a feast consisting of the meat of the raided sheep. If these animals are what it was all about, then their consumption is logical and fitting. But the quest motif is not the only layer of meaning in the episode. The raid on the Cyclops' flock reverberates with depredation elsewhere. There may be a pervasive similarity between the Cyclops and the Suitors, as we saw earlier, but once the story comes to its conclusion, with the escape under the bellies of the sheep and the theft of the Cyclops' flock, the dominant paradigmatic relation is between Odysseus/Companions and the Suitors. There is no suggestion in the text that entering the cave is for Odysseus and his men what

---

[26] Bremmer 2002: 142.
[27] Burkert 1979: 34. See Chapter 2 on the possible role of the Cyclops in this regard as "anti-donor" in the quest sequence.

entering Odysseus' house is for the Suitors. But once they are in, trapped by the master of the house, the similarity between their situation and that of the Suitors in their final hour becomes apparent. And the similarity continues into the final meal.

The Cyclops' animals are slaughtered as soon as Odysseus and his six remaining Companions have reached the opposite shore and rejoined the men who had remained behind. The wild goats are forgotten, and the sheep are divided according to the rules of the art, with Odysseus receiving the ram, under whose belly he reached safety, for himself alone. The language is that of the sack of a city (*Od.* 9.548–51; cf. *Od.* 9.41–2):

> μῆλα δὲ Κύκλωπος γλαφυρῆς ἐκ νηὸς ἑλόντες
> δασσάμεθ', ὡς μή τίς μοι ἀτεμβόμενος κίοι ἴσης.
> ἀρνειὸν δ' ἐμοὶ οἴῳ ἐϋκνήμιδες ἑταῖροι
> μήλων δαιομένων δόσαν ἔξοχα·
>
> And the sheep of the Cyclops we took out of the hollow ship
> and divided them so that no one was cheated of his share.
> The ram, to me alone my well-greaved Companions
> they gave it, above all the others when the sheep were being divided.

Unlike the wild goats, these domesticated sheep are sacrificed to the gods. Odysseus burns the thigh bones of the Cyclops' beloved ram to Zeus, but the god rejects the offering (*Od.* 9.553–5), a significant moment to which we will return in Chapter 7.

But in spite of the differences with the feast of the game animals the formula for "unlimited meat" used for that feast is used again (*Od.* 9.556–7):

> ὣς τότε μὲν πρόπαν ἦμαρ ἐς ἠέλιον καταδύντα
> ἥμεθα δαινύμενοι **κρέα τ' ἄσπετα** καὶ **μέθυ ἡδύ**
>
> So then all day long until the sun went down
> we sat there feasting on <u>unlimited meat</u> and <u>sweet wine</u>.

The formula for "unlimited meat" is nowhere else in the poem used for feasts consisting of domesticated animals and it marks the present meal as incongruous. The use of the formula here aligns the present meal with the feast of the wild goats and so points up its peculiar nature.[28] The Cyclops' carefully farmed sheep are not innumerable and their meat is "unlimited" only when consumed without restraint. Odysseus and the Companions have tasted the limitless plenty of paradise, and that experience now frames the present meal. That is, Odysseus and the Companions pretend that the

---

[28] See the Epilogue for discussion of the repetition within the wider framework of formulaic diction.

supply of meat of the stolen sheep of the Cyclops is as endless as that of the meat of the wild goats. What is more, they eat animals to which they have first assimilated themselves, the introduction of a theme that will be fully developed in the Circe episode (see Chapter 5).

The treatment of livestock – almost by definition a limited and bounded commodity – as limitlessly available is what further aligns Odysseus and the Companions with the Suitors as consumers of meat. If the Suitors create an illusory paradise out of the availability of meat animals that do not belong to them, then Odysseus and the Companions, having just experienced a real paradise of abundance, treat someone's bounded wealth as if nothing has changed. The meal, not sanctioned by Zeus, foreshadows the catastrophic consumption of much more rigidly counted livestock on Thrinacia, island of Helios the Sun, to which we turn in Chapter 6. In that feasting Odysseus will not participate. The Cyclops adventure, early as it happens in Odysseus' Wanderings, is a turning point for the hero. After it he will be able to refrain from meat consumption and to avoid other rash acts that endanger his *nostos* – a learning curve that will set him increasingly apart from his Companions in the adventures to come. The hero who played the role of the Suitors in the Cyclops episode and who likens the humiliation in his own house with the ordeal in the cave will be able to play yet another role: when his *nostos* draws to its climax, he will play the role of the Cyclops, meting out punishment to the intruders in a way of which Polyphemos would have been proud.

The master's return

The name Κύκλωψ (κύκλ-ωψ) is known to the Hesiodic tradition as referring to the single κυκλοτερὴς ὀφθαλμός, 'circular eye', lying in the Cyclopes' foreheads (Hes. *Theog.* 143–5). Modern comparative linguistics has proposed a different etymology: κύ-κλωψ, derived from *$p\hat{k}u$-klōps* (with an otherwise unattested reflex of Indo-European *$pe\hat{k}u$*): "cattle thief."[29] This etymology, if right, might link the Cyclops tale with the myth-type in which animals are stolen and hidden in a cave by a monstrous thief, necessitating a quest in which the animals are retrieved by a hero of the shaman-type who owns the cattle (Heracles, who has to deal with a variety of "cattle thieves" of this type, is the first example that comes to mind).[30] It would also illustrate the ease with which Odysseus and the Cyclops trade roles, not only in the Cyclops episode proper, but also across

---

[29] Thieme 1951: 177–8.   [30] Burkert 1979: 83–98.

the tale and its paradigmatic manifestation. The cattle thief takes on features of the "cattle thief," in particular, when Odysseus announces to Penelope, after their night of reunion, that he will resort to "raid and plunder" (ληΐσσομαι, *Od.* 23.357) in order to restore his stables after the Suitors' depredations.

We saw that Odysseus sees similarities between his patient suffering in his own house and the ordeal in the cave. But the paradigmatic alignment with his past self gives way to an altogether different role once the trap for the Suitors has been set. A preview of this role is offered when Odysseus is briefed by Athena (in the role of donor, see Chapter 2), on the situation in his house. In response to Odysseus' fatalistic reaction and wish that the goddess would assist him in the same way as she did at Troy, Athena replies (*Od.* 13.393–6):

καὶ λίην τοι ἐγώ γε παρέσσομαι, οὐδέ με λήσεις,
ὁππότε κεν δὴ ταῦτα πενώμεθα· καί τιν' ὀΐω
αἵματί τ' ἐγκεφάλῳ τε παλαξέμεν **ἄσπετον οὖδας**
ἀνδρῶν μνηστήρων, οἵ τοι βίοτον κατέδουσιν.

You bet that I for one will be there, and I will not lose sight of you
when you and I will be working on this job; and I look forward
to spatter <u>limitless ground</u> with blood and brain-matter,
of these Suitor men, who are devouring your livelihood

The remarkable phrase ἄσπετον οὖδας, 'unlimited ground', which recurs in the actual description of the massacre (*Od.* 22.269), resonates with the κρέα ἄσπετα of the Companions' Otherworldly feasts, linking unlimited bounty with death. But the entire speech Athena makes relates paradigmatically to the Cyclops episode, in which brain-matter is spattered when the Cyclops smashes Odysseus Companions to the ground (*Od.* 9.290). Athena's words have been found objectionable by some readers of the *Odyssey* (often in connection with a conception of different "layers" of religion in the poem) for their brutal, regressive violence, which one would prefer not to associate with an enlightened Olympian goddess.[31] But they are part of an elaborate strategy to fix the violent death of the Suitors in advance, and so create suspense of anticipation. In particular, they prepare Odysseus' alignment with the Cyclops as returning Master of Animals, who finds his house invaded by eating strangers. Athena's words are a strategic echo of the language of the Cyclops himself, the address to his favorite ram, which is about to carry Odysseus to safety (*Od.* 9.456–60):

---

[31] For example, Segal 1994: 222. See further Chapter 7.

εἰ δὴ ὁμοφρονέοις ποτιφωνήεις τε γένοιο
εἰπεῖν, ὅππῃ κεῖνος ἐμὸν μένος ἠλασκάζει·
τῶ κέ οἱ ἐγκέφαλός γε διὰ σπέος ἄλλυδις ἄλλῃ
θεινομένου ῥαίοιτο πρὸς οὔδεϊ, κὰδ δέ τ' ἐμὸν κῆρ
λωφήσειε κακῶν, τά μοι οὐτιδανὸς πόρεν Οὖτις.

If only you could think along with me and become communicative
so that you could tell me where that guy is skulking from my might;
then his brain-matter would be spattered through the cave in all
   directions
as he is beaten to the floor, and my heart would
get a relief from the suffering which non-valiant No-man gave me.

The position in which the Cyclops utters these words underscores the difference between him and his intended victim, whose escape, through *mētis*, will enable him not only to occupy the Cyclops' slot in a future allomorph of the tale, but also to improve on the latter's performance. The *megaron* of Odysseus' house, hermetically sealed, will serve as cave to the Suitors; the hero, standing on the threshold with his bow and his quiver, will not let anyone pass, unlike the Cyclops, who closed the entrance to his house "just as if he put the lid on a quiver" (*Od.* 9.314).

The similarity between the two situations is further marked by meaningful repetition of a half-line from the Cyclops episode (*Od.* 9.442–3):

τὸ δὲ νήπιος οὐκ ἐνόησεν,
ὣς οἱ ὑπ', εἰροπόκων ὀΐων στέρνοισι **δέδεντο.**

<What> he, clueless, did not grasp <was>
that they under the chests of the wool-fleeced sheep had been bound.

The Cyclops' ignorance is aligned with that of the Suitors, at the beginning of the carnage, after Odysseus has shot Antinoos through the throat (*Od.* 22.32–3):

τὸ δὲ νήπιοι οὐκ ἐνόησαν,
ὣς δή σφιν καὶ πᾶσιν ὀλέθρου πείρατ' **ἐφῆπτο.**

<What> they, clueless, did not grasp <was>
that at that point for all of them the ropes of their demise had been
   fastened.

The verbal similarities extend to the next line of each passage, which end on a pluperfect passive verb denoting binding, fastening (δέδεντο, ἐφῆπτο). There are multiple reversals and ironies here. The Suitors in their total lack of understanding of the situation in which they are trapped are likened to the Cyclops in his inability to keep his victims trapped. But the one who is really taking the role of the Cyclops is Odysseus, who does a far better job than the monster in keeping *his* victims imprisoned in his hall, whereas the Cyclops had to let his victims escape from his cave. Conversely, the Suitors, likened to the Cyclops in their ignorance, are in reality playing the role of Odysseus, but do much worse than he did. Both Odysseus and the Suitors enter into somebody's home uninvited and are helping themselves to the food supplies. But whereas Odysseus escaped triumphantly, the Suitors will be helplessly slaughtered in the hero's tightly locked *megaron*. The difference is ironically signaled by the two passive pluperfect verbs for fastening and binding. Odysseus' binding (under the sheep) is the way to survival, whereas the Suitors' binding, by the ὀλέθρου πείρατα, 'cables of destruction', is the seal of death.

Odysseus' first kill is Antinoos, whose blood, spouting in a thick stream from his nostrils, is characterized as ἀνδρομέοιο, 'human'. The rare adjective is Cyclopean, occurring three times in the episode (9.270, 347, 374) and nowhere else in the poem.[32] The Suitors' hour of reckoning begins as a hunt, as Odysseus kills them one by one with the arrows from the quiver (*Od.* 22.117–18). It may be pressing the evidence too far, but the text does specify, albeit indirectly, that the number of Suitors is identical to the number of wild goats killed in the hunt on Goat Island.[33] In addition, the "limitless meats" of the goats is echoed in the "limitless blood" (ἄσπετον ... αἷμα, 22.407) seen by Eurycleia after the slaughter and the "limitless ground" (ἄσπετον οὖδας) covered by the Suitors' bodies (22.269); but the spattering of their brain-matter over limitless ground, as foreseen by Athena (13.395), remains implicit, just as the Cyclops' own murderous vision does not become reality.

As the slaughter turns from a hunt into a battle, the Suitors are compared with domestic animals, a herd of cows spurred on by a gadfly in springtime (*Od.* 22.299–301). The ultimate alignment of Odysseus and the Cyclops, the consumption of the flesh of the intruders in the house, remains contained in similes: both Polyphemos and Odysseus become lions, in particular Odysseus, whose simile reverberates with the earlier cow simile (*Od.* 22.402–6; cf. 9.292):[34]

εὗρεν ἔπειτ' Ὀδυσῆα μετὰ κταμένοισι νέκυσσιν
αἵματι καὶ λύθρῳ πεπαλαγμένον ὥς τε λέοντα,

---

[32] This was pointed out to me by one of the two readers of the Press.
[33] According to the information Telemachos provides to Odysseus after the recognition scene, under the general heading ἀριθμόν, 'number'(*Od.* 16.246), there are 108 Suitors, as we can deduce from the addition of 52 Suitors from Doulichium, to 24 from Same, 20 from Zakynthus, and 12 from Ithaca itself.
[34] More on the significance of this simile in Chapter 8.

ὅς ῥά τε βεβρωκὼς βοὸς ἔρχεται ἀγραύλοιο·
πᾶν δ' ἄρα οἱ στῆθός τε παρήϊά τ' ἀμφοτέρωθεν
αἱματόεντα πέλει, δεινὸς δ' εἰς ὦπα ἰδέσθαι·
ὣς Ὀδυσεὺς πεπάλακτο πόδας καὶ χεῖρας ὕπερθεν.

Thereupon she [Eurycleia] found Odysseus among the dead corpses,
spattered and defiled with blood and gore, like a lion
who has feasted on a bull from the field and walks away from the slaughter.
All his breast and his cheeks on either side
are covered with blood; he is fearsome to look in the face:
Thus Odysseus was spattered and defiled, his legs and his arms above.

Odysseus, then, has much more in common with the Cyclops than he would have liked his audience to think when he presented the Cyclopes as lawless brutes without agriculture or political culture. Little did he know then that the situation in his own house would compel him to display Cyclopean behavior in order to win back his house and family, and we begin to appreciate the unintended irony in Odysseus' words when he declares that the Cyclopes make their own law for their wives and children, and do not care for each other (9.114–15, cited earlier). Indeed, Odysseus' Cyclopean behavior is forced on him by the Cyclops himself, who successfully prays to his father Poseidon that Odysseus may find "evil in his home" upon his return, having lost all his ships and his Companions. That prayer and its consequences will occupy us further in Chapter 7. Let us first follow Odysseus in his Wanderings, exploring the potential they have for putting the evil in his home in perspective.

CHAPTER 5

Feasting in the land of the dawn

"Will you not stop this woeful bloodshed? Don't you see
that you are devouring each other in the heedlessness of your *noos*?"
(Empedocles, *Fr.* B136 DK)

The adventure in the cave of the Cyclops creates a rift between Odysseus and his men the full impact of which will not become apparent until much later, and that will not concern us as such until Chapter 6. It is announced in Odysseus' mysterious explanation for Zeus' refusal to accept the sacrifice of the Cyclops' sheep: the god was already "pondering how they could all come to perish, the well-benched ships and my trusted Companions" (9.554–5). The next two adventures demonstrate the lines along which the Companions' demise will play out. The Aiolos episode has the Companions act in "heedlessness" (ἀφραδίῃσιν, 10.27), as they open the Bag of the Winds, having no access to the privileged information Aiolos had given to Odysseus alone: the hero comes to be separated from his crew as an individual facing a collective, just as he was presented to us in the poem's proem. This points ahead to the final stage of mutual alienation, the hero's solitude in the adventure of the Cattle of the Sun.

The Aiolos episode also continues the theme of unreal abundance, as Odysseus and his men are feasting for an entire month in Aiolos' hall, whose *dais* is perpetual (αἰεὶ ... δαίνυνται, 10.8–9). The detail that his house is κνισῆεν, 'filled with the steam of burning fat', suggests that the eternal, copious meal consists of beef, miraculously procured on this floating island.

The Laestrygonian episode highlights the new developments by copying essential features of the Cyclops adventure, over and above the paradigmatic features that the two episodes have in common (see Chapter 2). Once more Odysseus' Companions get eaten by monstrous cannibals and again an enclosed space plays an essential role: the ships are moored in a fjord-like harbor with steep cliffs on either side and a narrow entrance

74

(10.87–90),[1] recalling the Cyclops' cave. But whereas it was Odysseus who urged entrance into the fateful cave in the face of opposition from his Companions, here he is the only one who is prudent enough not to enter, mooring his ship outside.

For the crews of the other eleven ships the closed harbor becomes a death trap paradigmatically equivalent not only to the Cyclops' cave for the Companions who died there, but also to Odysseus' hermetically closed *megaron*, in which the Suitors were trapped in order to be massacred. The parallelism of the fate of both groups is underscored by similar imagery: in both cases the victims become fish caught in order to be consumed. The Laestrygonians destroy the ships with large boulders thrown from above and then, spearing them like fish, carry them away as a "joyless *dais*" (ἀτερπέα δαῖτα, 10.124); and the Suitors are likened to fish dragged in nets out of the water to die on the beach piled on each other (22.383–9) in a simile to which we will return in Chapter 6.

Hunting to survive

Being eaten is also a leading theme in the second of the three extended episodes in the Otherworld, even though no one actually gets eaten, at least none of Odysseus' Companions. Circe is often called a "witch" or a "sorceress," but a variety of anthropological perspectives, derived from diverse regions around the world, will allow us to be more precise than that and do more justice to this goddess' role and importance in the *Odyssey*. Circe, as Odysseus informs his audience at the beginning of his telling of the episode (10.137–9), is the daughter of Helios the Sun and the Oceanid Perse, and sister of Aietes, the "man of Aea." The latter family relation links her with the myth of Jason's quest for the Golden Fleece, which takes place at Colchis in the Caucasus. A detail provided later in the episode confirms that Circe has in fact to be located in the far east, since her island is where the "dancing-places of early-born Dawn" are located and where the "risings of Helios" occur (12.3–4).[2] She seems to be associated with the dawn in more than a mere spatial sense.[3]

---

[1] Identified by M. L. West (2005: 49–53), on the basis of earlier scholarship, with the Balaclava harbor in the Crimea.

[2] Nakassis 2004: 222–3; M. L. West 2005: 43–5, 2007 (seeing "dawn" in the etymology of Aea). Ballabriga 1998: 139–53 argues for actual geographical reflection in the *Odyssey*, and discusses the ambiguities of Circe's location along the east–west axis.

[3] M. L. West (1997: 408) brings out the solar connections of Circe through her name: the manifest connection with κίρκος, 'falcon', may reflect Egyptian iconography, where the Sun God is represented as a falcon, also in Phoenician art under Egyptian influence. In addition, the Hebrew word for 'falcon', he notes, is *'ayyah*.

In addition to the east–west axis, sources for the Circe episode have been located in the north and in the south (Mesopotamia).[4] Suggestive evidence, however, as we will see later in this chapter, comes from the very area where the *Odyssey* locates her.

Circe's solar connections, as daughter of Helios and a goddess associated with the dawn, are significant, since there is, as we will see, a contrastive relation between her island Aeaea and Thrinacia, island of the Sun and located in the far west. Moreover, both father and daughter are owners and protectors of animals, albeit in very different ways. But Circe has more functions. She can change humans into animals, has Underworld associations, is interested in having sex with the traveler who meets her, and is capable of procuring paradisiacal abundance. There is, as we will see, a common denominator to all these seemingly disparate functions.

The paradigmatic relations between the various instantiations of the basic story pattern as discussed in Chapter 2 point up further meanings. On Aeaea things are not what they seem to be, and the charms of the island's mistress belie the important characteristics she has in common with the monstrous Cyclops: both have received prophecies about Odysseus' coming (9.507–14; 10.330–2), both serve as the goal of a quest and at the same time helper, as part of a wider quest. Circe's role as helper, or "donor" in Propp's terminology, which, as we saw in Chapter 2, relates her to Siduri in *Gilgamesh*, consists in sending Odysseus to the Land of the Dead, where he is to consult Tiresias, and in providing directions for the continuation of the journey. But the most important link between Circe and the Cyclops is that both are Masters of Animals.

The Cyclops and Circe episodes stand out from the other instantiations of the quest/reconnaissance pattern in that both encounters are preceded by a hunt during which smoke is sighted, betraying the presence of the antagonist. This shared feature is striking, but so are the differences. On Goat Island the hunt was a collective undertaking: the entire company hunts a large number of animals out of an "unlimited" pool of game; on Aeaea it is Odysseus alone who hunts and his catch is a single, if enormous, animal. On both islands the game is presented as food for the Companions, but whereas on Goat Island, as we saw, the nymphs stir up the animals "so that the Companions could have a meal" (ἵνα δειπνήσειαν ἑταῖροι, 9.155), on Aeaea it is the hero who takes the initiative to "give the

---

[4] Carpenter 1956: 18–19 (north); Crane 1988: 61–75 (Mesopotamia).

Companions a meal" (δεῖπνον ἑταίροισιν δόμεναι, 10.155). Whereas the hero and his Companions were a coherent community in relatively good spirits on Goat Island, they are now divided, as the rift between Odysseus and his men begins to appear, into a passive and dejected collective, on the one hand, and an energetic but solitary hero, on the other.

Odysseus has to share agency with "some god" (10.157) who takes pity on the lonely hero in stirring up the large stag to cross his path. True to "Jörgensen's Law," which specifies that as a first-person narrator Odysseus has an experiential perspective different from that of the omniscient epic narrator,[5] the hero is ignorant of the identity of the god responsible for this piece of good luck. The text never reveals the identity of this god, but we may perhaps suspect Hermes, for reasons to be detailed later. In any case, the detail in which the kill – a heroic slaying, humanizing the victim – and especially the transportation of the carcass to the ship is described is striking; this is the largest catch that one man can take home.

When Odysseus has completed his mission, the resulting meal is described in exactly the same terms as the feast of the 108 goats: Odysseus and his men dine all day long on "unlimited meats (κρέα ἄσπετα) and sweet wine" (10.183–4). By this time meat has stopped being a hero's symbolic capital. The new feast is not even an attempt at culture as made by settlers in a remote outpost in the wilderness. During the consumption of this game animal no nearby presence of domesticated meat animals distracts the eaters, as it did on Goat Island. Meat, any meat, has become a matter of elementary physical survival, a need for proteins that typifies human life deprived of the trappings and resources of culture. Odysseus says as much when he invites the Companions to the feast (*Od.* 10.174–7):

> ὦ φίλοι, οὐ γάρ πω καταδυσόμεθ᾽, ἀχνύμενοί περ,
> εἰς Ἀΐδαο δόμους, πρὶν μόρσιμον ἦμαρ ἐπέλθῃ.
> ἀλλ᾽ ἄγετ᾽, ὄφρ᾽ ἐν νηΐ θοῇ βρῶσίς τε πόσις τε,
> μνησόμεθα βρώμης μηδὲ τρυχώμεθα λιμῷ.

> My friends, we are not yet going down, afflicted though we are,
> to the house of Hades, before the day of our death has arrived.
> Come on, as long as there is meat and drink in the swift ship
> let us get our strength from meat and let's not be worn out by hunger.[6]

Food is essential to sustain the life of mortals who are not yet ready to go down into Hades (although Odysseus and the Companions will go down

---

[5] Jörgensen 1904.   [6] For the translation of μνησόμεθα, see Bakker 2008a. See also Chapter 8.

there sooner than they now realize), and who delight in the light of the sun, the giver and sustainer of life, and food. The stag was said to be held by "the might of the sun" (δὴ γάρ μιν ἔχεν μένος ἠελίοιο, 10.160), a phrase that at the surface simply means that the animal was thirsty; but on the island of the daughter of Helios, giver of light and life and Master of Animals, things are not what they seem to be at first sight. The reference to Hades and death, furthermore, is more than merely ironic – Odysseus and the Companions will in fact go to Hades in the course of the Circe episode. Food, Odysseus is saying, is for the living, but little does he realize that the adventure in which he finds himself links food and eating with death.

If the homologous goats in the Cyclops episode are significant, we may wonder about the meaning of this stag. Some scholars stress the heroic way in which Odysseus kills it and thus see the episode, and Odysseus' resolve to "give the Companions a meal," as a confirmation of his heroic status and his ability to take responsibility for his men. Being a redistributor is after all, as we saw in Chapter 3, an important function of chieftains in the heroic world. But Aeaea is far beyond the confines of the heroic world, and different types of explanation have been proposed as well. The stag hunt has been seen in connection with folktale Underworld motifs: the hunter, in pursuing an animal of prey, arrives in the Underworld, or in an Otherworld. This assumes the existence of an earlier version in which Odysseus arrives at Circe's while pursuing the stag – or that Circe's world *is* in fact the Underworld, a possibility we will pursue below. Finally, the stag has drawn attention to itself as a kind of Actaeon, a hapless former hunter turned into the animal he presumably pursued. Metamorphosis into animal shape is explicitly suggested by Eurylochos, when he tries to dissuade Odysseus and the Companions from returning to the house of Circe, by saying that she will turn them all into the boars, wolves, and lions that guard her house (10.432–4). The stag, we may note, is referred to as πέλωρον, 'monstrous creature' (10.168), just like the fawning wolves and lions around Circe's palace (10.219).[7]

The mythical operation of metamorphosis is what has turned Circe into a folktale witch or a sorceress, her most common characterization both in popular and in scholarly literature as well as in the rich reception history of the episode. But what if we speak instead of *metempsychosis*? We do not hear

---

[7] Odysseus' confidence as an Iliadic hero: Schmoll 1987; Odysseus as responsible leader: Scodel 1994; Underworld: Alexander 1991; Actaeon: Roessel 1989: 32–3.

about the outlook of the stag, but Odysseus' men, when they have undergone their change of shape, retain a distinctly human psyche (*Od.* 10.239–40):

οἱ δὲ συῶν μὲν ἔχον κεφαλὰς φωνήν τε τρίχας τε
καὶ δέμας, αὐτὰρ νοῦς ἦν ἔμπεδος ὡς τὸ πάρος περ.

And they had the heads, voice, and hair as well as the build
of swine, but their *nous* had not changed from what it was before.

Metempsychosis – or metensomatosis, if we concentrate on the "incorporation" of the disembodied soul into its new body – is one out of several allegorizing ways in which the Circe episode has been read in the Neoplatonist milieu of late antiquity.[8] Homer is here typically seen as repository of philosophical concepts and ideas that are dear to the interpreter, expressed in riddling ways. In a passage quoted in Stobaeus (1.445.14–448.3), variously attributed to Porphyry and Plutarch,[9] the lines just quoted are interpreted allegorically as a poetic statement on the transmigration of souls, with Aeaea being the place where the souls of the dead arrive, bewildered and disoriented after losing the familiar surroundings of their former flesh and before the beginning of their next life, reincarnated into a lower mammal. The author of the fragment sees in Odysseus' words to the Companions upon returning with the stag to the camp a confirmation of this interstitial period (*Od.* 10.190–2):

ὦ φίλοι, οὐ γὰρ ἴδμεν ὅπῃ ζόφος οὐδ' ὅπῃ ἠώς,
οὐδ' ὅπῃ ἠέλιος φαεσίμβροτος εἶσ' ὑπὸ γαῖαν
οὐδ' ὅπῃ ἀννεῖται·

My friends, we do not know what way the dusk is, nor what way the dawn,
nor what way Helios who shines for mortals goes below the earth,
nor what way he rises.

But in another account, *De vita Homeri*, attributed to Plutarch, Odysseus is far less disoriented than the Companions, being able, due to Hermes (standing for *logos*, reason), to resist temptation and therefore to remain human and avoid the cycle of metensomatosis. The Companions, by contrast, succumb to gluttony and greed, and fall victim to the cycle of death and rebirth that Circe stands for (Ps.-Plut. *De vit. Hom.* 126):[10]

And the change of Odysseus' Companions into swine and similar animals is told in a riddling way: the souls of men who are devoid of sense and reason exchange

---
[8] See Lamberton 1986: 41–2, 106–7, 115–19; Bettini and Franco 2010: 106–10.
[9] Most recently (Helmig 2008) to the latter on stylistic grounds; translation in Lamberton 1986: 115–17.
[10] Cf. Lamberton 1986: 41; Bettini and Franco 2010: 107.

<their human bodies> for the shape of the body of wild animals. They fall into the cyclical rotation that is called "Circe." She is plausibly taken to be the daughter of the Sun and lives on the island Aeaea. This name comes from the verb *aiazein*, lamenting of humans at their deaths. By contrast, the man of sense and reason (ἔμφρων ἀνήρ), Odysseus himself, does not experience this kind of change, as he takes immunity from Hermes, i.e., from reason.[11]

In this allegorizing reading, then, the Companions are not so much changed into as *reborn* into swine. The reading is suggestive; punishment for the Companions as gluttons and reward for Odysseus as a rational and virtuous man are certainly in line with the moral thrust of the poem (see further Chapter 7). But a formal and developed theory of Pythagorean or Neoplatonist transmigration, which emphasizes the great divide between man and beast, seems less pertinent to the Circe episode – and the *Odyssey* – than a conception of transmigration based on the essential similarity between the two. And instead of the *Odyssey* foreshadowing the tenets of the philosophers of late antiquity, we may want to look at some of the ways in which the poem reflects belief systems of societies that preceded it. This leads us back to the context in which Odysseus kills the stag.

The inclusive society

As the *Odyssey* "remembers" the remote past in making Odysseus travel far beyond the world known to its Greek audiences, the hero must experience what those at Ithaca have "forgotten." Presumably the Greek world was once closer to hunting as a means of subsistence than it is at the time of the historical record, or even at the time depicted in epic. Odysseus is forced to survive in "nature." We saw in Chapter 4 that a natural environment, untouched by the demands imposed by culture (i.e., agriculture and pastoralism) can procure abundance unimaginable in the civilized world of domesticated nature. But here on Aeaea a further aspect of pre-cultural "nature" emerges.

Traditional hunting cultures are typically not likely to see the supply of game animals in the forest around them as an unlimited, inexhaustible resource any more than the farmers of archaic Greece thought of their

---

[11] Καὶ τὸ μεταβάλλειν δὲ τοὺς ἑταίρους τοῦ Ὀδυσσέως εἰς σύας καὶ τοιαῦτα ζῷα τοῦτο αἰνίττεται, ὅτι τῶν ἀφρόνων ἀνθρώπων αἱ ψυχαὶ μεταλλάττουσιν εἰς εἴδη σωμάτων θηριωδῶν, ἐμπεσοῦσαι εἰς τὴν τοῦ παντὸς ἐγκύκλιον περιφοράν, ἣν Κίρκην προσαγορεύει καὶ κατὰ τὸ εἰκὸς Ἡλίου παῖδα ὑποτίθεται, οἰκοῦσαν ἐν τῇ Αἰαίῃ νήσῳ· ταύτην δὲ ἀπὸ τοῦ 'αἰάζειν' καὶ ὀδύρεσθαι τοὺς ἀνθρώπους ἐπὶ τοῖς θανάτοις κέκληκεν. ὁ δὲ ἔμφρων ἀνήρ, αὐτὸς ὁ Ὀδυσσεύς, οὐκ ἔπαθε τὴν τοιαύτην μεταβολήν, παρὰ τοῦ Ἑρμοῦ (τουτέστι τοῦ λόγου) τὸ ἀπαθὲς λαβών.

The inclusive society

herds and flocks as a daily source of meat. The availability of game animals is often not guaranteed or self-evident, and success in the hunt cannot be taken for granted any more than gods in the Greek experience are obliged to accept the sacrifice offered to them. The hunt itself, in fact, may be framed as a sacrifice;[12] religious rules may apply to it that make the concept of "nature," as an objective reality untouched by man, problematic: the hunter and his prey are members of one and the same society that imposes rules on the interaction between them.

The idea that humans and the animals they prey on constitute a single natural society or "system" is attested for a wide variety of traditional hunting cultures. For example, the Tukano of the Vaupés territory of the northwest Amazon (Colombia) hold that the universe is the work of a Sun-Father, a masculine, energizing divinity that created only a limited number of animals (one is reminded here of Helios as the owner of strictly numbered cattle, to be discussed in Chapter 6). The amount of energy that the killing of an animal takes out of the cosmic system has to be restored and reincorporated back into the system by converting the animal into nourishment or ensuring that human energy, even in the form of loss of human life, is redirected to balance the system.[13] The task of overseeing such reciprocities falls to the shaman, or *payé*, who acts as broker between culture and nature, demand and supply, life and death, ensuring that the two remain intimately interconnected.[14]

For the Tukano the hunt is not only connected with a notion of balance and reciprocity, but also with the human life cycle. To replace the animals that are caught by the hunters, a number of the souls of the dead go to uterine storehouses teeming with life, where the prototypes of animals are kept, to replenish the energy lost in the killing of prey animals and to be converted into new animals that will go on to inhabit the forest to be caught by new hunters.[15] These animal storehouses, located under rocky outcrops or in deep river pools, are where *Vaí-mahsë* lives, a spiritual being who is in some respects (animal shape, sexual appetite) very similar to the Greek satyrs.[16] He acts as Master of Animals (or Master of Fish), being

---

[12] Valeri 1994.   [13] Reichel-Dolmatoff 1976: 309–11; Jackson 1983: 208–9.
[14] Reichel-Dolmatoff 1971: 125–35; Jackson 1983: 196–7.
[15] Reichel-Dolmatoff 1971: 65–6; Jackson 1983: 206–7.
[16] Hybridity is typical of Masters of Animals as they control humans' interactions with the animal world, e.g., Nordenskiöld 1924: 278 (Maya); Baumann 1938: 224 (Hausa, West Africa); Röhrig 1959: 108 (Russia); H. P. Duerr 1984: 278 (Inuit); Valeri 2000: 28, 318 (Huaulu, Moluccans). In this connection one may wonder about the numerous hybrid beings in Greek mythology. (I owe the references in this footnote to J. Duerr 2010.)

responsible for the animals' procreation, but he is also a hunter himself.[17] *Vaí-mahsë* has to be visited by the shaman, whose task it is to negotiate who in the community has to die and in what numbers, in order to ensure a successful new hunting season.[18] The consequence of such recycling of vital energy is that killing and eating the forest's wildlife is not only a matter of moderation and restraint, but also of considerable anxiety.

A natural consequence of such reciprocal relations between humans and their environment is a conception of humanity as being an integral part of the total class of mortal beings. In a wide variety of unrelated cultures the dividing line between human and animal tends to be blurred, in a belief that there is more than meets the eye beneath the surface reality of biological diversity: human and animal blend together, especially in the defining event of the hunt. The quest for food brings hunter and hunted together as competitors on an even plane. Thus, the Makuna, an eastern Tukano group, hold that in their essential aspect, human beings and animals are undifferentiated, all belonging to the comprehensive category of *masa*, 'people'. Within this "inclusive society," humans can become animals, animals humans, in an encompassing circulation of energy and vitality.[19] What matters is not the individual virtue cherished by the Neoplatonist philosopher, but the balance and harmony of the world.

For the Huaulu, who live in the forests of the Moluccas in eastern Indonesia, the reciprocity is enacted in the pivotal and performative event of the hunt, which is conceived as double: a visible hunt, in which human hunters prey on deer, wild pigs, and cassowaries, inexorably joined with an invisible hunt, in which the lord of the land preys on the human hunters, using their own prey animals as his hunting dogs.[20] Animals are further humanized in this culture by the prescription that the hunt be conducted as human warfare (compare the description of Odysseus killing the stag), a struggle that can always end in the adversary's favor.[21] What heroizes the human humanizes the animal.

The complex of interrelated beliefs and conceptions we are investigating as background for understanding Circe and her world also comprises sexuality, in conjunction with human life and death and the integration of human and animal life cycles. *Vaí-mahsë*, the Tukano Master of Animals, takes a keen sexual interest in humans. He may follow women

---

[17] Reichel-Dolmatoff 1971: 80–4. Other cultures have similar conceptions of subterranean dwellings full of wildlife, e.g., the sub-Arctic Cree; cf. Tanner 1979: 175–6.
[18] Reichel-Dolmatoff 1971: 130–1; cf. 81–2.   [19] Århem 1996: 188.   [20] Valeri 1994: 117; 2000: 305.
[21] Valeri 1994: 115.

who walk alone in the forest and cause them to fall into a deep sleep, during which he has intercourse with them; the victim experiences the intercourse only as a dream, but she dies after a short time.[22] He has also a daughter, who appears along riverbanks and seduces young boys – much like Greek nymphs.[23] In both cases an abundance of game animals is produced in return for the sexual favor. But the sudden abundance may be dangerous, as it may cause the death of more people in return for the animals.[24] The sexual relations between the Master of Animals and women is mirrored in the sexual symbolism of the hunt, in which the game animal has to be "seduced" into allowing itself to be killed, the kill being an act of sexual domination.[25] This symbolism underlies the elaborate prescriptions and taboos, attested for a wide variety of hunting cultures, of sexual purity and abstinence, and ritual purity of the hunter's body and his weapons.

A variant on this sexual symbolism is the "mystic marriage" that the hunter or the shaman may have to contract in the spiritual world. The Buryat, situated in central Siberia to the west of Lake Baikal, know a "spirit of the forest," a giver of game who appears most often in the form of a large cervid, whose daughter, beautiful and nude, seduces the hunter and leads him on into the forest, giving game animals in return. She is indispensable for any success in the hunt, but predictably dangerous.[26]

A particularly suggestive case of the interconnected set of conceptions under study here is the goddess Dæl of the Svans, who inhabit the highlands of northwest Georgia, to the east of the Black Sea.[27] Dæl is the divine "shepherd" of the ibex and other large horned mammals of the high mountains. She appears as a woman of exceptional beauty with long golden-colored hair, but can also change her shape into one of the animals under her protection. This Mistress of Animals protects her flock, ensuring that no individual hunter can kill and bring home more than one animal (Odysseus and the stag come to mind), but she is generous to the hunter

---

[22] Similarly for the Huaulu: Valeri 2000: 305.
[23] The complex of conceptions discussed here may well underlie what is in the study of Greek religion known as "nympholepsy," on which, see recently Pache 2011.
[24] Reichel-Dolmatoff 1971: 84; similar sexual predation is attested for the Master of Animals of the Huaulu: Valeri 2000: 305.
[25] Reichel-Dolmatoff (1971: 220) notes that the Tukano verb for hunting can be translated as "make love to the animals." Special relations between hunter and game animals also underlie conceptions of the hunt for the Mistassini Cree hunters (sub-Arctic Canada); see Tanner 1979: 136–52.
[26] Hamayon 1990: 378. The shaman in this culture owes his status to a mystic alliance with this spirit being; see Hamayon 1990: 454ff.
[27] Tuite 2006.

she has selected as her lover, granting him success as long as he is faithful to her. She demands purity; a hunter is polluted if a woman in his household is having her period or is in childbirth. And in one story she orders her human lover to avoid all contact with his wife or any mortal woman.[28] Again, the successful hunt is construed as sexual consummation in the spiritual world.

Dæl, furthermore, is associated with the morning star and dawn.[29] The Svan hunter must be at the hunting grounds when the morning star is still visible in the sky (note that Odysseus' stag hunt also takes place at dawn, 10.144). Dæl is further worshipped on New Year's night, the moment of the completion of a full year and the beginning of a new one. A link with the dead is suggested by Dæl's homologue Samdzimari (from northeast Georgia), who has hypochthonic origins and is entrusted with the trajectory of the souls after their death.[30]

Dæl and Samdzimari each have an antagonist and counterpart in, respectively, Jgëræg and Giorgi. This divinity is equated with St. George by name, but he antedates the Georgian Orthodox tradition. His function is to exploit the very spaces that Dæl protects: he is the patron of beekeepers, hunters, travelers, even cattle-raiders, in short, all those involved in activities that take men out of their village into the wilds in order to further their own interests or to secure the well-being of their community. It is not difficult to see in this ancient Georgian divinity traits of Hermes, Circe's antagonist in the *Odyssey* who ensures Odysseus' survival and makes sure his quests succeeds.

The parallels between Circe and Dæl (protection of animals, sexual predation, dawn and New Year associations, on which see below, male divine counterpart and adversary) are in fact so striking that we may be tempted to posit direct borrowing beyond mere typological similarity. This may seem perilous, but the intriguing fact remains that the Svan territory is located near what is Colchis for the Greeks, and apart from Circe the exchanges between the Caucasus and the Greek world have been well documented.[31]

---

[28] Tuite 2006: 166.
[29] Tuite 2006: 166–7, 178–9; the name Dæl has been connected with Georgian *Dila* 'morning', but that etymology is disputed (Tuite 2006: 165).
[30] Tuite 2006: 168–74.
[31] Charachidzé 1986; Tuite 1998. Tuite (2006: 175) further notes that the Svan territory has been inhabited "continuously since the Bronze Age, with no archeological, ethnographic or toponymic evidence to indicate that the Bronze Age inhabitants ... were other than the ancestors of the current residents."

The yearlong feast

But just as important as the possible local sources for the Circe story are the coherence and wide distribution of the interrelated notions and beliefs under study (hunting, the blurring of the dividing line between human and animal, transmigration, sexuality, and protection of game animals). This complex and its typological importance enable us to bring to bear on the episode features that can be gathered from remote and manifestly unrelated traditions and societies. Circe is an elemental force of nature, surrounded by nymph servants who are "born from sources, groves, and sacred rivers" (10.350–1); she is presumably an important nymph herself,[32] to continue the discussion of this kind of divinity from Chapter 4. Her dwelling place on the paradise island, surrounded by a variety of large mammals, can be seen as something comparable to the uterine storehouses of animal life where the Tukano locate regeneration and the abundance they contrast with the reality of their hunting grounds. Approaching those places in the forest is dangerous, as Circe's house is dangerous to Odysseus' unsuspecting Companions, who follow the Mistress of Animals into her house out of "ignorance" (ἀϊδρείῃσιν, 10.231) of the land and its dangers.

What happens inside is a two-stage process. First, the victims are made to "lose the fatherland from their mind" (λαθοίατο πατρίδος αἴης, 10.236), so that they enter an induced state of cultural alienation. We may note that in formulaic grammar this is the state Odysseus himself is in, in spite of his resisting the charm at first, when after a full year of feasting the Companions have to remind him of his fatherland (ἤδη νῦν μιμνῄσκεο πατρίδος αἴης, 'and now put the fatherland in your mind', 10.472). Like people in the anthropological record who have come in contact with the Master of Animals, the Companions lose awareness of their surroundings, origins, and community. But whereas the Companions are dehumanized in the first stage of Circe's charm, in the second stage, after their "death" as humans they are humanized as animals: the lines quoted earlier (10.239–40) specify that the hogs that Circe engenders have human knowledge and perception.

Pigs not only have minds; they also have flesh that can be eaten. When Odysseus after the first lovemaking with Circe is seated before a copious meal, he displays a strongly negative reaction to the food put before him by Circe's servants, "having thoughts other <than appetite>" (ἀλλοφρονέων, 10.374) and his "spirit suspecting evil things" (κακὰ δ' ὄσσετο θυμός,

---

[32] Larson 2001: 27–8.

10.374). When Circe asks him about his aversion to the food offered, the hero replies as follows (*Od.* 10.383–7):

ὦ Κίρκη, τίς γάρ κεν ἀνήρ, ὃς ἐναίσιμος εἴη,
πρὶν τλαίη **πάσσασθαι ἐδητύος ἠδὲ ποτῆτος**,
πρὶν λύσασθ' ἑτάρους καὶ ἐν ὀφθαλμοῖσιν ἰδέσθαι;
ἀλλ' εἰ δὴ πρόφρασσα πιεῖν φαγέμεν τε κελεύεις,
λῦσον, ἵν' ὀφθαλμοῖσιν ἴδω ἐρίηρας ἑταίρους.

Oh Circe, what man, any man who has any sense of decorum,
could ever bear <u>to taste of this food and drink</u>,
<u>before he had set free his Companions</u> and seen them with his own
   eyes?
No, if you really are asking me with the best intentions to eat and drink,
then set them free, so that I can see with my own eyes my faithful
   Companions.

The text does not specify what Odysseus has before him on his plate.[33] But we may safely assume Odysseus suspects it might be pork. His concern is not made explicit and is often overlooked.[34] We saw that the episode has been allegorized as a dramatization of Pythagorean transmigration; and in the context of the quest story pattern, in which the retrieval of the Companions is pivotal, it would make sense to think of the reincarnation of *individual* souls with the concomitant urge for vegetarianism out of fear of eating the flesh of someone one knows.

But with respect to the wider themes of the poem a less specific kind of anxiety emerges. The quest pattern dramatizes the dangers of and anxieties about eating meat in general, especially meat that is (too) readily available. Eating meat, as we saw, can easily be conceived of as linked with human death; hunting brings hunter and prey closer to each other in more ways than just in physical space.

If we assume, with the Tukano and other hunting cultures as reviewed earlier, that humans are an integral part of the animal kingdom, then pigs and humans can be said to form an exclusive subgroup within which the dividing line between human and animal is further weakened. Pigs are neither ruminants nor carnivores, but omnivores, just like humans; the two are thus capable of eating each other. They have very similar digestive tracts and may compete for the same food.[35] Circe gives the swine

---

[33] The food Circe offers Odysseus is referred to as σῖτον (10.371, 375), which properly means "bread." But the other terms used, εἴδατα (10.372), ἐδητύος (10.384), and βρώμης (10.379), are all capable of referring to food as meat (and βρώμης links the present meal with the meat of the stag: 10.176).
[34] The only mention known to me of the food anxiety in the passage is Roessel 1989: 36 n. 21.
[35] On pig physiology, see Swindle and Smith 2000.

she has created acorns to eat, a reminder that the pig is originally a woodland species, though in other circumstances pigs may get wheat, or other food suitable for human consumption to eat.[36] Moreover, within the poetic world of the *Odyssey*, the conditions suitable for survival of a human deprived of clothing and tools, that is, reduced to an animal state, are similar to the shady lair of the wild boar, as is formulaically expressed in the identical description of Odysseus' shelter on Scheria and the lair of the wild boar of the hunting expedition on Mount Parnassus (*Od.* 5.478–83; 19.440–3).

But most uncannily to the point is that human flesh and pork are very similar in taste and smell. Within the ancient world a suggestive formulation comes from the second-century physician and philosopher Galen (*On the Properties of Foodstuffs*; 6.663 Kühn):[37]

> The flesh of swine is very similar to that of man, as can be inferred from the fact that people who have eaten human flesh served to them as pork (criminal innkeepers have been known to do this) did not have any suspicion as to the taste and smell of it.

More recent evidence includes the Polynesian practice of referring to human flesh as "long pig" (in addition to eating it) and the "testimony" of individual cannibals in the Western world.[38]

If human flesh tastes like pork, then pork tastes like human flesh. Circe's actions have not only laid bare man's nature as an eating animal, but have also drawn attention to the dangers of eating. No overt cannibalism takes place, since Circe does as Odysseus asks and releases the Companions. When they have regained their human flesh, their looking "much more beautiful and bigger" (10.396) suggests a genuine rebirth. Circe's power over human and animal shape is in reality a power over the human life cycle. She has effected not so much a metamorphosis as an accelerated metempsychosis, a recycling of human flesh and energy. The goddess' associations with death and the Afterlife, as suggested by the

---

[36] Harris 1985: 75–6 attributes the religious taboo on pork in Jewish and Muslim cultures to deforestation in the Middle East and the subsequent deterioration of the resulting farming and grazing lands to desert, pigs having been more popular as domestic meat animals before. Raising pigs, which are forest animals needing shade and humidity, would have become unsustainable under the new ecological conditions.

[37] τῆς δ' ὑείας σαρκὸς τὴν πρὸς ἄνθρωπον ὁμοιότητα καταμαθεῖν ἔστι κἀκ τοῦ τινας ἐδηδοκότας ἀνθρωπείων κρεῶν ὡς ὑείων οὐδεμίαν ὑπόνοιαν ἐσχηκέναι κατά τε τὴν γεῦσιν αὐτῶν καὶ τὴν ὀσμήν· ἐφωράθη γὰρ ἤδη που τοῦτο γεγονὸς ὑπό τε πονηρῶν πανδοχέων καὶ ἄλλων τινῶν.

[38] Most notorious recently (2001) is the case of the German Armin Meiwes, who reportedly said in an interview (held in prison) that the flesh of his victim tasted like pork. Less recent (1925) is the case of Karl Denke of Ziębice, Poland, who pickled the flesh of his victims and sold it as pork.

ethnographical evidence reviewed above, are closely linked with her function as provider of game animals and their meat.[39]

Just as in the various accounts of the sexual encounters of hunters with Masters of Animals, Odysseus' sexual union with Circe results in an unreal abundance of food, which can be enjoyed safely, or so one thinks, once the Companions have regained their human flesh. When Odysseus returns to Circe's house with the remaining half of his crew, the newly reborn humans are already dining (10.452). From then on everything Odysseus and his men do or experience on Aeaea revolves around eating. Once more the unlimited meat formula is used, but this time the feast lasts not "an entire day till the setting of the sun," but a full year till the completion of all the seasons (*Od.* 10.467–70):

ἔνθα μὲν ἤματα πάντα τελεσφόρον εἰς ἐνιαυτὸν
ἥμεθα, δαινύμενοι **κρέα τ' ἄσπετα** καὶ μέθυ ἡδύ·
ἀλλ' ὅτε δή ῥ' ἐνιαυτὸς ἔην, περὶ δ' ἔτραπον ὧραι,
μηνῶν φθινόντων, περὶ δ' ἤματα μακρὰ τελέσθη . . .

There for all the days toward the completion of a full year
we sat there feasting on <u>unlimited meat</u> and sweet wine;
but when the whole year was there, and the seasons had turned around,
the months dwindling, and the long days had come to fulfillment . . .

The completion of a year is emphatically and elaborately expressed in terms of *telos* ('goal', 'end', 'completion'), with the year, the seasons, the months, and the days all coming full circle. Within the context of Circe and her world we might think of a more than merely temporal designation: an entire life cycle has been completed, with death and rebirth coming full circle. And recall that Dæl, Circe's putative Caucasian homologue, is associated with the New Year. But equally important is the parallel with another feast, enjoyed at Ithaca, that continued through the year until another meaningful temporal boundary was reached.

Rethinking the *Necyia*

The designation of the yearlong feast is grammatically a subclause framing significant action on the part of the Companions: they call out to Odysseus, reminding him of the need to move on and be mindful of *nostos* (*Od.* 10.471–4):

καὶ τότε μ' ἐκκαλέσαντες ἔφαν ἐρίηρες ἑταῖροι·
"δαιμόνι', ἤδη νῦν μιμνήσκεο πατρίδος αἴης,

---

[39] For Underworld associations of Circe, see Crane 1988: 31; Alexander 1991: 523; Nagler 1996: 145–9.

εἴ τοι θέσφατόν ἐστι σαωθῆναι καὶ ἱκέσθαι
οἶκον ἐϋκτίμενον καὶ σὴν ἐς πατρίδα γαῖαν."

And then calling out to me they spoke, my trusted Companions:
"Strange man, bring now your fatherland back to your mind,
if it is ordained that you will safely reach
your well-built house and your fatherland."

Whereas the Companions lost the fatherland from their mind as a prelude to their transmigration into the bodies of swine, it is now Odysseus' turn, presumably in and through the feasting, to be culturally alienated. His yearlong forgetful state of mind can be seen as the mental equivalent of the bodily experience of the Companions, though a foreshadowing of the situation at Ithaca is in play as well: in both cases the hero is pitted against a collective of actual or potential competitors for the favors of the local insular queen.[40] Departure from Aeaea, however, is not immediate. Not only does yet another full day of feasting on "unlimited meats" follow (10.476–7); Circe also tells Odysseus that he "has first to complete another journey" (ἄλλην χρὴ πρῶτον ὁδὸν τελέσαι, 10.490) and reach the house of Hades in order to consult the shade of Tiresias. This trip, known as the *Necyia* 'Song of the Dead', is commonly seen as a new episode in the Wanderings, in spite of the fact that after completing the mission Odysseus and his men return to Aeaea. In light of the preceding discussion of Circe and her island, in fact, there is reason to consider the *Necyia* as being an integral part of the Circe episode.

The *Necyia* is a semantically multilayered episode whose meaning and function are not confined to any single stage in the diachronic development of the *Odyssey*.[41] In Chapter 1 we saw how the episode contributes to the hero-singer theme in allowing Odysseus to perform a *Catalogue of Women*; and the visit to the Underworld is the traditional high point of any hero's biography – Odysseus has some illustrious predecessors in this regard. But the fact that the expedition to Hades is launched from Circe's island is significant, as is the fact that it is the goddess herself who announces, quite unexpectedly, its necessity to Odysseus. Circe's order is made, in the terms developed in Chapter 2, at the point where Circe turns from being the hero's adversary in his quest into being his helper or donor in a new quest. The preceding discussion of Circe as a force presiding over the human life cycle allows us now to put some semantic flesh on these

---
[40] Also Louden 1999: 15.
[41] S. West (2012: 135) speaks of "an unusually strong sense of work-in-progress."

syntactic bones. Circe's role as guide to the Underworld is a natural outgrowth of the function she has on her island.

The journey to Hades is presented by Circe to Odysseus as a necessary consultation of Tiresias (10.490–5), who, Circe goes on to say (10.539–40), "will tell you the way and the measures of your path and your *nostos*, how you will travel over the sea rich in fish." But, as it turns out, when the company has returned from the dead, Circe herself has more detailed things to say to Odysseus about the perils of the return journey (12.37–141) than the seer.[42] The new quest seems less a consultation than a symbolic *catabasis*, a death and rebirth orchestrated by Circe. Circe greets the returning company with the address δισθανέες, 'twice-deceased ones' (12.22), an epithet that applies to the successfully completed *nostos* of the Hades quest, but is valid as well for the transmigration experience that she has already effected herself.

Viewed as rebirth, then, the *Necyia* is a duplication of what has already happened on Aeaea. Earlier, analytically inclined, scholarship has tended to see the *Necyia* as a separate composition inserted later in the sequence of Odysseus' Wanderings, based on the relative uselessness of Tiresias' prophecy for Odysseus' *nostos* and some perceived awkward adjustments in the main story to accommodate the insert.[43] There is in itself enough reason to suppose that the *Necyia* episode is diachronically stratified and that we have to allow for modifications and accretions over time, due to evolving poetic intentions and needs.[44] But the older analyst idea of the insertion of an independently composed episode leaves unexplained why the *Necyia* has been attached to the Circe episode in particular, and we may consider seeing the *Necyia* as an outgrowth of Circe's specific functions. There is diachronic pressure on her, too, after all: at the time when the *Odyssey* reached its present form, the Mistress of Animals may already have metamorphosed into the sorceress we know from later tradition. At some point in the ongoing composition and recomposition of the poem the need may have

---

[42] As also noted by Focke 1943: 202–3.
[43] For example, Focke 1943: 199–247; Page 1955: 21–51. Among the traces of perceived imperfect adjustment are the wording of Circe's instructions at 10.531–2 (δὴ τότ' ἔπειθ' ἑτάροισιν ἐποτρῦναι καὶ ἀνῶξαι | μῆλα, τὰ δὴ **κατάκειτ'** ἐσφαγμένα νηλέϊ χαλκῷ) as quoted from Odysseus' actual narrative (11.44–5), where the past tense of κατάκειτ' is more natural. The hasty departure before burying the body of Elpenor (ἐπεὶ πόνος ἄλλος ἔπειγε, 11.54) has also been adduced as anomalous. Finally, insertions have also been suspected in the body of the *Necyia*, such as the *Catalogue of Women* at 11.225–330.
[44] In a recent discussion S. West (2012: 134–5) posits four "strata" for the composition of Book Eleven: an original conjuration of his mother's ghost; an actual journey to the edge of Hades in order to perform necromancy; a consultation of Tiresias in order to make peace with Poseidon; and an actual *catabasis*.

been felt for the death and rebirth motif to be "reinforced" through the voyage to Hades when metempsychosis had changed into metamorphosis.

Finally, we may in this connection also think of Elpenor the "Hope man," whose death was caused by the preparations for the expedition (10.552–60), but whose proper burial and hence successful transition to the Afterlife was ensured by that same expedition, as Odysseus carries out the wishes that Elpenor's soul communicates to him (11.51–80; 12.8–15). In a sense Circe effects Elpenor's transition to the Afterlife by sending Odysseus on his quest, and the episode may reflect a function of the goddess akin to the Underworld functions ascribed to her Georgian counterpart Dæl/Samdzimari. Or is Elpenor's death to be understood as payment for the animals/persons consumed on Circe's island?

The feast of the ghosts

It is unlikely that there is in the *Odyssey* a direct cultural awareness of the kind of anxieties that make the Tukano and other traditional hunting peoples a suggestive comparandum for what happens on Aeaea. The Circe story may, in fact, show a decreasing awareness in that many of the semantic features discussed earlier are not immediately obvious and possibly less prominent than in earlier versions of the tale. But the events on the island, whatever their origin or cultural provenance and whatever their contemporary cultural experience, provide, poetically, powerful parallels to the feasts of the Suitors, whose vicious but mundane crimes come to be seen against the backdrop of the cycle of human life, and death, that has been acted out on Aeaea.[45]

The repetition of the quest sequence and the paradigmatic relations between its many multiforms in the poem as traced in Chapter 2 brings out, first of all, similarities between Circe and Eumaios.[46] The former has solar associations as daughter of Helios and with a dwelling place at the "risings of the Sun"; the latter comes from an island Syria, which lies close to the "turnings of the Sun" (τροπαὶ ἠελίοιο, *Od.* 15.404), a specification that might suggest a location opposite Circe's, in the far west.[47] Eumaios'

---

[45] On the Suitors and the Companions in connection with Circe and Aiaia, see also Louden 1999: 32–46, who notes parallelism between Elpenor and Leodes.
[46] On the name Εὔμαιος (as derived from μαῖα), see Dumont 2003.
[47] Eumaios' island is said to be "above Ortygia" (Ὀρτυγίης καθύπερθεν, *Od.* 15.404), which in Hellenistic poetry and scholarship was thought to refer to Delos (e.g., Callim. Hymn 2.59; Ap. Rh. *Arg.* 1.419); this would then give Syros as referent for Syria (Str. 10.5.8). But earlier poetry seems to have located Ortygia in the west; the oracle about the foundation of Syracuse (Paus. 5.7.3)

island, moreover, is "rich in cattle (or pastures), rich in sheep" (εὔβο(τ)ος εὔμηλος, 15.406), which conceivably would make it capable of producing "unlimited meats" just like Circe's.[48]

Not only Eumaios' origins, but also his present situation align him with Circe. Their houses are linked by formulaic phraseology, being both located "in a place sheltered from the winds" (περισκέπτῳ ἐνὶ χώρῳ, 10.211; 14.6);[49] and the savage dogs, "similar to wild animals" (14.21) guarding Eumaios' compound recall the large drugged wild carnivores around Circe's house. Both are also swineherds, of course. Eumaios' animals are consumed without anxiety, until the Suitors' feasting reaches its completion.

A striking detail is that the number of boars that Eumaios keeps in an enclosure outside the compound proper – a practice of keeping male animals outside that he shares with the Cyclops[50] – is specified as 360 (14.20), the number of days in the solar year. This seemingly gratuitous detail has been mentioned, quite plausibly, in connection with another intriguing figure, 350, as the number of cattle and sheep of Helios at Thrinacia,[51] on which more in Chapter 6. But the link with Circe is at least as important. The number of days in the solar year is, as we saw, emphatically the duration of the company's feast on Aeaea. The Suitors, for whose table the boars are fattened, indulge in feasting of very similar duration, as appears from Eumaios' complaint to the beggar (*Od.* 14.92–4):

> κτήματα δαρδάπτουσιν ὑπέρβιον, οὐδ' ἔτι φειδώ.
> ὅσσαι γὰρ νύκτες τε καὶ ἡμέραι ἐκ Διός εἰσιν,
> οὔ ποθ' ἓν ἱρεύουσ' ἱερήϊον, οὐδὲ δύ' οἴω.

> They devour his possessions in wanton ways, without any restraint.
> As many nights and days as there are from Zeus,
> never do they butcher <just> one victim, nor even two.

---

apparently "reads" Eumaios' passage and places Ortygia "above Thrinacia" (Θρινακίης καθύπερθεν), thus locating it in the far west. An association of Eumaios' island with the Island of the Sun is suggestive within the perspectives explored in this book (see further Chapter 6). On possible Western realities for (some of) the mythical geography of the *Odyssey*, see, e.g., Ballabriga 1998; Malkin 1998. Nakassis 2004 draws attention to the "gemination" (east and west mirroring each other) involved in the imagination of the edges of the world in early epic.

[48] Syria, furthermore, provides Golden Age conditions to its inhabitants, who die a gentle death, without diseases and hit by Apollo's and Artemis' arrows in old age (15.407–11), much like Hesiod's humans of the Golden Age, who die in their sleep (*W&D* 116). See also Louden 1999: 54, who, however, stresses the paradigmatic relationship between Eumaios and Alkinoos and their respective islands.

[49] Note that 14.5–6, ἔνθα οἱ αὐλή | ὑψηλὴ δέδμητο applies also to the Cyclops' dwelling (9.184–5). On the treatment of formulas in this way, see the Epilogue, below.

[50] *Od.* 9.238–9 and 14.16.   [51] Austin 1975: 134.

The Suitors' feasting takes on features of the Companions' experience at Aeaea. After Eumaios has changed from goal into donor (see Chapter 2), he acts as intermediary between his pig farm and Odysseus' palace, located just like Eumaios' farm and Circe's house "in a place sheltered from the winds" (περισκέπτῳ ἐνὶ χώρῳ, 1.426), and once the scene is set there a whole new set of paradigmatic relationships comes into play. The old dog Argos acts as multiform of Eumaios' savage watchdogs and Circe's lions and wolves,[52] and most importantly Penelope acts as an Ithacan Circe, who holds the collective Suitors in thrall during an extensive, yearlong feast.[53]

Penelope is no Circe and does not effect metamorphosis or metempsychosis, at least not consciously. But just as on Aeaea there is more than meets the eye in Odysseus' hall, particularly when a seer is contemplating the situation. When Telemachos has announced that he will no longer delay Penelope's marriage, the Suitors go wild and are seized by supernaturally uncontrollable laughter mixed with tears (*Od.* 20.345–9):

> ὣς φάτο Τηλέμαχος· μνηστῆρσι δὲ Παλλὰς Ἀθήνη
> ἄσβεστον γέλω ὦρσε, παρέπλαγξεν δὲ νόημα.
> οἱ δ' ἤδη **γναθμοῖσι** γελώων **ἀλλοτρίοισιν**,
> **αἱμοφόρυκτα** δὲ δὴ κρέα ἤσθιον· **ὄσσε δ' ἄρα σφέων**
> **δακρυόφιν πίμπλαντο, γόον δ' ὠΐετο θυμός**.
>
> So he spoke, Telemachos; and for the Suitors, Pallas Athena
> stirred up unquenchable laughter and led their wits astray,
> and they were now laughing <u>with jaws belonging to others</u>,
> and <u>blood-defiled</u> were the meats they ate; <u>their eyes</u>
> <u>filled up with tears, and</u> <their> *thumos* <u>foresaw lamentation</u>.

A dislocation of the Suitors' conscious awareness seems to have taken place, a split of the self into body and soul entirely separate from each other – very atypical indeed for the Homeric conception of man as an inseparable unity of body and soul.[54] Eating and laughing are performed mechanically as mindless functions performed by an "external" body, whereas *thumos* has a disjointed premonition of impending doom. The disembodied spirit also has an altered perception of the meats on the table: the Suitors' meal is meant to be a *dais* (20.279–83), but is revealed here as a

---

[52] A detail also seen by Powell 1977: 40, although he also aligns Argos with animals eaten in the Otherworld, such as the wild goats, the stag, or the Cattle of Helios.
[53] The link between Circe and Penelope is stressed by Nagler 1996; but in relation to the two companies involved, the Companions and the Suitors, the most elaborate discussion is Louden 1999, where the young men at Scheria as suitors of Nausicaa and competitors of Odysseus are discussed as a third instance of the pattern.
[54] Clarke 1999.

display of carnivorous frenzy. What appeared to be cooked steaks are now revealed to be bloody chunks of flesh, as expressed by the rare adjective αἱμοφόρυκτα, 'blood-defiled', used only here in extant Greek. This is food for predators[55] – or cannibals.

The Suitors' temporarily disembodied state of their *thumos* not only foreshadows the slaughter of their bodies the next day; it is also reminiscent of the predicament of the Companions in Circe's hall, who have the body and the physical reflexes of swine with a *nous* that is intact and human (10.239–40). The line in which the tearful eyes and the forebodings of *thumos* are mentioned repeats a line from the description of Eurylochos' reaction to the fate of his companions (*Od.* 10.246–8):

> οὐδέ τι ἐκφάσθαι δύνατο ἔπος, ἱέμενός περ,
> κῆρ ἄχεϊ μεγάλῳ βεβολημένος· <u>ἐν δέ οἱ ὄσσε
> δακρυόφιν πίμπλαντο, γόον δ' ὠΐετο θυμός.</u>
>
> And he could not utter a word, much as he wanted to,
> his heart stricken with great grief; <u>and his eyes
> filled up with tears and <his> *thumos* foresaw lamentation.</u>

The Suitors' disembodied premonitions are a step beyond the speechless perplexity of Eurylochos' *thumos*, just as the Companions' metempsychosis is a step beyond the ecstatic awareness of the Suitors' *thumos* at the *dais*; but the three scenes are interrelated in ideas and articulation. The Suitors are facing death stricken with perplexity at the sight of the mistress whose animals they consume in the most sacrilegious way possible. Their vision of blood-defiled chunks of meat becomes reality when it is their own blood that pollutes the food, as expressed with the verb from which the adjective αἱμοφόρυκτος derives: σῖτός τε κρέα τ' ὀπτὰ φορύνετο, 'the bread and roasted meats were polluted' (*Od.* 22.21).[56] The blood is Antinoos', ringleader of the Suitors and Odysseus' first victim. It is fitting that it is his blood that brings up the suggestion of implicit cannibalism.

The scene of hysterical laughter over blood-dappled pieces of meat is articulated in ways beyond the Suitors' expressive powers by a seer on the

---

[55] Consider also the use of δαρδάπτω, 'devour', for the eating habits of the Suitors (14.92).
[56] The verb φορύνω is just as rare as the adjective, occurring in poetry only here and in Quintus of Smyrna, in obvious imitation of Homer.

scene, Theoklymenos, who has an embodied vision encompassing present and future (*Od.* 20.3512–7):[57]

> ἆ δειλοί, τί κακὸν τόδε πάσχετε; νυκτὶ μὲν ὑμέων
> εἰλύαται κεφαλαί τε πρόσωπά τε νέρθε τε γοῦνα,
> οἰμωγὴ δὲ δέδηε, δεδάκρυνται δὲ παρειαί,
> αἵματι δ' ἐρράδαται τοῖχοι καλαί τε μεσόδμαι·
> εἰδώλων δὲ πλέον πρόθυρον, πλείη δὲ καὶ αὐλή,
> ἱεμένων Ἔρεβόσδε ὑπὸ ζόφον· **ἠέλιος δὲ
> οὐρανοῦ ἐξαπόλωλε**, κακὴ δ' ἐπιδέδρομεν ἀχλύς.

Ah, wretches, what evil is this here that you suffer? In night your
heads are covered, your faces and your knees below;
a wail flares up, cheeks are soaked with tears,
spattered with blood are the walls and beams;
of ghosts the portico is full, full is the court,
all striving down to Erebos in the gloom; <u>and Helios
has vanished from the sky</u>; an evil mist has come upon you.

The seer seems to foresee a solar eclipse as reaction to the sacrilegious behavior he witnesses. The Suitors have come to the end of their yearlong feasting; theirs was a paradise that was false, an illusion of carefree abundance in which the *dais*, the heroic symbolism of meat *par excellence*, was perverted into a predatory feeding frenzy in which the boundary between eater and eaten, human and animal, became blurred. The cycle of nature requires painful compensation for this excess. Theoklymenos reveals it all as a prelude to a visit to Hades, a journey that the Companions have already made; indeed, that they have made twice. In Chapter 6 we will look into the prelude to the Companions' second, and final, death.

---

[57] The scholiast believes that Theoclymenos is the only one to see.

CHAPTER 6

The revenge of the Sun

"Bright-shining Helios, how you have destroyed me . . .
Apollo is what you are rightly called among mortals,
whoever knows the silent names of the gods."

(Euripides, Phaethon)

The festival of the New Moon

The return of Odysseus was once understood in terms of solar symbolism serving as fuel for allegorizing interpretations. In scholarship now only vaguely remembered much less practiced, Odysseus was one of the numerous mythological figures in whom was seen hiding an erstwhile sun god, his twelve ships standing for the twelve months of the year, Penelope for the earth whom the Sun struggles to reach after the cold of winter, and the number of the Suitors for the days of the winter months.[1] In more recent times, Norman Austin has drawn attention to the real details about the seasonal cycle that the poem provides.[2] He traces the astronomical and meteorological phenomena that accompany Odysseus' voyage from Calypso's island Ogygia till his arrival at Ithaca and beyond.

The hero sets sail on his raft "watching the Pleiades and late-setting Boötes" (*Od.* 5.272), an astronomical detail that, as Austin shows, must refer to a moment late in the sailing season; this would mean that Poseidon's storm in which Odysseus' raft is shipwrecked with the hero barely surviving is the first of the winter storms.[3] Signs of winter, such as long cold nights and a moonless night (νύξ ... σκοτομήνιος, *Od.* 14.457), are evident during Odysseus' first days on Ithaca, when he enjoys Eumaios' hospitality and relocates to the palace. When the final phase of Odysseus' *nostos* has started, however, winter begins to give way to spring, as Austin observes. Among the

---

[1] Menrad 1910. See the literal-minded critique in Scott 1917.   [2] Austin 1975: 239–53.
[3] Austin 1975: 240–3. Also referring to Hes. *W&D* 619–22.

The festival of the New Moon

details he notes are Penelope speaking about herself as a nightingale in spring (19.518–19), the string of Odysseus' bow "singing beautifully, similar in sound to the swallow" (21.411), and Athena taking on the shape of the swallow at the climax of the fight with the Suitors (22.240). Moreover, the hero's archery has the effect of a gadfly goading a herd of cows "in the Spring season, when the days are long" on the Suitors (22.299).[4]

But more precise than general, if suggestive, indications of a change of seasons is the declaration of the beggar Odysseus, twice repeated, that the return of the king is nigh. In it Odysseus uses one of the most enigmatic terms in the *Odyssey* (*Od.* 14.161–2 = 19.306–7):

τοῦδ' αὐτοῦ **λυκάβαντος** ἐλεύσεται ἐνθάδ' Ὀδυσσεύς,
τοῦ μὲν φθίνοντος μηνός, τοῦ δ' ἱσταμένοιο

This very same *lukabas* he will come here, Odysseus,
as the one month is waning and the other waxing.

The word λυκάβας, which in later epic and in epigraphic sources is always meant to refer to a "year," has in these two Homeric instances been variously interpreted as day, month, or year.[5] It may denote not so much a period as a point in time that defines a period, a seasonally recurring moment. The explanatory apposition "as the one month is waning and other waxing" suggests that the word is an obscure term for the New Moon. But the later meaning of "year" suggests that the term originally designated a specific New Moon, the one that is the beginning not just of a new month, but of a new year.[6] It has even been suggested that the reference is to the Great New Year, the coincidence of the solar and lunar cycle, which occurs every nineteen years.[7] The coincidence would then also be with the total duration of Odysseus' absence as well as with the coming of age of his son, Telemachos' reaching the ἥβης μέτρον, 'measure of youth'.[8] There is place for the idea of initiation in Odysseus' return on other grounds as well, as we will see.

---

[4] Austin 1975: 246–50; cf. Borthwick 1988. Levaniouk 2011: 93–108 discusses Odysseus' third Cretan Lie, addressed to Penelope, in terms of renewal and rebirth. She notes (p. 206) that Penelope, upon hearing the tale, "melts" like ice in spring in the high mountains.
[5] Koller 1973 sees the origin of the term in the coalescence of a petrified word combination (functioning as temporal modifier) *λύκα βάντα, 'the going of the (moon)light', i.e., the moonless night of the New Moon (cf. ἥλιον καταδύντα, 'the setting of the Sun'). Other solutions proposed are based on λυκ-, 'wolf': "the time of the running of the wolves"; this would fit in with the idea of initiation, on which see below. See further, Chantraine 2009 *s.v.* See also Levaniouk 2011: 204 n. 15.
[6] Wilamowitz-Moellendorff 1927: 44; Austin 1975: 246.   [7] Auffarth 1991.
[8] At *Od.* 19.530–4 we hear about the temporal frame set on Penelope's authorized remarriage as the moment of Telemachos' initiation.

The timing of Odysseus' return as seen against the background of the revolving seasons can involve the idea of the return of the Sun in the sense of a mythical representation of lengthening days and strengthening light. But the typical role for the Sun in connection with Odysseus' *lukabas* is not presence and growth, but absence. The seer Theoklymenos' mantic vision prompted by the Suitors' supernatural laughter includes, as we saw, what seems to be a solar eclipse (ἠέλιος δὲ | οὐρανοῦ ἐξαπόλωλε, κακὴ δ' ἐπιδέδρομεν ἀχλύς, 'and the sun has perished utterly from the sky and an evil mist has come upon you', *Od.* 20.356–7). The vision has more than one application within the poetic system of Odysseus' return. At one level, we can see it as a perceived cosmic outrage over human transgression, a traditional conception of solar eclipses as portents of calamities to come.[9] At another level the eclipse has less to do with the Suitors and their crimes than with the timing of Odysseus' return. The allegorizing scholar Heraclitus states that Theoklymenos' eclipse implies a precise moment for the action at this point in the poem, since solar eclipses occur only at the time of the new moon, the νουμηνία, the last day of the month that was called ἕνη τε καὶ νέα in Athens.[10] In other words, Theoklymenos' solar eclipse is tied up with Odysseus' *lukabas*.

Helios thus comes to play a role in the location of Odysseus' return in cyclical time, an important function, but not one that exhausts all his significance, as we will see. But of more immediately relevant thematic importance than Helios in the timing of Odysseus' return is Apollo. The seasonally recurring moment that Odysseus seems to be referring to with the term *lukabas*, in fact, is ritually marked by a festival in honor of Apollo. The mentions of this festival in the poem are unobtrusive, but hard to miss. First, Eurycleia, early in the day of the bow contest, urges her maidservants to clean the house; the Suitors will come early, she says, since today is a "public festival" (πᾶσιν ἑορτή, 20.155–6). The scholion on these lines, citing the authority of the fourth-century historian Philochorus, declares that the festival is that of Apollo Noumenios, Apollo of the New Moon, which would align Odysseus' statement about the return of the king with a public event in his kingdom.[11]

---

[9] For example, Pind. *Pae.* 9.2–5; Arch. 122W, Mimn. 20W; Stesich. 271 *PMG* – all mentioned by Plut. *De fac. In orbe lun.* 931e.
[10] Heracl. *Quest. Hom.* 75; cf. Wilamowitz 1927: 43–4; Austin 1975: 246. On the Athenian ἕνη καὶ νέα, see Mikalson 1975: 8–9.
[11] Schol. 20.155; cf. Eustath. *ad loc.*; Schol. Aristoph. *Plut.* 1126, and Schol. Pind. *Nem.* 3.2. For Apollo festivals on this day, see Detienne 1998: 57.

The festival of the New Moon

A little before Eurycleia's mention of the festival the narrator informs us that Telemachos visits the "assembly of the well-greaved Achaeans" (20.146). He is equipped with a spear and accompanied by two hunting dogs (20.145, just as when he was ready to join the earlier assembly at Ithaca (2.10–11). Spears are for travelers (1.104) or warriors, not for civilians attending a peacetime meeting, and swift dogs are for hunting – could it be that Telemachos is dressed and equipped for rituals of initiation? In any case, he looks much like his father on *his* initiatory hunting trip (*Od.* 19.429–38).[12] No further details are given, but the text informs us that an assembly is held on the island, which is ostensibly the festival of which Eurycleia spoke earlier (*Od.* 20.276–8):

> κήρυκες δ' ἀνὰ ἄστυ θεῶν ἱερὴν ἑκατόμβην
> ἦγον· τοὶ δ' ἀγέροντο **κάρη κομόωντες Ἀχαιοὶ**
> ἄλσος ὕπο σκιερὸν ἑκατηβόλου Ἀπόλλωνος.

> Heralds were leading through the city the sacred hecatomb
> of the gods; and they came to the assembly, <u>the long-haired Achaeans</u>
> in the shady grove of far-shooting Apollo.

In oral-formulaic theory the epithetic phrase κάρη κομόωντες (Ἀχαιοί) 'long-haired (Achaeans)' may be part of a system of noun–epithets for "Achaeans,"[13] but in the *Odyssey* its distribution is limited to the two Ithacan assemblies that mark the departure and return of Telemachos and his "long-haired companions" (κάρη κομόωντας ἑταίρους, *Od.* 2.408), the assembly in Book Two and the one here in Book Twenty. We may wonder whether the *Odyssey* is using the formula here in its literal (and proper?) sense of unshorn (ephebic and uninitiated) male.[14] And if this is so, the possibility emerges that formal initiation is part of the Apollo festival that is being celebrated on the island. Telemachos and the crew that accompanied him on his trip to Pylos and Sparta could then be the *agélē* 'herd of young males' that are entered into the ranks of adult men; and the assembly at Ithaca, held at the time of the festival of the god who is the divine representation of the male initiand, could then be an event similar to the festival of the *Apellai* at Delphi, which has been associated with the very name of the god.[15]

---

[12] See also Petropoulos 2011: 70; 105–28. [13] Parry 1971: 101.
[14] The common formula κοῦροι Ἀχαιῶν in the *Iliad* may well reflect an underlying reality of the Trojan War itself as an initiatory expedition of roving bands of youths, e.g., Dowden 1992: 111–12; Gottschall 2008.
[15] Burkert 1975; on Apollo as the patron of the *nostos* of the male initiand, see Versnel 1993: 313–19. Levaniouk 2011: 93–108; 166–89 draws attention to the initiatory overtones of Odysseus' Cretan Lie to Penelope as well as of the boar hunt at Parnassus.

A public Apollo festival on the island revolving (at least in part) around initiation puts in high relief the diseased situation in Odysseus' house, where the Suitors' private obsession keeps them from participating in society's seasonally marked progression and intergenerational renewal, marking their own initiation as a failure.[16] But a festival in honor of Apollo the archer god at the same time casts Odysseus in the striking role as the archer of the day. His arrows will in fact accomplish what Penelope's wished for the previous day, when Antinoos had thrown a footstool at the head of the beggar: "Would that Apollo famous for his bow strikes you yourself like this," she says to the Suitor (*Od.* 17.494), referring to Apollo's power to bring about "sudden death" in the *megaron*.[17]

An Apollo role for Odysseus also lends further depth to Telemachos' newly acquired status of manhood, since it places father and son in a relation of ritual antagonism. "Three times," the narrator tells us, "Telemachos strained himself to string the bow, three times he was wanting in strength; he would have succeeded in stringing the bow in his fourth effort, but Odysseus nodded and held him back, eager though he was" (*Od.* 21.125–9). The father, who himself had his initiation into manhood in the boar hunt on Mount Parnassus, the mountain of Apollo (19.394–466), stands to his son as Apollo to the Iliadic Diomedes (*Il.* 5.436–44; cf. *Il.* 16.702–9), another young hero who had to live up to the specter of a father he had never seen. Telemachos' name gains in semantic richness when seen in this connection: this is the son of the "far fighter" (*tēle-mach*), the hero who "fought far away" at Troy and who now shoots his enemies from a distance, just like Apollo *hekēbolos*, the god who strikes from afar. The young hero, through his name, both embodies Apollo and aligns his father with the god.[18]

We may wonder whether Apollo's widely attested function as cattle owner in myth and cult has played a role in his inclusion in the complex semantics of Odysseus' return. This could align him in the *Odyssey*'s plot with Helios, though the *Odyssey* does not show any sign of the later conflation of the two divinities. There is solar and light imagery for

---

[16] At *Od.* 21.258–9 Antinoos breaks off the Suitors' futile attempts at stringing the bow with a reference to the festival at hand, which he calls "pure" (ἑορτὴ | ἁγνή). Detienne 1998: 58–9 draws attention to the Suitor's absurd intention to sacrifice to Apollo the next day (a day after the festival), when the Suitors will reconvene to resume the contest.

[17] See also Melanthios' earlier wish (17.251–2) that Apollo strike Telemachos dead. Penelope herself utters the wish (18.202) to suffer a "soft death" at the hands (arrows) of "pure Artemis," the equivalent death for women.

[18] Note also the wordplay in Odysseus' speech to the unfaithful maidservant Melantho at *Od.* 19.83–8, with ἕκητι (86) playing on Apollo's essential epic epithet ἑκήβολος and τηλίκος (88) on Telemachos' own name.

Odysseus, as we will see, which has tended to be folded into the *lukabas*–spring complex.[19] But the semantics of Odysseus' return is sufficiently complex in order for both gods, Apollo and Helios, each to make their separate contribution, alongside that of the Cyclops (see Chapter 4). Helios is implicated in the revenge on the Suitors since his herds were violated in ways that make them paradigmatically relevant to the animals slaughtered in Odysseus' hall.

Eating in the land of the Sun

Helios is an important owner of livestock in the Otherworld, though as a Master of Animals he is more distant to his flocks and herds than Polyphemos the dedicated shepherd. Helios just enjoys watching his animals as he goes on his daily course (*Od.* 12.379–81), leaving the actual care of the animals to his daughters, the nymphs Phaethousa and Lampetie (*Od.* 12.131–6), half-sisters of Circe, we may note. Helios' herds and flocks on Thrinacia are not an isolated phenomenon in Greek mythology or in actual religious practice. The Sun god, along with Apollo, is owner of livestock in various places: the Cretan sailors in the Homeric *Hymn to Apollo* pass Helios' precinct at Cape Tainaron, where his eternal flock of "deep-fleeced sheep" is grazing (*HH. App.* 410–13). In the Homeric *Hymn to Hermes* the newborn god finds in Pieria, in the foothills of Mount Olympus, "the immortal cattle of the blessed gods, grazing in lovely, pristine meadows" (71–2). And Herodotus (9.92–5) tells a story revolving around sacred sheep of Helios in the town of Apollonia, which in being a multiform of the Cyclops story provides a curious link between the first and last of the three great eating adventures of Odysseus in the Otherworld.[20]

The *Odyssey*'s historical audiences must also have been familiar with sacred cattle from sources other than the epic tradition.[21] The epigraphic record shows sacred herds and flocks in a number of sanctuaries, among which are Tegea (Athena), Delphi (Apollo), and Delos.[22] Such animals have to be distinguished from meat animals that are part of a sanctuary economy: they are not sacrificed or sold, and their function is to provide pleasure and company to the divinity who owns them, much as Helios rejoices in his cows when he rises up on his daily journey into the sky and comes back from it.

---

[19] Austin 1975: 282–3 n. 16.   [20] On this story, see Griffiths 1999.
[21] Other literary mentions include Theoc. 25.129ff., Pol. 4.18.10, Paus. 10.35.7, Porph. *De Abst.* 1.25.8.
[22] See Isager 1992; Chandezon 2003: 286–93.

The language that Tiresias, and later Circe, use for the warning concerning Helios' sacred cows (both syntax and vocabulary) must also have been familiar to the audience, as it echoes prohibitions in the real world (*Od.* 11.110–12 = 12.137–9):

τὰς εἰ μέν κ' **ἀσινέας** ἐάᾳς νόστου τε μέδηαι,
ἦ τ' ἂν ἔτ' εἰς Ἰθάκην, κακά περ πάσχοντες, ἵκοισθε·
εἰ δέ κε **σίνηαι**, τότε τοι τεκμαίρομ' ὄλεθρον.

These <cows> if you leave them <u>unharmed</u> and remain mindful of
  nostos,
surely you may still reach Ithaca in spite of much suffering.
<u>But if you harm them</u>, I ordain destruction for you at that moment.

The verb σίνομαι, used as here in a prospective subjunctive conditional, seems formulaic in inscriptions dealing with prohibitions concerning land (whether or not sacred) and the animals and plants on it, for example:

αἰ δέ κα **σίνηται** ἀποτεισάτω τὰ ἐπιτίμια [ὁ] σι[νό]μενος κατὰ τὸς
νόμος τὸς ἑκατέρη κειμένος.
  (*Inscriptiones Creticae* III.4; Crete, second century BCE)

<u>and if someone causes harm or damage</u>, let the one who does harm
  pay the fine according to the laws of either city.

αἰ δέ τίς κα ἐπιβῆι ἢ νέμει ἢ φέρει τι τῶν ἐν τᾶι hιαρᾶι γᾶι ἢ τῶν
δενδρέων τι κόπτηι ἢ θραύηι ἢ πρίωι ἢ ἄλλο τι **σινήται**, hο
μεμισθωμένος ἐγδικαξῆται hως πολίστων.
  (*Inscriptiones Graecae* XIV.645; Heraclaea, Magna Graecia,
                                    fourth century BCE)

And if someone enters or puts livestock to graze or carries away
  something from what belongs to the sacred precinct, or cuts or
  shatters or saws one of the trees, or causes harm in any other way,
  the lessee shall prosecute for compensation to the maximum[23]
  extent.

The potential of harm being done is the principal factor involved when humans enter sacred spaces or when access to property is regulated by laws or decrees. Tiresias' prophecy (filling in the details of the Cyclops' prayer; see further Chapter 7) reads as a mythical intensification of such injunctions in the real world: the animals are literally immortal, the crime is not an infraction of the rules of a sanctuary or for the management of sacred

---

[23] Πολίστων = πλείστων (cf. Homolle 1891: 627–8). The otherwise unattested form looks like an ad hoc analogical creation ("muchest").

Eating in the land of the Sun

land, but a direct, personal offense to an important divinity, and the punishment is not a fine, but total annihilation.

In addition to Thrinacia being a sacred precinct with animals exempt from sacrifice or consumption there may be a deeper significance to Helios being the owner of the place and its animals. The Sun is giver and owner of light and life in many different cultures, including the Amazonian Tukano we met earlier.[24] Herodotus' report (3.17–18) on the mysterious Table of the Sun in the land of the Aethiopians may reflect religious conceptions of this kind. In the Thrinacia episode, the Sun is not creator, source, or provider of meat animals caught in the wild, but this primordial function has been subsumed in his function as patron of farmed, domestic, animals. His herds are somehow an emblem of all cattle of all times and places, their immortality reflecting the essentiality of farmed animals for human civilization, not only as meat, but also as wealth. Using these prototype animals for the kind of feasts that are usual in the heroic world is to touch on the essence, the root of all things, with irrevocable consequences for both man and beast, eater and eaten.

The Cattle of Helios are intimately connected with Circe. Not only is Circe Helios' daughter; she also, as Helper in the quest pattern we reviewed in Chapter 2, sets out the terms and conditions for the company's stay on Thrinacia. In so doing she repeats Tiresias' earlier prophecy, confirming that the Journey to the Dead is a symbolic death related to the stay on her island, rather than an independent quest for consultation (see Chapter 5). Circe expands on Tiresias' prophecy with details about the numbers of Helios' possessions (*Od.* 12.127–31):

Θρινακίην δ' ἐς νῆσον ἀφίξεαι· ἔνθα δὲ πολλαὶ
βόσκοντ' Ἠελίοιο βόες καὶ ἴφια μῆλα,
ἑπτὰ βοῶν ἀγέλαι, τόσα δ' οἰῶν πώεα καλά,
πεντήκοντα δ' ἕκαστα· γόνος δ' οὐ γίγνεται αὐτῶν,
οὐδέ ποτε φθινύθουσι

You will reach the island Thrinacia; there numerous
cows of Helios are pasturing and fat sheep,
seven herds of cattle, as many flocks of sheep, beautiful,
and fifty animals each; offspring does not come from them,
nor do they ever decay or waste away.

Circe's own animals (mentioned mostly as the countless meats consumed by the company) and those of her father at Thrinacia are antithetically opposed to each other in strict complementary distribution: unlimited

---

[24] See also Harrod 2000: 25–6 on the Blackfeet Indians of Montana; Eliade 1949: 117–18.

abundance of the κρέα ἄσπετα of presumably innumerable animals contrasts with a limited, precise number. While the feast on Aeaea was endless in terms of duration, consumption, and available resources, eating meat on Thrinacia will mean causing irreparable harm to a whole that is intact and significant. The adventures on Aeaea and Thrinacia taken together, moving from the unproblematic plenty of wild game to owned wealth consisting of farm animals and the possibility of property crime, reflect on a larger scale the progression in the Cyclops episode, which moves, as we saw in Chapter 4, from the unlimited abundance of the wild goats to the theft of Polyphemos' sheep. As indicated before, both the limitless bounty and the transgression involving owned animals are mythically amplified foils for what the Suitors do at Ithaca, pushing the two major aspects of the Suitors' destructive feast to the limit: treating someone's vast but bounded wealth as a limitless resource.

Masters of Animals like to count their herds or flocks as something that is of limited supply and comes for a price. The Tukano Sun Father, as we saw in Chapter 5, created only a limited number of game animals, whose count remains balanced with that of their human hunters; the Georgian hunting goddess Dæl, as we saw also in Chapter 5, does not allow hunters to bring back more than one animal for each hunter. And within the poem itself we can observe that Proteus, the Master of Seals (in Menelaos' tale), counts his animals as they come on shore to bask in the sun (ἀριθμήσει, *Od.* 4.411; cf. 451); the number of the doves whose job it is to bring Zeus his ambrosia is kept constant, as the god sends in a new one each time one is caught in the Planctae, the "Wandering Rocks" that destroy all ships that try to pass them, as Circe explains to Odysseus (*Od.* 12.62–5). All these herds or flocks are immortal only in their number, as a collective: each animal that is missing will be replaced to fill out the requisite number of the total.[25] Helios' Thrinacian herds are different in that the collective is immortal, not through exchange or substitution, but in the very immortality – and sterility – of their constitutive individuals.

The scholiast notes that according to Aristotle the number of Helios' animals, seven herds of fifty animals each, has symbolic significance as the number of days in the lunar year.[26] But the text does not actually say 350 (as it gives 360 as the number of boars in the enclosure in front of

---

[25] On this conception of a herd, see Vidal-Naquet 1986: 196–7; see also Bakker 2002a: 18–20 on the notion of time involved.
[26] Schol. *Od.* 12.129: Ἀριστοτέλης φυσικῶς τὰς κατὰ σελήνην ἡμέρας αὐτὸν λέγειν φησὶ τί οὔσας. τὸν γὰρ πεντήκοντα ἀριθμὸν ἑπταπλασιάσας εἰς τὸν τριακοστὸν πεντηκοστὸν περιεστάναι εὑρήσεις. See also Austin 1975: 134.

Eumaios' pigsty; see Chapter 5), and we may look for the significance of the component numbers of fifty and seven. The first number in fact recurs frequently in relation to farmed domestic animals. The sows inside Eumaios' stables are divided into twelve groups of fifty each (14.13–15), and since that number is later included in Eumaios' catalogue of his master's wealth (14.101) along with twelve herds of cattle, twelve flocks of sheep, and twelve of goats, we may perhaps infer that the size of Odysseus' herds and flocks was fifty head as well. Fifty is also the number of cows that the newborn Hermes steals from his brother Apollo (*HH. Herm.* 74).[27] In the epigraphic record in the real world we hear of a gift of fifty cows from the citizens of Tyros, a borough of Sparta, to the sanctuary at Delphi,[28] and, in the secular sphere, of a grant, free pasturage for fifty cows, of the city of Akraiphia to a citizen to whom it owed a debt.[29] Finally, the Demosthenic corpus contains a speech in which the theft of fifty "soft-fleeced sheep that were being herded" (πρόβατα ποιμαινόμενα μαλακά, [Dem.] 47.52) is mentioned.

Why fifty animals? Two details may help us answer this question. First, the number fifty for livestock applies to groups of female animals; and second, Apollo in the Homeric *Hymn to Hermes* finds that all that is left of his herd is a bull, which apparently was closely related to the herd of females (*HH. Herm.* 195–6). We can conclude, it seems, that fifty is the size of a breeding unit, an observation that is in agreement with both ancient and modern evidence and practice. Varro (*Res Rust.* 2.5.18) states that one bull could suffice for sixty to seventy cows, a figure that is rather high, but that could be explained by the fact that ancient husbandry was less focused on maintaining a high birth rate than is cattle breeding in the modern age. Modern manuals give as appropriate for a mature bull a number of up to fifty and, significantly, specify that no increase in fertility rate can be achieved by having two or more bulls serve the same cows – in fact, the arrangement is presented as counterproductive in view of possible fights in competition over females.[30] Very similar figures are given for the ratios of ewes to a ram in breeding manuals for ovicaprid farmers.[31]

It appears, then, that Helios' herds are modeled on self-contained farming units in the real world, whose size is required and constrained

---

[27] Note that this Hymn uses the notion of "herd" (ἀγέλη) in a slightly different way, in specifying that Hermes cut off fifty cows from a larger "herd" (πεντήκοντ' ἀγέλης ἀπετάμνετο βοῦς ἐριμύκους, *HH. Herm.* 74, cf. 192–3), whereas in Homer ἀγέλη applies to the unit of fifty animals itself.
[28] *Syll.³* No. 407; see also Isager 1992: 16; Chandezon 2003: 54–5.   [29] *SEG* 24.439.
[30] For example, Hamilton 2006; Perry and Patterson 2007. An eighteenth-century handbook, on the other hand, Ringsted 1800: 34, gives twenty as the requisite number of cows for one bull.
[31] Schoenian 2006.

by the realities of breeding. This puts extra emphasis on the animals' immortality and sterility: they stand for birth and death, renewal and change, all processes in which they themselves do not participate. This makes their consumption an act that is all the more irrevocable. Eating the sacred cows is not the invigoration and renewal of life, but the depletion of nonrenewable resources and so a sure invocation of death.

The meal has been described as a pious attempt at approximating a ritually correct sacrifice, but seems better characterized as a travesty of sacrifice. The Companions are trying in vain to imitate correct sacrificial ritual by substituting water and wild oak leaves for the ritually required wine and grains of barley (12.353–63).[32] Eurylochos presents the consumption of the cows as an exchange with Helios in which a rich temple on Ithaca will be given in return to the god (12.345–7). But sacrifices are gifts to the gods for which one expects favors in return, not loans to be paid back later. Helios' own words (to be cited in full later in this chapter) underscore the perversion in his use of the term ἀμοιβήν (12.382), which is part of the language of reciprocity in human–divine relations involving sacrifices and dedications, both in myth and in the real world. Athena (impersonating Mentor) uses it in the characteristic formulaic collocation δίδου χαρίεσσαν ἀμοιβήν, 'give a requital rich in grace and gratitude' (*Od.* 3.58), in a prayer to Poseidon in which favors are asked from the god in return for the magnificent bull sacrifice he has just received from the Pylians.[33] Helios in his complaint to Zeus turns the requital from return favor into the death and destruction of the would-be sacrificers.

The Companions' consumption of the sacred cows is also a perversion of the heroic *dais*, being a feast falsely enjoyed by people who fundamentally misunderstand their present situation. Heroes do not share beef that is not theirs in the *dais*; the meat is theirs by force or possession, and when table companions are forced to promise restitution to the rightful owner, then something is very wrong with the meal, both as a *dais* and as a sacrifice. The Suitors, too, in the speech of Eurymachos at 22.55–9, will promise restitution and compensation to Odysseus, marking their previous feasting as illicit and aligning it with the ill-conceived feast at Thrinacia.

The Companions give in to criminal indulgence for which the poem has reserved in its programmatic proem, as noted above, the essential term

---

[32] See Vernant 1979: 242–3, who further notes that the way the animals to be butchered are caught and rounded up confuses sacrifice with the hunt. Contrast Fenik 1974: 213, taking the sacrifice as genuine and well intentioned ("preserving all the ritual of sacrifice as far as they can").
[33] The formula is also epigraphically attested (e.g., McCabe 1984, 441; *CEG* 326).

Eating in the land of the Sun

ἀτασθαλία, 'culpable recklessness'. The etymology of this word is unclear and controversial, but in the poetic system revolving around abundance and excess that we are studying, we may notice the striking collocation (even if it is etymologically unsound by the standards of modern comparative linguistics) of ἄτη, 'disastrous blinding', and θαλίη, 'abundance', or θάλεια, 'rich, plentiful'.[34] The latter is used exclusively for modifying δαίς when the religious component of the feast is explicitly stated (e.g., θεῶν ἐν δαιτὶ θαλείῃ, 'during the plentiful feast of [i.e., shared with] the gods').[35] The criminal recklessness inherent in the compound ἀτασθαλίαι would then specifically be an abuse of abundance, in particular the blasphemous and criminal consumption of abundantly available meat.

The Companions' illicit and disastrous feast is paradigmatically related to the Suitors' depredations, but the outrage of which each feast consists is a matter of complementary distribution: whereas the Suitors in the real world with its constraints and limitations create an Iron Age illusion of paradise, a paradise of heroic (Bronze Age) or even pre-cultural (Golden Age) abundance, the Companions in their paradisiacal setting create the illusion of ordinary human reality.

Their fateful feast is the climax of a process of separation between Odysseus and his men that has its roots in the Cyclops adventure and that is first felt in the Aiolos episode immediately following, when the Companions open the Bag of the Winds and so destroy an early, if already painful, *nostos*. The process reaches an early climax on Aeaea, when Eurylochos challenges Odysseus' leadership as he voices his objections to going back to Circe's house (10.431–7; see Chapter 7). At Thrinacia, Odysseus, alone against the majority, is unable to persuade his Companions to avoid the island: "You overpower me, since I am alone" (με βιάζετε μοῦνον ἐόντα, 12.297) says Odysseus, using a verb that is more appropriate for physical combat than for rational argument, and effectively admitting the failure of his leadership (more on which in Chapter 7).

Eurylochos, who had earlier answered Odysseus' command to stay clear of the island with a "hateful speech" (στυγερῷ ... μύθῳ, 12.278) is now

---

[34] The linguistic objection to this etymology is that the first syllable of ἄτη is long, whereas the first syllable of ἀτασθαλίαι is short. Some etymologies based on this collocation stress the direct vegetal metaphor in –θαλ(λ), e.g., the gloss in Hesychius, ἀτασθαλίαι· ἁμαρτίαι, ἀπὸ τοῦ ταῖς ἄταις θάλλειν, 'flourishing in blinding' or, taking the adjective ἀτάσθαλος as basis, Schwyzer's (1922: 14) ἄτας θάλλων, 'making disaster flourish'. Other etymologies are based on θάλεια, e.g., Ath. *Deipnosoph.* 1.21 (crimes during the feasts of early humans). Note that at Hes. *W&D* 231 the two terms are juxtaposed (the absence of ἄτη during the θάλεια).
[35] Cf. *Od.* 3.420 θεοῦ ἐς δαῖτα θάλειαν, where the god is Poseidon and the banquet the enormous sacrifice that is in course when Telemachos and Athena-Mentor arrive at Pylos.

the *de facto* new leader. He underscores the new situation by arrogating Odysseus' own formulaic address of the Companions as their leader, which the hero had used shortly before (12.271) when attempting to dissuade the company from disembarking on the island (*Od.* 12.340):

> κέκλυτέ μευ μύθων, κακά περ πάσχοντες ἑταῖροι.
>
> Listen to my words, my Companions in the woes that you are suffering.

The consequence is that *epos*, the traveler's tale, which throughout had been an experiential and first-person narrative, now turns into a third-person narrative, the vehicle for *aoidē*. The leader becomes bystander and the internal narrator becomes external as the Companions seal their fate and act out the poem's theological program (*Od.* 12.397–400):

> ἑξῆμαρ μὲν ἔπειτα ἐμοὶ ἐρίηρες ἑταῖροι
> δαίνυντ' Ἠελίοιο βοῶν ἐλάσαντες ἀρίστας·
> ἀλλ' ὅτε δὴ ἕβδομον ἦμαρ ἐπὶ Ζεὺς θῆκε Κρονίων,
> δὴ τότ' ἔπειτ' ἄνεμος μὲν ἐπαύσατο λαίλαπι θυίων.
>
> For six days thereafter my faithful Companions
> were feasting after driving off the best of the cattle of Helios;
> but when Zeus who is son of Kronos had set up the seventh day,
> then thereafter the wind stopped raging like a hurricane.

These lines stand in marked contrast to the earlier first-person plural accounts of the company's feasts in paradise. The god's best cows occupy the place of the *krea aspeta* of Circe's island and Helios is now not a mere temporal specification measuring the duration of the feast (ἐς ἠέλιον καταδύντα, 'till the setting of the Sun'), but owner of the meat consumed and agent in the destruction of its eaters. Seven days is the duration of the new feast and we may perhaps think here of the number of herds on the island. Would the integrity of each of the seven herds have been compromised?[36] At any rate the punishment is swift and the company's annihilation total. The Companions perish without a trace in the domain of fish, the food that they had spurned in favor of what they mistook for the dish of heroes.

---

[36] Note that 12.397–8 (ἑξῆμαρ ... δαίνυντ') recur at *Od.* 14.249–50 in Odysseus' first "liar tale," equally as a prelude to disaster for the Companions, even though the six-day feast there is not in itself wrong. The two remaining instances of ἑξῆμαρ occur in the formulaic line ἑξῆμαρ μὲν ὁμῶς πλέομεν νύκτας τε καὶ ἦμαρ, once (10.80) as prelude to the Laestrygonian episode. It seems, then, that the formulaic frame "for six days ... on the seventh day ..." acts as the staging for disaster to happen. By contrast, the "for nine days ..., on the tenth day" frame acts more neutrally as a linking device between two episodes, e.g., *Od.* 7.253; 9.82; 12.447.

Archery in the light of the Sun

If Odysseus' revenge on the Suitors is polysemous, so is the solar eclipse that Theoklymenos sees as part of his mantic vision of the Suitors' demise. The vision is repeated here for convenience from the end of Chapter 5 (*Od.* 20.352–7):

> ἆ δειλοί, τί κακὸν τόδε πάσχετε; νυκτὶ μὲν ὑμέων
> εἰλύαται κεφαλαί τε πρόσωπά τε νέρθε τε γοῦνα,
> οἰμωγὴ δὲ δέδηε, δεδάκρυνται δὲ παρειαί,
> αἵματι δ᾽ ἐρράδαται τοῖχοι καλαί τε μεσόδμαι·
> εἰδώλων δὲ πλέον πρόθυρον, πλείη δὲ καὶ αὐλή,
> ἱεμένων Ἔρεβόσδε ὑπὸ ζόφον· **ἠέλιος δὲ
> οὐρανοῦ ἐξαπόλωλε**, κακὴ δ᾽ ἐπιδέδρομεν ἀχλύς.

> Ah, wretches, what evil is this here that you suffer? In night your
> heads are covered, your faces and your knees below;
> a wail flares up, cheeks are soaked with tears,
> spattered with blood are the walls and beams;
> of ghosts the portico is full, full is the court,
> all striving down to Erebos in the gloom; <u>and Helios
> has vanished from the sky</u>; an evil mist has come upon you.

We saw earlier in this chapter that the solar eclipse can have a place in the astronomical timing of Odysseus' return. But the parallelism between the Suitors' transgressions and those of the Companions in the Otherworld suggest a possible paradigmatic function for Helios' vanishing as well. Theoklymenos' vision combines the perspectives of the living, who are faced with a sunless, gloomy world, and the dead, the ghosts of the Suitors as they are hurtling toward the gloom of Erebos. The combination of the Sun, the dead, and the living resonates with a curious moment in the story of Odysseus' Wanderings, which was beyond his mortal range of experience and perception; it came to him mediated through Calypso and Hermes (12.389–90). This earlier mention is not an actual solar eclipse, but the threat of one. Helios himself, when his cows have been slaughtered, complains to Zeus and announces that he will stop shining among the living, transferring his activity instead to Hades and the dead (*Od.* 12.377–83):

> Ζεῦ πάτερ ἠδ᾽ ἄλλοι μάκαρες θεοὶ αἰὲν ἐόντες,
> τεῖσαι δὴ ἑτάρους Λαερτιάδεω Ὀδυσῆος,
> οἵ μευ βοῦς ἔκτειναν ὑπέρβιον, ᾗσιν ἐγώ γε
> χαίρεσκον μὲν ἰὼν εἰς οὐρανὸν ἀστερόεντα,
> ἠδ᾽ ὁπότ᾽ ἂψ ἐπὶ γαῖαν ἀπ᾽ οὐρανόθεν προτραποίμην.

> εἰ δέ μοι οὐ τείσουσι βοῶν ἐπιεικέ' ἀμοιβήν,
> δύσομαι εἰς Ἀΐδαο καὶ ἐν νεκύεσσι φαείνω.
>
> Father Zeus, and the other blessed gods who are always:
> take revenge on the companions of Laertes' son Odysseus,
> who killed my cows with wanton arrogance, the animals in which
> I used to rejoice when moving up the sky rich in stars,
> as well as when I would turn back to the earth from the sky.
> If they do not pay in fair reciprocation for my cows,
> I will go down into Hades and shine among the dead.

Zeus prevents such an unthinkable cosmic disaster from happening by utterly destroying the Companions in the supernatural storm that he sends as soon as Odysseus and the company have left Thrinacia. But perhaps the disaster did happen, not as cosmic event at the level of myth in Odysseus' *epos*, but as one of the ways in which that *epos* resonates with the events of Odysseus' return in the real world.

When Odysseus has strung the bow and shot the arrow through the row of standing axes, he becomes – among many other things – the poet who is present at every aristocratic banquet, enlivening the feast with his song. Odysseus himself says so with grim humor as he is about to play his deadly lyre. What is perhaps less often observed is that Odysseus specifies that the meal he will accompany will take place in the light of the Sun (*Od.* 21.428–30):

> νῦν δ' ὥρη καὶ δόρπον Ἀχαιοῖσιν τετυκέσθαι
> **ἐν φάει**, αὐτὰρ ἔπειτα καὶ ἄλλως ἑψιάασθαι
> μολπῇ καὶ φόρμιγγι· τὰ γάρ τ' ἀναθήματα δαιτός.
>
> Now it's the moment to prepare the Achaeans a meal
> in the sunlight; and thereafter to amuse ourselves in other ways,
> with song and the lyre; for those are the delights of the banquet.

In the Companions' feasts in the Otherworld Helios was the temporal limit to the *dais* (ἐς ἠέλιον καταδύντα, 'till sunset'), but here he is the feast's notional essence. Helios is the one "who sees all and hears all" (ὃς πάντ' ἐφορᾷ καὶ πάντ' ἐπακούει), precisely the quality in which the god is presented as owner of the immortal cattle.[37] Here he witnesses the massacre that is going to take place. We are now reminded that he also witnessed the entrance of another Suitor into the house of an absent husband: Ares in his illicit lovemaking with Aphrodite in Demodokos' tale (*Od.* 8.302). But the perception of that Suitor is different, as Helios does not have the same

---

[37] *Od.* 11.109 (Tiresias speaking); 12.323 (Circe). At *Il.* 3.277 the formula, adjusted for grammatical person, is performed to invoke Helios as witness to an oath.

Archery in the light of the Sun

interest in the transgression involved. Helios is mentioned by name at the end of the scene of Odysseus' gruesome revenge, when the Suitors' entire company has been killed. The arresting image of their massacre is that of fish piled high on a beach (*Od.* 22.383–9):

> **τοὺς δὲ ἴδεν** μάλα πάντας ἐν αἵματι καὶ κονίῃσι
> πεπτεῶτας πολλούς, ὥς τ' ἰχθύας, οὕς θ' ἁλιῆες
> κοῖλον ἐς αἰγιαλὸν πολιῆς ἔκτοσθε θαλάσσης
> δικτύῳ ἐξέρυσαν πολυωπῷ· οἱ δέ τε πάντες
> κύμαθ' ἁλὸς **ποθέοντες** ἐπὶ ψαμάθοισι κέχυνται·
> τῶν μέν τ' **ἠέλιος φαέθων ἐξείλετο θυμόν**·
> ὣς τότ' ἄρα μνηστῆρες ἐπ' ἀλλήλοισι κέχυντο.

> And he saw them, all of them, lying in blood and dust,
> fallen in great numbers, like fish that fishermen
> have dragged out onto the hollow beach away from the grey sea,
> in their net with many holes, and all of them,
> craving the waves of the sea, lie poured out on the sand;
> Helios, the Shining Sun, has taken out their *thumos*.
> This is how then the Suitors had then been heaped on each other.

The importance of Helios extends beyond his obvious role in the simile as source of heat, just as in the story of the stag on Circe's island Helios is more than the cause of the animal's thirst. Helios kills the fish by shining, that is, gazing at them. Helios' proverbial all-seeing gaze becomes just as deadly to the fish as were Odysseus' arrows to the Suitors. In this light it becomes significant that the spectacle of the Suitors' bodies piled on each other is strikingly presented as the object of Odysseus' gaze (τοὺς δ' ἴδεν, 'and he saw them', 22.383). It is not clear whether the hero focalizes also the image of the bodies of the Suitors as dead fish, but his seeing the bodies is analogous to Helios seeing the fish.

It appears, then, that after all Helios' threat did come true. He did shine among the dead in Hades, the disembodied souls of the Suitors at the time of their physical death in Odysseus' *megaron*. During the time of their presence in Odysseus' house the light went out for those who remained faithful to the absent master. Eumaios, who, as we saw in Chapter 5, was born on an island with solar associations, has to yield to Melanthios 'the Black One', the evil goatherd who gave up his animals much too easily to the Suitors' hungry company. His sister is Melantho, equally 'Black', the most evil of the maidservants in Odysseus' house and lover of Eurymachos.

When on the eve of the festival the blackness of dusk has arrived and the maidservants are busy lighting torches, Odysseus intervenes. Ordering the maids to their womanly tasks, he says: "I will provide light to all those present here" (αὐτὰρ ἐγὼ τούτοισι φάος πάντεσσι παρέξω, *Od.* 18.317). After Melantho has insulted the beggar for the first time, the maids disperse when Odysseus threatens them with punishment at the hands of Telemachos. He then stands close to the light (*Od.* 18.343–4):

αὐτὰρ ὁ πὰρ **λαμπτῆρσι φαείνων αἰθ**ομένοισι
ἑστήκειν ἐς πάντας ὁρώμενος·

But he, shining beside the burning lighters
he stood there visible to all.

The light-words are prominent and evoke the names of Phaethousa and Lampetie, daughters of Helios and as guardians and shepherdesses witnesses to the slaughter of the Thrinacian cows.[38] The root *aith-* is connected with Aithon, 'Burning One', the name that Odysseus will give to himself later that night in his Cretan Lie to Penelope, his last one (19.183), though as we shall see in Chapter 8, the *aith*-words evoke not so much light as burning desire. The spectacle of the beggar with the light reflecting on his bald head is another opportunity for crude humor on the part of the Suitors when Eurymachos says that the beggar "surely did not come to the house of Odysseus without the help of divinity" (οὐκ ἀθεεί, *Od.* 18.353). Eurymachos is right, but little does he realize that Helios' universal visibility has an obverse in his all-embracing gaze.

The play on "black" and light can find a place in a symbolizing reading of Odysseus' return as the return of the Sun after the winter months, and there is independent evidence for the beginning of spring in the poem, as we have seen. But supplementing the celestial superstructure of the hero's Homecoming there is the pervasive parallelism between the events at Ithaca and those in the Otherworld as mediated through the interplay of *aoidē* and *epos*, the poet's tale and the hero's. In the simile cited earlier, the immediate focus is on the position and condition of the beached dead fish as a vivid rendering of the carnage in Odysseus' *megaron*. Through the simile, the Suitors die, deprived (ποθέοντες, 22.387) of the sea water, the very element that is the cause of the Companions' death on the high seas. The two mass killings are contrasting and complementary, in line with the complementary and contrasting feasts for which both companies are punished. The idea of fish dredged to the shore also reactivates the memory of the earlier mass killing at Telepylos of the Laestrygonians,

---

[38] See also Austin 1975: 282–3. On light imagery, further Clarke 1967: 73–5 (cited by Austin). Other significant references to Helios: 19.234; 21.226.

when Odysseus' Companions were speared like fish trapped in a space as close and constricted as the *megaron* at Ithaca (or the cave of the Cyclops).

We may note further that the massacre in the *megaron* is followed by a scene of cleansing and purification: sulfur is used to fumigate the *megaron* (22.481, 482, 494), recalling the smell of sulfur that fills Odysseus' remaining ship when the Companions are washed into the sea in the terrible storm with which Zeus avenges the slaughter of Helios' cattle (12.417).

If the Suitors' depredations are linked with the Companions' consumption of the divine cattle at Thrinacia, then Odysseus and Helios come to be linked too, as the wronged and outraged Masters of the Animals. Eumaios the swineherd has been earlier aligned with Circe and Alkinoos, but we may now link him as well to the solar nymphs Lampetie and Phaethaousa, subservient guardians who were unable to save the herds and flocks that were placed under their protection. Eumaios is too gentle a master of the animals; he and his colleague the cowherd Philoitios have to wait in darkness until the return of their master, the real Master of Animals, who unleashes cosmic energy in his revenge on the eaters destroying his wealth. The destruction of the Companions is carried out by Zeus on behalf of Helios, that of the Suitors by Odysseus in the role of Helios on behalf of Zeus (22.411–16). This complementarity, however, real as it is, leaves out of account a player who is not present on the Ithacan scene, but who casts a long shadow over what is happening there. This is Poseidon, the god whose wrath was the reason why Odysseus' household had to remain in darkness for so long. In Chapter 7 we will assess the role Poseidon has in compromising the success of Odysseus' return.

CHAPTER 7

The justice of Poseidon

"Right now, may I myself among humans not be 'just'
nor my son, since it is bad for a man to be just."
(Hesiod, *Works and Days* 270–1)

The demise of Odysseus' Companions after their consumption of the cattle of Helios gains in meaning, as Chapter 6 argued, when seen in connection with the lethal punishment that Odysseus metes out to the Suitors. Both groups of eaters meet with their doom due to their own reckless behavior, for which the poem has the "technical" term ἀτασθαλίη. The contexts in which this term is used in the *Odyssey* favor a specialized sense of criminal behavior due to human inability to deal with abundance. The passages are well known, but worth repeating here.

When the killing of the Suitors is over, Odysseus, who has just taken gruesome revenge on those who invaded his property, rejecting ample material compensation (see Chapter 8), casts himself as the instrument of the enlightened justice of Zeus, patron of strangers and guests (*Od.* 22.413–16):[1]

> τούσδε δὲ μοῖρ' ἐδάμασσε θεῶν καὶ σχέτλια ἔργα·
> οὔ τινα γὰρ τίεσκον ἐπιχθονίων ἀνθρώπων,
> οὐ κακὸν οὐδὲ μὲν ἐσθλόν, ὅτίς σφεας εἰσαφίκοιτο·
> τῶ καὶ **ἀτασθαλίῃσιν** ἀεικέα πότμον ἐπέσπον.

> These men, the doom of the gods subdued them as well as their own awful deeds, for they would not honor anyone of the earth-dwelling humans, neither base nor noble, whoever would come in contact with them. This is why through their criminal recklessness they met with this unseemly doom.

Odysseus obscures once more the boundary between poet and hero, *aoidē* and *epos*, in adopting a stance properly belonging to the poet, who (in dialogue

---

[1] Odysseus' language is Hesiodic (e.g., *W&D* 238–42; for the opposite, treating both locals and visitors justly, see *W&D* 225).

with Odysseus' words; see Chapter 1) formally aligns the Companions' doom with that of the Suitors at the very beginning of the poem (*Od.* 1.4–9):

πολλὰ δ' ὅ γ' ἐν πόντῳ πάθεν ἄλγεα ὃν κατὰ θυμόν,
ἀρνύμενος ἥν τε ψυχὴν καὶ νόστον ἑταίρων.
ἀλλ' οὐδ' ὣς ἑτάρους ἐρρύσατο, ἱέμενός περ·
αὐτῶν γὰρ σφετέρῃσιν ἀτασθαλίῃσιν ὄλοντο,
νήπιοι, οἳ κατὰ βοῦς Ὑπερίονος Ἠελίοιο
ἤσθιον· αὐτὰρ ὁ τοῖσιν ἀφείλετο νόστιμον ἦμαρ.

Many <were the> woes on the high seas <that> he suffered in his spirit,
as he was striving for his own soul and the homecoming of his Companions.
Yet not even so could he save the Companions, much as he wanted:
through their very own culpable recklessness they perished,
ignorant fools, who devoured the cattle of Hyperion the Sun;
but he, he took away the day of their return.

The alignment could not be more formal and conspicuous. Yet the death of the Companions and the nature of their punishment has puzzled many scholarly readers of the *Odyssey*. It is true that the offense of eating the Cattle of the Sun is much more serious than scholarship has tended to acknowledge, especially when the cosmic importance of Helios' herds and the existence of sacred cattle in real life is given due consideration, as was done in Chapter 6. Still, the punishment could be found to be unduly harsh in view of what is presented as a genuine theodicy at the very beginning of the poem.[2] In a clear reference to the proem and its singling out of the guilt of the Companions in the Thrinacia episode, Zeus in the Assembly of the Gods brings up the case of Aigisthos, a successful Suitor in the house of Agamemnon, who is clearly meant to be aligned with Penelope's Suitors as well as with the Companions (*Od.* 1.32–43):

ὢ πόποι, οἷον δή νυ θεοὺς βροτοὶ αἰτιόωνται.
ἐξ ἡμέων γάρ φασι κάκ' ἔμμεναι· οἱ δὲ καὶ αὐτοὶ
σφῇσιν ἀτασθαλίῃσιν ὑπὲρ μόρον ἄλγε' ἔχουσιν,
ὡς καὶ νῦν Αἴγισθος ὑπὲρ μόρον Ἀτρεΐδαο
γῆμ' ἄλοχον μνηστήν, τὸν δ' ἔκτανε νοστήσαντα,
εἰδὼς αἰπὺν ὄλεθρον, ἐπεὶ πρό οἱ εἴπομεν ἡμεῖς,
Ἑρμείαν πέμψαντες, ἐΰσκοπον Ἀργεϊφόντην,
μήτ' αὐτὸν κτείνειν μήτε μνάασθαι ἄκοιτιν·
ἐκ γὰρ Ὀρέσταο τίσις ἔσσεται Ἀτρεΐδαο,

---

[2] "The oldest Greek theodicy" (Jaeger 1926: 84); see Clay 1983: 216; Friedrich 1987: 375 with further references; Nagler 1990; Cook 1995, 1999: 15.

> ὁππότ' ἂν ἡβήσῃ τε καὶ ἧς ἱμείρεται αἴης.
> ὣς ἔφαθ' Ἑρμείας, ἀλλ' οὐ φρένας Αἰγίσθοιο
> πεῖθ' ἀγαθὰ φρονέων· νῦν δ' ἀθρόα πάντ' ἀπέτεισε.
>
> Oh my, how mortals are always blaming us gods;
> for they claim that their woes come from us. But they themselves,
> through their own criminal recklessness also come to undue grief.
> Just as now Aigisthos beyond what was due has married
> the wedded wife of Agamemnon, and him he killed when he returned,
> in full knowledge of his own steep perdition, since we had told him in advance,
> sending Hermes, ever-vigilant slayer of Argos,
> not to kill him, nor to woo his spouse.
> For from Orestes the retribution for Agamemnon will come,
> when he has grown to manhood and starts longing for his fatherland.
> Thus spoke Hermes; but not did he persuade the mind of Aigisthos,
> for all his good intentions. And now he has massively paid for everything.

The gods, Zeus seems to say, act as "good cops," trying to keep humans away from crime and transgression by giving them full and fair advance warning. Whatever sin is committed under this scenario is a matter of full human responsibility and any punishment of it is accordingly fully deserved. Such just treatment seems perfectly appropriate for the Suitors in both Agamemnon's and Odysseus' homes; Aigisthos, as Zeus says, has been adequately warned, and the way in which the Suitors disregard sound advice and ignore signs of doom, from the eagles over the Ithacan assembly and Halitherses' interpretation of it (2.146–76), to Theoklymenos' dire prophecy (20.351–7; see Chapters 5 and 6), is one of the leading themes of the poem. In these cases, divinity, it seems, really sought to prevent crime or tried to stop it.

But what about Odysseus' Companions? They are certainly forewarned, through the instructions that Odysseus receives from both Tiresias and Circe; they are even made to swear an oath to stay away from the herds and flocks on Thrinacia, the island that Odysseus has been advised to avoid (12.297–304). But divinity can hardly be said to have done its best to prevent the forbidden meat consumption: during the first night that Odysseus and company spend on the island Zeus sends strong winds that prevent the ship from leaving the island the next morning (12.312–16), a situation that lasts for a month till the crew have run out of the supplies that Circe had provided them with.[3] The rest is history, when the crew succumb to the needs of the belly and allow themselves to be persuaded by

---

[3] Friedrich 1987: 385–9, in an effort to diminish the case for a vindictive and malevolent Zeus, who forces humans to commit sins for which they are subsequently punished, argues that Odysseus

Eurylochos, who continues and completes the pattern of insubordination he had started earlier. The winds do not stop until the crime has been committed and the integrity of Helios' herds has been irrevocably compromised.

The consequences for Odyssean scholarship have been substantial.[4] The poem's unmistakable efforts to align the Companions' transgression with that of the Suitors as comparable cases of ἀτασθαλίη have been met by efforts to minimize the Companions' guilt, with even more serious consequences for the interpretation of the poem. For the less we think of the consumption of the cattle as a real crime,[5] comparable with the Suitors' transgression, the more glaring will be the gap between the Zeus of the first divine assembly, the enlightened god who cares for human ethics and morality, and the seemingly vindictive, capricious Zeus of the Thrinacia episode, who virtually forces humans to commit the crime for which they are then harshly punished.

The resulting theological discrepancy has been dealt with in various ways. In the German analyst tradition, multiple authorship has been assumed, with a "younger" poet, responsible for the proem and its enlightened theology, being unable to reconcile the differences with the work of an older poet, who was "still" working within an older, more primitive conception of divine agency.[6] The Unitarian version of this idea would be the poem's own representation of the transition from primitive to advanced religion, much as in some readings of the *Oresteia*.[7] Alternatively, the seeming mismatch between Zeus' words in the assembly and his deeds at the end of the Wanderings has been attributed to the diachronic nature of oral tradition and its typical collocation of archaic with more recent and innovative elements: just as epic language cannot be reduced to a single synchronic plane, so epic's theology – in addition to epic society and

---

 simply cannot know that the winds were sent by Zeus, having attributed other storms to Zeus that came from other gods (*Od.* 5.303–5).

[4] On the Thrinacia episode and its theological problems, see, among others, Focke 1943: 156–61, 347–54; Heubeck 1950: 72–8; Schadewaldt 1960; Fenik 1974 Clay 1983: 218–20; Friedrich 1987; Segal 1994: 195–227; Cook 1995, 1999; Danek 1998: 261–5; Schmidt 2003.

[5] Focke 1943: 249: "Übergriff, zu dem äußerste Lebensnot trieb"; Clay 1983: 230: "fundamental innocence." Fenik 1974: 212 seems to imply that only a good reason for not killing the cattle (which he apparently thinks has not been provided) would have justified the punishment of the Companions.

[6] Jaeger 1926; Focke 1943: 25–31; Schadewaldt 1960. Underlying such conceptions is the tacit assumption that the *Odyssey*, assumed to be "later" than the *Iliad*, is expected to have a more advanced moral-religious outlook than the earlier poem against the general backdrop of the progressive development of Greek culture.

[7] Segal 1994: 218–20.

warfare, etc. – displays disparate, even conflicting elements, since it draws on centuries of religious thought.[8]

The Companions are guilty, of course. They are not forced, as some scholars think, to commit the crime for which they will be punished.[9] And only common-sense reasoning can turn the religious offense of eating the Cattle of the Sun into innocent behavior. The Companions' alignment with the criminal Suitors goes much deeper than the mere fact that both groups are linked to Zeus' theodicy as presented through the example of Aigisthos. This complex paradigmatic relation also puts in perspective the notion of "primitive" gods, for if the wrath of Zeus–Helios is "primitive," then Odysseus' Zeus-sanctioned revenge on the Suitors must be primitive, too, a thought that does not sit well with those who see in Odysseus' victory over the Suitors a higher justice that prevails over rancorous vendetta.[10]

The idea of personal vendetta as opposed to formal justice reminds us of the important fact that Zeus (whether or not linked to Helios) is not the only god in play. It might even be asked why it is Zeus at all who acts on the transgression of Odysseus' Companions in the Thrinacia episode. Was it not Poseidon under whose wrath Odysseus was laboring? His wrath has to yield to Zeus' plan for Odysseus' return (*Od.* 1.77–80), but that does not mean that Poseidon stops having an impact on the Homecoming. And what is the role and importance of Poseidon in the question of the guilt of the Companions? Their demise in any case figures prominently in the Cyclops' prayer to his father Poseidon. So let us now examine that prayer, bearing in mind, in the face of all the criticism of the lack of a unified moral and religious outlook, that the *Odyssey* is not a theological treatise but a narrative, a time-space in which human experience of divine intent may be very different from that in real life, and in which even the gods are constrained in their actions by the requirements of the story in which they find themselves.

The prayer and the sacrifice

A theodicy such as the one presented by Zeus in the first divine assembly in Book One may be a transparent affair from the perspective of the gods who determine the crime and mete out its punishment, but the human

---

[8] Fenik 1974: 218–19. This solution from the perspective of oral poetry has been criticized (e.g., Clay 1983: 220–1; Friedrich 1987: 384) as ultimately equivalent to analyst scholarship in explaining away discrepancies, instead of attempting to resolve them through interpretation.
[9] See also Friedrich 1987.   [10] For example, Segal 1994: 195–227.

The prayer and the sacrifice

perspective is not so clear. Even the sinners themselves do not always know what is in store for them, lacking the personal divine warning that Aigisthos received through the intervention of Hermes himself. Those who do not sin are even more in the dark. The members of Odysseus' household who suffer from the Suitors' invasion in the master's absence do not always have an unshakeable belief in divine providence. There is a feeling of random luck and suffering according to the whims of Zeus. "Singers are not to blame," says Telemachos to his mother when she objects to Phemios' song about the homecoming of the Achaeans, "no, it is Zeus who is responsible for everything; he gives mortals their share just as it pleases him" (*Od.* 1.347–8). Less placid is Philoitios the faithful cattleman, when he exclaims that no god is "more baneful" (ὀλοώτερος) than Zeus, who pitilessly tangles mortals up in misery and grievous suffering (20.201–2). Only *post factum*, with hindsight, can one know for certain that justice has been dealt and the wicked have received their deserved punishment. "Father Zeus," old Laertes exclaims when he has learned of the killing of the Suitors, "I see now that you gods are still there on great Olympus, if it is true that the Suitors have paid for their reckless violence" (ἀτάσθαλον ὕβριν, 24.351–2). Only *post factum* can one know whether or not prayers have been answered.[11]

The narrator of such events and his audience are in a better position. They know, being in the future of the events recounted, whether or not prayers or sacrifices are successful. Being at a safe temporal distance makes it easy to perceive and understand the designs of the gods. Toward the end of the Cyclops episode there are two events that put Odysseus as narrator in a good position to display such knowledge, events which involve communication with the two principal gods involved: first, the prayer of Polyphemos to his father Poseidon, and not much later Odysseus' sacrifice to Zeus of the Cyclops' ram.

After Odysseus' last taunt from his ship, the Cyclops raises his arms to the sky and utters a prayer (*Od.* 9.528–36):

κλῦθι, Ποσείδαον γαιήοχε κυανοχαῖτα·
εἰ ἐτεόν γε σός εἰμι, πατὴρ δ' ἐμὸς εὔχεαι εἶναι,
δὸς μὴ Ὀδυσσῆα πτολιπόρθιον οἴκαδ' ἱκέσθαι,

---

[11] Cf. the image of Zeus' jars in *Iliad* 24 and on the theodicy, see Versnel 2011: 151–225, who discusses, among many other things, Solon's great elegiac *Hymn to the Muses* (Solon 13W). Gagné 2009 shows that the poem's alleged lack of "unity" is in fact a juxtaposition of the two perspectives involved: the incomplete vision of lived humanity versus the memory of the poet who contemplates human action from the vantage point of hindsight.

> υἱὸν Λαέρτεω, Ἰθάκῃ ἔνι οἰκί' ἔχοντα.
> **ἀλλ' εἴ** οἱ **μοῖρ'** ἐστὶ φίλους τ' ἰδέειν καὶ ἱκέσθαι
> οἶκον ἐϋκτίμενον καὶ ἑὴν ἐς πατρίδα γαῖαν,
> ὀψὲ κακῶς ἔλθοι, ὀλέσας ἄπο πάντας ἑταίρους,
> νηὸς ἐπ' ἀλλοτρίης, εὕροι δ' ἐν πήματα οἴκῳ.
> ὣς ἔφατ' εὐχόμενος, τοῦ δ' ἔκλυε κυανοχαίτης.

> Hear me, Poseidon, you who hold the earth, dark-haired one:
> <u>if</u> truly I am your son, and you proclaim yourself to be my father,
> grant that "Odysseus, sacker of a city," will not come home,
> "son of Laertes, having his home in Ithaca."
> But, <u>if it is given</u> to him to see his own people,
> and come back to his strong-founded house and to his own fatherland,
> <u>may he come home late, in bad shape</u>, having lost all his
>   Companions,
> on board a foreign ship, and may he find evils in his house.
> Thus he spoke in his prayer, and the dark-haired one listened to him
>   with benevolence.

Polyphemos actually utters two prayers in this single utterance, each framed with a conditional clause. First, comes the standard *if*-clause in which the praying agent (human or otherwise) states conditions that entitle him to the favor requested, for example, past services rendered to the divinity, or, as here, family relationship.[12] The *if*-clause is not hypothetical but factual, presenting what is presumed to be the case as basis for the request, typically, as here, articulated with aorist imperatives (δὸς μὴ ... οἴκαδ' ἱκέσθαι, 'give that ... will not return home'). The request is simply the elimination of Odysseus' *nostos* (in the sense of both homecoming and survival, see Chapter 2), now that Polyphemos is no longer in a position to kill Odysseus himself.

But then, interrupting himself with ἀλλά, Polyphemos makes a new start in his prayer. The mentioning of Odysseus' name had reminded him of the old prophecy made to him by the seer Telemos son of Eurymos, who foretold him Odysseus' visit and the blinding (9.507–12). If Odysseus' present feat was preordained, Polyphemos seems to reason, then more of his guest's biography may already have been fixed, and so he portentously introduces the notion of *moîra* as a frame for his alternative wish. The second conditional, now hypothetical rather than factual, reverses the desired outcome of the previous prayer as a frame for the second: let *nostos* be impossible for him, but *if* it is possible, let it be maximally painful. This is not a request based on presumed entitlements, but a wish contingent

---

[12] For example, *Il.* 1.37–42; *Od.* 20.98–101; Sapph. 1.5–25. On Greek prayer, see Depew 1997 with further references.

The prayer and the sacrifice

on a single important condition, and the imperative is replaced with optatives of wish. It is easy to see that Polyphemos' modified wish/prayer will come true – in fact, Odysseus, in reperforming it, is contributing to its fulfillment: mentioning the "foreign ship" before his Phaeacian hosts, whose escort home he is trying to secure, will help to persuade them now that they see that their help has been prophesied.[13]

For a prophecy is what Polyphemos' prayer turns out to be, without the speaker realizing it. The term for such a speech act in the *Odyssey* is φήμη. In the tragedians and Herodotus this term denotes intentional prophetic or oracular utterance or the coming true of divine signs such as dreams.[14] In the *Odyssey*, on the other hand, φήμη is an unintentionally prophetic utterance, as in Polyphemos' case.[15] Nor is Odysseus aware of the power of the words of Polyphemos, who presumably owes his name to this prayer.[16] Polyphemos' *phēmē* will be confirmed and specified through Tiresias' prophecy, on which more later. By the time he recounts the Cyclops tale, having heard Tiresias' prophecy, Odysseus can round off the speech, in the manner of a true *aoidos* who has the knowledge of hindsight, with the formulaic τοῦ δ' ἔκλυε κυανοχαίτης, 'and he heard him, the Black-haired one'. Polyphemos' *phēmē* takes effect immediately, unbeknown to the speaker, who will turn out, within an even wider temporal frame, to be the hero's most important "donor" in the sense discussed in Chapter 2: he will enable a quest that is nothing less than the poem as a whole.

One final linguistic feature of Polyphemos' portentous prayer can be seen in connection with Odysseus' sacrifice to Zeus, the second moment in the episode in which contact with the divine is attempted. All the painful aspects of Odysseus' return wished for by the Cyclops, the late Homecoming, the evil in his house, are expressed as finite optative verbs

---

[13] See Bakker 2002b: 146–9.
[14] For example, Soph. *OT* 42–3 (θεῶν φήμην), 723 (φῆμαι μαντικαί); Hdt. 1.43.3 ἐξέπλησε τοῦ ὀνείρου τὴν φήμην.
[15] At *Od.* 20.105 a servant in Odysseus' house utters the prayer to Zeus that this should be the Suitors' final day; the speaker is unaware of the fact that she is being used as a sign from Zeus to Odysseus (σῆμα ἄνακτι, 20.111), who had explicitly asked for it (φήμην τις μοι φάσθω, 20.100).
[16] See Bakker 2002b for more on the name Polyphemos and its poetics. The combination of prophetic insight with blindness is well attested generally, and it is explicitly present in an unexpected multiform of the Odyssean Cyclops tale, Euenios and the flocks of Helios in Apollonia (Hdt. 9.92–5). The ubiquitous explanation of "Polyphemos" as "famous" (e.g., Burkert 1979: 153 n. 11; Bergren 1983: 49, 69 n. 27; Cook 1995: 94; Higbie 1995: 12; Louden 1995: 41–3; Ahl and Roisman 1996: 109. Bremmer 2002: 144 sees Polyphemos as calque on Theoklymenos) is at odds with the meaning of φήμη in the *Odyssey* (the word does not occur in the *Iliad*). Note, furthermore, that the *Odyssey* distinguishes φήμη from φῆμις, 'rumor, gossip', which elsewhere in the epic corpus (Hes. *W&D* 760–4) is expressed as φήμη. On the play with both φήμη and φῆμις in the semantics of Polyphemos' name, see Bakker 2002b.

(ἔλθοι, εὕροι), except for one element, the loss of the Companions. This item is expressed as a participial clause (ὀλέσας ἄπο πάντας ἑταίρους, 'having lost all his Companions'), a phrase that recurs in the prophecies of other speakers as well.[17] Here in Polyphemos' prayer the loss of the Companions is backgrounded with respect to the main clause, which specifies the lateness and the misery of the Return (ὀψὲ κακῶς). It looks as if Polyphemos takes the loss of the Companions for granted as part of Odysseus' *moira*, keeping it out of the string of events he asks his father to accomplish. Perhaps Poseidon is not supposed to be responsible for the loss, which falls within the domain of another god.

The loss of the Companions is the central element in Zeus' response to Odysseus' sacrifice, which is the centerpiece of the heroic *dais* that Odysseus and his men try to create out of the stolen sheep of the Cyclops (*Od.* 9.548–55):

μῆλα δὲ Κύκλωπος γλαφυρῆς ἐκ νηὸς ἑλόντες
δασσάμεθ᾽, ὡς μή τίς μοι ἀτεμβόμενος κίοι ἴσης.
ἀρνειὸν δ᾽ ἐμοὶ οἴῳ ἐϋκνήμιδες ἑταῖροι
μήλων δαιομένων δόσαν ἔξοχα· τὸν δ᾽ ἐνὶ θινὶ
Ζηνὶ κελαινεφέϊ Κρονίδῃ, ὃς πᾶσιν ἀνάσσει,
ῥέξας μηρί᾽ ἔκαιον· ὁ δ᾽ οὐκ ἐμπάζετο ἱρῶν,
ἀλλ᾽ **ἄρα** μερμήριζεν ὅπως ἀπολοίατο πᾶσαι
νῆες ἐΰσσελμοι καὶ ἐμοὶ ἐρίηρες ἑταῖροι.

And the sheep of the Cyclops we took out of the hollow ship
and divided them so that no one was cheated of his share.
The ram, to me alone my well-greaved Companions
they gave it, as a special honor, when the sheep were being divided.
    And him, on the beach,
to Zeus of the Black Clouds, Kronos' son, who rules over all,
I burnt his thighbones in sacrifice; but Zeus did not care for the offerings;
no, (as I now know), he started pondering on how everything
could be destroyed, my well-benched ships and my Companions
so faithful to me.

This sacrifice has raised many questions.[18] Let us first observe that Odysseus speaks again with the knowledge of hindsight, violating "Jörgensen's Law" in stepping out of the limited perspective of the first-person experiential narrator.[19] We can see in Odysseus' use of the "evidential" particle ἄρα that his knowledge now in telling the story is different from

---

[17] *Od.* 2.174 (Halitherses), 11.114 (Tiresias), 12.141 (Circe), 13.340 (Athena).
[18] See, e.g., Focke 1943: 160–1; Fenik 1974: 222; Segal 1994: 212–14.
[19] Also noted by Friedrich 1991: 16.

The prayer and the sacrifice

his ignorance then, when he tried to communicate with Zeus.[20] He now knows, as opposed to his original ignorance, having learned from Calypso (12.389–90), that Zeus was responsible for the Companions' destruction after Thrinacia.

But why would that punishment, just though it may have been, be prepared now? In Chapter 4 we looked at the context and occurrence of the sacrifice, observing that the sheep have been obtained through an unprovoked raid and are being consumed as if their meat is as limitlessly plentiful as that of the wild goats. This is a transgression, paradigmatically linked with that of the Suitors, and, more importantly in the present context, foreshadowing the slaughter of the Cattle of the Sun. But observing this will only increase, it seems, the conflict between the benign Zeus of the proem with his advanced theodicy and the malevolent Zeus who, it has been held, pursues mortals who have been trapped into committing a sin. The Companions may have been forewarned in the later adventure, but here there has been no divine intervention explaining that the sheep of the Cyclops were not to be touched – unless the supernaturally easy and plentiful hunt of the wild goats, given by "a god" (9.158), was an oblique warning not to look for food elsewhere.

The Companions cannot be blamed for the events of the Cyclops adventure. The blame for entering the Cyclops' cave rests squarely with Odysseus, whose inquisitiveness and desire for "gifts of hospitality" landed them in this situation, as Odysseus himself admits (*Od.* 9.228–30). In fact, the charge of ἀτασθαλία, squarely on the side of the Companions in the Thrinacia episode, is directed at Odysseus in connection with the Cyclops adventure. The accuser is Eurylochos, who considers Circe's house a duplicate of the Cyclops' cave (*Od.* 10.431–7):

> ἆ δειλοί, πόσ' ἴμεν; τί κακῶν ἱμείρετε τούτων;
> Κίρκης ἐς μέγαρον καταβήμεναι, ἥ κεν ἅπαντας
> ἢ σῦς ἠὲ λύκους ποιήσεται ἠὲ λέοντας,
> οἵ κέν οἱ μέγα δῶμα φυλάσσοιμεν καὶ ἀνάγκῃ,
> ὥς περ Κύκλωψ ἔρξ', ὅτε οἱ μέσσαυλον ἵκοντο
> ἡμέτεροι ἕταροι, σὺν δ' ὁ θρασὺς εἵπετ' Ὀδυσσεύς·
> τούτου γὰρ καὶ κεῖνοι **ἀτασθαλίῃσιν** ὄλοντο.

> Ah, poor wretches, where are we going? Why do you long for these evils?
> To go down into Circe's hall, who will turn us,
> all of us, into swine or wolves, or lions,
> so that we can guard her big house whether we want it or not.

---

[20] On the semantics of ἄρα, see Bakker 1993: 15–25; 2005: 97–101.

> Just as the Cyclops shut them in, when they came to his enclosure,
> our companions, and with them came that brazen one, Odysseus;
> it is through that man's <u>culpable recklessness</u> that these too perished.

There is irony, for Eurylochos himself will be, as leader of a collective, the perpetrator of the much more destructive ἀτασθαλία at Thrinacia. But the charge pointedly assigns exclusive agency to Odysseus: as leader he treated the lives of the men under his command with reckless carelessness.[21] The Cyclops adventure and the Thrinacia episode in this way bookend the Wanderings in a contrasting way: in the former case Odysseus stands apart from the collective as undisputed leader who has unrestrained control over the lives of his Companions, whereas in the latter case he stands apart as outsider who has lost all control and is ignored by the collective. The charge of ἀτασθαλία has passed from the individual to the group.

Odysseus' reckless leadership, coupled with his taunts and boastful addresses to the Cyclops from the relative safety of his boat, have led to the supposition that Zeus rejects the sacrifice because he wants to punish Odysseus' "hubris," acting in this way in concert with his brother Poseidon.[22] But visiting the punishment for this crime on the Companions, who are guilty neither of the cave invasion nor of the provocations of the Cyclops, would contradict Zeus' theodicy, which emphasizes human responsibility, not the need to die for the sins of someone else.

Zeus and Poseidon

We can now begin to investigate how Zeus' plan (which as Odysseus now knows began at this moment, just after Polyphemos' prayer) is related to Poseidon's wrath. The presence of two vindictive gods has been seen as a compositional and esthetic liability for the poem, as we saw earlier. But there is more than one reason for divine persecution and it appears that Zeus and Poseidon each have their own agenda. The poem informs us repeatedly and through various speakers (Zeus, 1.69; Tiresias, 11.103; Athena, 13.343) that the blinding of the Cyclops is the sole reason for Poseidon's vindictive wrath, even though modern scholars have tended to see the mutilation as a necessary act of self-defense.[23] But modern notions of guilt, legal liability, or legitimate self-defense are perhaps not the right

---

[21] In this way the expedition into the cave is similar to Hector keeping his troops outside the walls of Troy, a decision for which the hero takes full responsibility by directing the charge of ἀτασθαλία to himself (*Il.* 22.104).

[22] Friedrich 1991, building on Reinhardt 1996: 82–3 [1948: 85–6].   [23] Schmidt 2003: 25.

lenses through which to view the wrath of Poseidon and the primitive world in which it is a meaningful force. Indeed, Greek religion in general is uninterested in adducing attenuating circumstances when it comes to defining human guilt. It seems best therefore to take the poem at face value; and Odysseus' boastful and blasphemous gloating provokes the god even more – these words are in fact what prompts Polyphemos to utter his fateful prayer in the first place (*Od.* 9.523–5):[24]

> αἴ γὰρ δὴ ψυχῆς τε καὶ αἰῶνός σε δυναίμην
> εὖνιν ποιήσας πέμψαι δόμον Ἄϊδος εἴσω,
> ὡς οὐκ ὀφθαλμόν γ' ἰήσεται οὐδ' ἐνοσίχθων.

> I wish I could rob you of your soul and your very life,
> and send you down in the House of Hades,
> just as he will not heal your eye, not even the Earth-Shaker.

The god most likely to be enraged by such words is Poseidon himself, not Zeus. And Poseidon is more likely to target Odysseus personally than to harm or kill his Companions. He and his son Polyphemos are interested in the Companions only insofar as their death will make the hero's Homecoming disgraceful and difficult. The Companions are pawns in the god's game, and they are not the only ones, as we will see.

The case of Zeus, on the other hand, is more complex. When Odysseus opens his taunting and boastful exchange of words with the Cyclops, he claims to have the divine protector of hospitality on his side (*Od.* 9.475–9):

> Κύκλωψ, οὐκ ἄρ' ἔμελλες ἀνάλκιδος ἀνδρὸς ἑταίρους
> ἔδμεναι ἐν σπῆϊ γλαφυρῷ κρατερῆφι βίηφι.
> καὶ λίην σέ γ' ἔμελλε κιχήσεσθαι κακὰ ἔργα,
> σχέτλι', ἐπεὶ ξείνους οὐχ ἅζεο σῷ ἐνὶ οἴκῳ
> ἐσθέμεναι· τῶ σε Ζεὺς τείσατο καὶ θεοὶ ἄλλοι.

> Cyclops! Now you can see that you were not going to eat the Companions
> of a defenseless man with your brute force in your hollow cave.
> Bad things were going to hit you, you terrible brute,
> since you did not stand back in awe from eating the strangers in your house. That is why Zeus has taken revenge on you and also the other gods.

So just as he did after the killing of the Suitors (see above) at the end of the Cyclops adventure, Odysseus casts himself as the instrument of Zeus'

---

[24] Schmidt 2003: 32 sees in these very words, not in the actual blinding, the fundamental cause for Poseidon's wrath, citing the boasting of Locrian Ajax, for which Poseidon smashed his ship on the rocks (*Od.* 4.502–11).

justice, aligning, as if he were Zeus' spokesman, the Suitors and the Cyclops as sinners who came to grief and deserved punishment through their own wicked deeds. Odysseus is probably right. But he is not an externally positioned divine agent looking in from a lofty perspective on human affairs. And so he finds himself implicated in the justice he himself metes out.

The punishment that Zeus has in store for Odysseus is very different from Poseidon's wrath, but there is overlap. In the plans of each god the Companions have to die, but whereas in Poseidon's vision of revenge the Companions are merely disposable as pawns in the game, to be sacrificed as an expedient way to make Odysseus suffer and compromise his *nostos*, for Zeus the Companions are part of a plan to make Odysseus look better than would have been the case if Poseidon had been the only god in play.[25] We have to believe Odysseus at face value when he says that Zeus in refusing to accept the sacrifice was already plotting the death of the Companions and the loss of the ships. There is a clear causal thread leading from the prayer to Zeus to the consumption of the cattle of Helios. The missing link is the prophecy of Tiresias, which is not a φήμη but the conscious voice of an oracle to be consulted.[26]

Tiresias provides an indispensable specification to Polyphemos' tentative scenario for Odysseus' future (*Od.* 11.100–18):

νόστον δίζηαι μελιηδέα, φαίδιμ' Ὀδυσσεῦ·
τὸν δέ τοι ἀργαλέον θήσει θεός. οὐ γὰρ ὀΐω
λήσειν ἐννοσίγαιον, ὅ τοι κότον ἔνθετο θυμῷ,
χωόμενος ὅτι οἱ υἱὸν φίλον ἐξαλάωσας.
ἀλλ' ἔτι μέν κε καὶ ὥς, κακά περ πάσχοντες, ἵκοισθε,
αἴ κ' ἐθέλῃς σὸν θυμὸν ἐρυκακέειν καὶ ἑταίρων,
ὁππότε κεν πρῶτον πελάσῃς εὐεργέα νῆα
Θρινακίῃ νήσῳ, προφυγὼν ἰοειδέα πόντον,
βοσκομένας δ' εὕρητε βόας καὶ ἴφια μῆλα
Ἠελίου, ὃς πάντ' ἐφορᾷ καὶ πάντ' ἐπακούει.
τὰς εἰ μέν κ' ἀσινέας ἐάας νόστου τε μέδηαι,
καί κεν ἔτ' εἰς Ἰθάκην, κακά περ πάσχοντες, ἵκοισθε·
εἰ δέ κε σίνηαι, τότε τοι τεκμαίρομ' ὄλεθρον
νηΐ τε καὶ ἑτάροισ'. αὐτὸς δ' εἴ πέρ κεν ἀλύξῃς,
ὀψὲ κακῶς νεῖαι, ὀλέσας ἄπο πάντας ἑταίρους,
νηὸς ἐπ' ἀλλοτρίης· δήεις δ' ἐν πήματα οἴκῳ,
ἄνδρας ὑπερφιάλους, οἵ τοι βίοτον κατέδουσι
μνώμενοι ἀντιθέην ἄλοχον καὶ ἕδνα διδόντες.
ἀλλ' ἦ τοι κείνων γε βίας ἀποτείσεαι ἐλθών.

---

[25] For a different view of the two gods' plans relative to each other, see Marks 2008: 42–5.
[26] Cf. χρησομένους, 10.492.

> You are seeking your return sweet as honey, glorious Odysseus:
> Yet a god will make that very difficult for you; I do not think
> you will be unaware of the Earthshaker, who has put anger in his spirit,
> enraged because you blinded his dear son.
> But even so, your company can still reach home in spite of grievous suffering,
> if, that is, you are willing to hold back your craving and that of your Companions,
> when first you bring your well-built ship close
> to the island of Thrinacia, having escaped the dangers of the violet sea,
> and find grazing there the cattle and vigorous sheep
> of Helios the Sun, who sees everything and hears everything.
> Those herds, if you leave them unharmed and are mindful of your return,
> then your company may still reach Ithaca, in spite of suffering evil.
> <u>But if you hurt them</u>, I guarantee you destruction that very moment
> for your ship and your Companions; yourself, if you escape at all,
> <u>you will come home late and in bad shape, having lost all your Companions,
> on a foreign ship, and you will find evils in your home</u>,
> overbearing men, who eat up all your wealth,
> wooing your godlike spouse and offering her wedding-gifts.
> Still, it is true that you will take revenge on them upon your return.

Polyphemos' tentative framing conditional, specifying a *nostos* required by *moîra* as constraint on his desire to see Odysseus come to grief, has here been replaced with a prospective subjunctive conditional, specifying the conditions under which a sure prediction will come true.[27] Helios' immortal herds of cattle have now been introduced as the fundamental test on which the *nostos* of Odysseus and company depends. And they have different functions for different gods.

Of central importance is the second-person singular of the pivotal verb, σίνηαι, whose meaning in the real world of sanctuaries and sacred land we discussed in Chapter 6. Odysseus is the person addressed, but of course he will not hurt Helios' cattle. The Companions will. Their doing so qualifies as a transgression of Odysseus. As leader he is responsible for the actions of his men. But his leadership, steadily eroding in the course of the Wanderings, has at this point vanished completely. Eurylochos as the *de facto* new leader successfully brings the Companions, unified now in opposition to Odysseus, to commit acts that Odysseus has explicitly warned them against. The beginning of this process of growing distrust goes back

---

[27] For the semantics of this kind of conditional, see Bakker 1988b.

precisely to the Cyclops episode. Looking back to it when questioning Odysseus' leadership in the Circe episode, Eurylochos accuses Odysseus of ἀτασθαλία (see above), the most serious crime the poem knows. The accusation makes Odysseus very angry, but it accurately reflects the way in which he and Polyphemos trade qualities and share guilt from their first encounter to the end of the poem (see Chapter 4).

The breakdown of Odysseus' leadership, beginning after the Cyclops adventure and culminating in Thrinacia, is Poseidon's side of the matter. Odysseus' inability to restrain his men is a disgrace that will haunt him until his return to Ithaca, and beyond. Coming back without any of the men he took with him to Troy is a social, political, and demographic disaster, the elimination of an entire generation of males in a small and close-knit community.

Zeus' interest in the Thrinacia episode, on the other hand, is very different. Notwithstanding the objections of some modern scholars, Zeus turns the inevitable, the loss of Odysseus' Companions as decreed by *moîra*, into a showcase of the moral policy he presents in the divine assembly at the beginning of the poem. He turns from Odysseus to the Companions and subjects their actions to the rule of human responsibility. In doing so he creates for Odysseus a more positive outcome than would otherwise have been the case. Odysseus lost his men, an embarrassing outcome for a leader, but they owed their doom to themselves. They were forewarned. The crime that they committed against Helios' divine animals turns Odysseus from the victim of Poseidon's wrath into the single just and virtuous human, the sole survivor of the punitive Flood. Odysseus is the only one who can resist the urges of the belly, the human organ that was so painfully tested in this episode (ἔτειρε δὲ γαστέρα λιμός, 'hunger was wearing out the belly', *Od.* 12.332). In this scenario, created by Zeus, the Companions become not merely a *loss* to Odysseus (as intended by Poseidon), but rather the *cause* of his late Homecoming; they are responsible not only for their own demise, but also for the long suffering and delayed *nostos* of their king.

The Companions fall victim to the temptation of food. This may seem merely unheroic, not criminal, to some,[28] but they not only ignore divine warnings, they also violate a divine taboo and lay their hands on divine property. Nor is their ultimate transgression unprepared in the narrative. A number of seemingly unimportant and irrelevant details, some of which we noticed in previous chapters, become meaningful retroactively in light of the Thrinacia episode:

[28] For example, Fenik 1974: 215.

9.45–6 (Cicones episode): "Then much wine was drunk and many sheep they slaughtered and many cattle with rolling gait and curvy horns."

9.86 (Lotophagoi episode): "And forthwith they took their meal by the swift ships, my Companions."

9.154–5 (Goat Island episode): "And the Nymphs, daughters of Zeus who holds the Aigis, stirred up goats born in the mountains, so that my Companions could have a meal."

10.57 (Aiolos episode): "And forthwith they took their meal by the swift ships, my Companions."

10.153–5 (Circe episode): "And this way it seemed to me to be more profitable as I was thinking, first to go back to the ship and the shore of the sea, and to give the Companions their meal."

Some of these mentions of meals and eating are innocent by themselves, but taken together they suggest a pattern running through the Wanderings. Long before the rift in the company comes explicitly to the fore in Thrinacia, Odysseus and the Companions are opposed to each other in relation to food, as already encoded in grammar by the third-person plural through which the narrator excludes himself from the action. The Companions' nutritional needs are no greater than Odysseus', but they are mindlessly compulsive eaters, prone to error due to their cravings and extremely vulnerable to temptation. They can handle neither scarcity nor abundance (Thrinacia presents both), and so are certain to commit the fundamental abundance-related crime of *atasthalia*.[29]

The situation at the other end of the paradigmatic axis between the Companions and the Suitors is very similar. The Suitors are depicted as responsible agents – more so than the Companions, some scholars would say; they die, as per Odysseus' words cited earlier, through "their own awful deeds, for they would not honor anyone of the earth-dwelling humans, neither base nor noble, whoever would come in contact with them. This is why through their criminal recklessness they met with this unseemly doom" (*Od.* 22.413–16). Odysseus is certainly justified in casting himself, once again, as the instrument of Zeus' justice. The Suitors clearly deserved their death, persisting in their actions in the face of numerous warnings and portents.

But that does not make Odysseus' Homecoming any less ugly. The slaughter of the Suitors may be a case of the justice of Zeus in action, but the relatives of the dead will disagree. Here is what Eupeithes, the father

---

[29] One is reminded of the elegiac wisdom that a surfeit of riches leads to *hybris* and *atē*, e.g., Theogn. 153; Solon 4.34–5; 6.3; cf. Aesch. *Pers.* 821–2.

of Antinoos has to say on this in a speech that we may perhaps take as the voice of the Ithacan community at large (*Od.* 24.426–9):

> ὦ φίλοι, ἦ μέγα ἔργον ἀνὴρ ὅδε μήσατ' Ἀχαιούς·
> τοὺς μὲν σὺν νήεσσιν ἄγων πολέας τε καὶ ἐσθλοὺς
> ὤλεσε μὲν νῆας γλαφυράς, ἀπὸ δ' ὤλεσε λαούς,
> τοὺς δ' ἐλθὼν ἔκτεινε Κεφαλλήνων ὄχ' ἀρίστους.
>
> Oh, my friends, what a terrible thing this man has devised for the Achaeans:
> leading away the others, many of them and good men, in the ships,
> he lost the hollow ships and destroyed our people.
> And now he is back and has killed these ones, by far the best of the Cephalonians.

Odysseus' revenge on the Suitors, the consequence of his coming home "late," and alone, is an act of extreme violence, Cyclopean in its brutality, and a cause of nothing less than *stasis*, civil strife, in the city. Odysseus himself knows this, in spite of his satisfaction in his victory (*Od.* 23.118–22, speaking to Telemachos):

> καὶ γάρ τίς θ' ἕνα φῶτα κατακτείνας ἐνὶ δήμῳ,
> ᾧ μὴ πολλοὶ ἔωσιν ἀοσσητῆρες ὀπίσσω,
> φεύγει πηούς τε προλιπὼν καὶ πατρίδα γαῖαν·
> ἡμεῖς δ' ἕρμα πόληος ἀπέκταμεν, οἳ μέγ' ἄριστοι
> κούρων εἰν Ἰθάκῃ· τὰ δέ σε φράζεσθαι ἄνωγα.
>
> Even someone who has killed <just> one man in the community –
> a man who doesn't have many to avenge him after his death –
> even so he goes into exile, leaving his kinsmen and his fatherland behind;
> but we, we have killed the very mainstay of the city, the elite
> of all the young men in Ithaca; this I'm asking you to consider.

The presence of Suitors in Odysseus' house, and the need to kill them, is the work of Poseidon; the Suitors are the πήματα οἴκῳ, 'evils in his house', of Polyphemos' prayer, with Tiresias' prophecy filling in the details (see above). They have been in the house for three years (*Od.* 13.377). This means that if the Companions had refrained from harming Helios' cattle, Odysseus would have arrived home in time to prevent the situation in Ithaca that motivated the invasion of his home (i.e., the social conflict discussed in Chapter 3: the presumed widow who refuses to remarry). As it is, when the Suitors entered, he was marooned on Calypso's island at the navel of the sea (1.50). The assembled gods' intention to free Odysseus from Calypso's embrace and so to expedite his *nostos* coincides with their desire that Poseidon let go of the wrath he holds against Odysseus

(*Od.* 1.74–9). We may conclude that Odysseus' prolonged stay on Ogygia was indeed the work of Poseidon, who in this way effectively allowed the "evils" to enter Odysseus' house, so fulfilling his son Polyphemos' prayer.

Before the poem has properly explained the tangle of divine wraths and motivations, the listener is offered a preview of Poseidon's mentality and of the nature of the farther reaches of his wrath. This happens indirectly, through the song of Ares and Aphrodite, sung by Demodokos before the Phaeacians and their mysterious guest. Poseidon, in opposition to Hermes and Apollo – gods favorable to Odysseus – takes the side of the Suitor and is in favor of offering legal assistance to Ares, the Suitor caught *in flagrante delicto*. He proposes that Ares pay a fine and not be subjected to further harm or humiliation – precisely the solution that Odysseus will emphatically reject in his own house when the moment of reckoning has arrived and Eurymachos wants to strike a deal (22.60–7, see Chapter 8).[30]

The revenge of the returning king, then, is a case of the justice of Zeus in practice only in a very limited sense. The "evil in the house" is not just something that Odysseus has to overcome; by killing the Suitors he becomes effectively part of it. In order to overcome the intruders Odysseus will need to have recourse to bestial savagery, decimate the human resources of the Ionian islands, and create conditions of *stasis* and civil war on Ithaca.[31] On the morning after his reunion with Penelope Odysseus – who has told Penelope "how many sorrows he had put on people" (23.306–7) – sets out on a raid to recover the sheep he had lost (αὐτὸς ἐγὼ ληΐσσομαι, 23.357), refraining from the dispute-settling and counseling he had accused the Cyclopes of lacking. Indeed, Odysseus would have wiped out yet another generation of Ithacans in combat, if Athena had not brought as *dea ex machina* an end to the strife at the close of the poem (24.528–36). Even so Odysseus can be stopped in his battle rage only when Zeus himself intervenes and sends forth the blazing thunderbolt (24.537–40). The self-proclaimed instrument of the justice of Zeus as protector of hospitality is deeply implicated in the barbarism he claims to avenge. The hand of Poseidon is visible until the very end of the poem. Peace and prosperity are perhaps going to come back to Ithaca (cf. Tiresias' words at 11.136–7), but not in the

---

[30] Segal (1994: 205) offers a diametrically opposed reading of this episode (seeing Poseidon as a "dignified, effective peacemaker").
[31] See also Nagler 1990: 341, 351, who interprets Odysseus' words at 22.6 (νῦν αὖτε σκοπὸν ἄλλον, ὃν οὔ πώ τις βάλεν ἀνήρ) as a sign of Odysseus' own awareness of his ambiguous role.

action depicted in our poem. The justice of Zeus is so compromised as to become a justice of Poseidon, a case of right by might avenging right by might. Ithaca has become a place where it is, to paraphrase Hesiod, "bad for a man to be just and just to be bad."[32]

Justice for Odysseus

The persona of Odysseus that results from this narrative scenario, a contradiction between the just man who can resist temptation and the brutal avenger who destroys his own people, can in itself be seen as a case of the traditional ambiguity of the epic hero.[33] Both problem and solution, savior and destroyer, Odysseus, the hero who suffers and who causes suffering, fits in well with the pattern. But this does not in itself explain the tension between the plans of two divinities, one forcing Odysseus to be bad, the other allowing him to be good.

This chapter has argued that far from being an esthetic liability or an unfortunate consequence of oral composition or dual authorship, the presence of two divine wraths is motivated by the nature of Odysseus' *nostos* as a complex compromise, the result of Zeus' and Poseidon's partly coinciding and partly conflicting intentions. The solution I have proposed bears equally on a related problem that scholars have seen in the *Odyssey*'s theology, the coexistence of different religious systems and conceptions of human responsibility and divine motivation. I conclude the chapter by adding a further consideration.

Poseidon's wrath is primitive. Or rather we should say that Poseidon and his son represent a non- or pre-Olympian element in the poem.[34] This is neither the unintentional presence of an older layer of religion, nor the deliberate representation of a rise of more advanced religion out of primitive antecedents, but an integral part of the narrative. Odysseus and his men have not only drifted far away from home, but have also regressed in time and degree of civilization. They have drifted far away from the places where heroic glory can be won, and sung. The Cyclops does not

---

[32] Hes. W&D 271–2 (κακὸν ἄνδρα δίκαιον | ἔμμεναι).
[33] See Cook 1999 in terms of "active and passive heroics." This contradictory personality fits in with the semantics of Odysseus' name ("the Hating/Hated one," *Od.* 19.407–9, with word play at 1.62 and 9.415), on which, see Dimock 1956; Clay 1983: 27–9, 54–68; S. West 1988: 83, and further references at Cook 1999: 151 n, 10. Odysseus' homologue in heroic ambiguity is, of course, Achilles, whose name is equally significant in this regard; see Nagy 1979: 69–93; 2004: 131–7.
[34] The Cyclopes, along with the Phaeacians, are associated with the Giants (7.59) and Polyphemos' mother is Thoosa, a daughter of the pre-Olympian sea god Phorkys. See further Segal 1994: 203–4.

literally live in the age of Kronos, but as many have noticed, his habitat has clear Golden Age features, as have other lands that Odysseus has to visit. And Odysseus is, paradoxically, below the Cyclopes in cultural attainment, as we saw in Chapter 4, having not yet reached the level of civilization of the sedentary pastoralist and being obliged to survive by hunting in the abundance provided by nature.

Odysseus' punishment is to have to live in this pre-civilized, non-epic state, free of the constraints of culture and the limits imposed by law and community, but removed also from heroic society and its rituals. To survive in this world is not to be so strong and heroic that one earns one's share at the *dais*, but to be able to resist the temptation of food, to understand that heroic rituals and routines are inappropriate, sometimes even deadly.

Zeus is not actually absent from the world in which Odysseus is forced to travel, but this is not Zeus' world, nor his moment, but Poseidon's. Athena admits as much when she answers Odysseus' reproach that he has not seen her by his side since the Trojan War: she did not want to "wage war" with Poseidon (13.341). In the space thus created Poseidon, standing apart from the other gods (*Od.* 1.20), takes on clear pre-Olympian qualities. The biggest mistake in Poseidon's world, a mistake made first by Odysseus and the Companions, later by the Companions alone, is to pretend that the normal rules with regard to heroism and the relations with the gods apply. In fact, each attempt at creating normalcy in the Otherworld fails. The sacrifice of the Cyclops' ram is rejected by Zeus, not because he wants to punish Odysseus for any hubris, but because sacrifice is as such inappropriate at this moment and in this place. And the sacrifice to Helios is at various levels a travesty of religious behavior by pseudo-worshippers who are already doomed.

These attempts are complemented by reverse attempts back in Ithaca, where the Suitors create perverted Golden Age conditions, by treating themselves to (unsustainable) meat abundance, without any sacrifice being performed, and suppressing all expression of civic life, in particular assemblies and councils, emphatically absent in the Cyclops community as well (9.112). They get their deserved punishment when their artificial Golden Age turns into the brutal reality of a Hesiodic Iron Age.

The idea of "primitive" layers of religion, then, is deeply integrated in the themes of the poem. There is no inconsistency in religious outlook, nor a neat division into primitive revenge in the Wanderings and enlightened justice in the Return.[35] Here, too, the deep structural unity of the two, as outlined in Chapter 2, applies. What primitiveness there is derives

---

[35] For example, Clay 1983: 236; Segal 1994: 196.

from a conflict between two divine visions through which Odysseus' return is negotiated. The seeming incomparability of the Companions' unheroic weakness and the Suitors' hardened criminality does not give us two versions of Zeus, a malevolent and a just one. The punishment of these two groups of eaters is collateral damage of Zeus' efforts to turn the hero's return, decreed by fate, into a more honorable one than would otherwise have been the case.

It is as if the *Odyssey*, through Zeus' actions, is answering epic traditions in which Odysseus is more negatively depicted. The Epic Cycle, where Odysseus kills Astyanax, and the Trojan plays in the corpus of Athenian tragedy, with their wily, scheming Odysseus, who readily betrays friends or reneges on promises when it suits his interests, give us some idea of what such an Odysseus might have been. The Homeric *Odyssey*, in giving a positive turn to such negative tendencies, pits Zeus against Poseidon in a conflict that remains unresolved throughout the poem, two gods dramatizing the competition between traditions of heroic poetry.[36]

This observation remains ultimately unverifiable, though it will give suggestive background to an as yet unexplored role of Odysseus in his climactic battle with the Suitors. We will investigate this role in Chapter 8, where we will see Odysseus emerge as a new Achilles, rivaling the most heroic – and most ambiguous – hero of the Iliadic tradition. For here, we may note that the opposition between benevolent and malevolent divinity, and in particular the inconsistency in the characterization of Zeus, can be explained as a consequence of the apparent attempts of the *Odyssey* tradition to cast its hero in a more positive way. It is not possible to be a benign god when attempting to modify the schemes of a malevolent one. After all, Zeus, too, has to live with the justice of Poseidon.

---

[36] On possible scenarios of interaction between the Homeric *Odyssey* and competing and/or epichoric traditions, see Marks 2008: 83–111.

CHAPTER 8

Remembering the gastēr

οὐδὲ ἡρωϊκὸν τὸ παράγγελμα γαστρὶ εἴκειν
"The imperative to yield to the belly is not heroic."
(Schol. *Od.* 7.216)

"Each type of human activity has its own appropriate reward;
the shepherd, the plowman, the bird trapper and he whom the sea nourishes:
everyone is bent on warding off nagging hunger from the belly."
(γαστρὶ δὲ πᾶς τις ἀμύνων λιμὸν αἰανῆ τέταται)
(Pindar, *Isthmian Ode* 1.47–9)

At Thrinacia Odysseus survives the crucial ordeal by resisting the essential heroic urge to eat roast meat; the Companions, in sharp contrast, stop fishing and hunting birds (10.330–1) and yield to the temptation posed by Helios' cattle that are grazing nearby.[1] "Hunger distressed the belly" (ἔτειρε δὲ γαστέρα λιμός, *Od.* 12.332), says Odysseus about the moment before he retires to pray to the gods, and the Companions will make their fateful decision. The annihilation of Odysseus' Companions is due to the implacable needs of the human belly. The belly is naturally the human organ most closely associated with food, and it comes as no surprise that in a poem as concerned with food as the *Odyssey* the idea of *gastēr*, 'belly' – Odysseus' belly, as it turns out – figures prominently, beyond the ultimate crime of the Companions.

Just as food in the *Odyssey* is more than proteins or carbohydrates, so *gastēr* is more than the digestive organ. In fact, in the most graphic case of food ingestion in the poem, it is not his *gastēr* that the Cyclops fills with the flesh of Odysseus' men, but his *nēdus* (9.296).[2] The discussion in this

---

[1] This chapter is a rewritten and extended version of Bakker 2010, a contribution in honor of the work of Pietro Pucci, whose work has been an inspiration for this part of the study. I am grateful to the publisher, Walter de Gruyter, for permission to reuse the material.
[2] As does Kronos when he swallows the stone he takes to be Zeus (Hes. *Th.* 487).

135

chapter of *gastēr* in the *Odyssey* will reveal that this concept plays a key role in the self-reflexive, metapoetic, and "interformulaic"[3] aspects of Odysseus' return. A study of *gastēr* will lead to a confrontation between Odysseus and Achilles as well as between their poems, an encounter that will be negotiated through food and the needs of the belly.

Bellies and beggars

In a detailed study of *gastēr* in the *Odyssey*[4] Pietro Pucci observes that the concept (and term) is used – by the narrator as well as by the hero himself, we may add – especially when Odysseus is disguised as a beggar (or perhaps, more generally, when he is not recognized by his interlocutors). Pucci aligns this with a social distinction: opposed to the heroic notion of *thumos*, "heart," "spirit" (of which in Pucci's system *gastēr* is both a "synonym" and an antonym, as we will see), *gastēr* cannot be applied to figures of high social status in the societies depicted in the *Odyssey*.[5] Even the Suitors, who of all the poem's characters most pathologically indulge in the needs of the belly, are never characterized in terms of *gastēr*. The word, it seems, can be used only of beggars and other needy and hungry people, the disguise that Odysseus has adopted.

We can map this limited distribution of *gastēr* onto the poem's narrative structure. Remarkably, given the emphasis on food throughout, Odysseus does not use *gastēr* anywhere in the story of the Wanderings, until the fatal moment at which the Companions give in to their cravings. But as soon as Odysseus has set foot in Scheria, his *gastēr* begins to be mentioned frequently throughout the narrative of the Return, up to the point when the hero sheds his disguise and goes on to kill the Suitors and regain his possessions. No mentions of *gastēr* occur after Odysseus' true identity has been revealed and his heroic status reasserted.

In terms of the dynamics and construction of epic fame, a subject in which the *Odyssey* takes a keen interest, what we could call the *gastēr* period falls between a time when *kleos* is unattainable or even dangerous and a time when Odysseus comes to be reintegrated in the network of epic *kleos*. Numerous elements in the story of the Wanderings point to a temporary suspension of the hero's conventional epic status. We have only to mention Odysseus' futile self-presentation to the Cyclops as an associate of Agamemnon (9.259–65), his equally futile stand against Scylla, facing

---

[3] This term will be explained in the Epilogue.
[4] Pucci 1987: 157–87. On *gastēr*, see also Svenbro 1976: 50–9.   [5] Pucci 1987: 179, 182.

the monster in full heroic panoply (12.228–30), and, most importantly for the poem, his failed attempt to turn his encounter with the Cyclops into a source of *kleos*, when he urges his opponent to tell others about the blinding of his eye by Odysseus king of Ithaca (9.502–5). And as we have also seen, normal sacrifice is impossible in this pre-epic world of monsters and paradise. By contrast, Odysseus' memorable revenge on the collective Suitors in his *megaron* will soon make the round of the royal courts, just as did the failed *nostos* of Agamemnon and the successful revenge of his son Orestes (*Od.* 1.298–300).

Mentions of Odysseus' *gastēr*, in other words, are confined to the transitional period between the Wanderings and the successful completion of the final *nostos*, an event with full epic connectivity. This is a time of disguise and hiding, for which *gastēr* is an apt symbol; *gastēr* can be a deceptive outward appearance, as in the trick with which Prometheus tries to deceive Zeus (Hes. *Theog.* 539). Odysseus' *gastēr* period is also a time in which elementary survival instinct can give way to desire and longing, desire first to get home, and, once there, to take revenge on the Suitors. Odysseus' "belly" begins to develop real cravings precisely when food is neither a lack nor a temptation. The *gastēr* in the *Odyssey*, it seems, craves something other than mere food.

Bastards and burning ones

In light of the pervasive parallelism between *aoidē* and *epos* – the poet's tale and the hero's – that we encountered in earlier chapters, it comes as no surprise that the concept of the beggar's hungry, needy *gastēr* is aligned with comparable ideas in the hero's self-presentation. Odysseus' so-called Cretan Lies, which he presents to Athena (*Od.* 13.256–86), Eumaios (*Od.* 14.192–359), and Penelope (*Od.* 19.172–202) are typologically equivalent to the tale of the Wanderings by the principle presented in Chapter 2: all are the hero's verbal interactions with the future helper or donor in the quest pattern repeated throughout the poem, and all are self-serving explanations of the stranger's present beggarly condition. The stories provide an interesting corrective to the heroic code as presented by Sarpedon in the *Iliad* (see Chapter 3). That code, as we saw, is built on the interplay of privileges and obligations, with the availability of wealth and luxury goods (including meat) for participation in a prestige economy of gift exchange taken for granted.

Odysseus' Cretan Lies show a very different picture. This is a world not of established heroes, whose first preoccupation is *kleos* and the need to live up to the reputation of their fathers, but of restless adventurers and self-made men. For these figures wealth is not to be taken for granted, but has to be actively pursued, and acquired with ingenuity and resourcefulness. *Mētis* is for these people in the margins of the heroic world more important than *biē*, mind more important than might. In this connection, Olga Levaniouk has recently drawn attention to the peculiar way in which Odysseus casts himself in the Cretan Lies, in particular the one he tells Penelope.[6] In the tale to Eumaios he is the bastard son of a rich Cretan, Castor son of Hylax, and does not receive much of the inheritance (*Od.* 14.200–10); and in the tale to Penelope he is the younger son of Deucalion son of Minos, with Idomeneus as the older, and "better," brother (*Od.* 19.181–4). In the second case Odysseus significantly names himself Aithōn, "Burning" (19.183), a name signifying unfulfilled desire and need for adventurous action.[7]

It is possible to pursue, as Levaniouk does, the mythical and ritual implications of such a self-characterization.[8] Second sons have to make room for themselves alongside their "older and better" brothers.[9] An important mythical template that comes to mind in this connection is the position of the newborn Hermes vis-à-vis his rich older brother Apollo, a situation that requires trickery and resourceful intelligence in order to secure Hermes a position in the Olympian family. In this way Hermes becomes a mythical model for Odysseus, whom he crucially assisted as donor in the Circe episode and with whom he shares not only the epithet *polumētis*, but also the much more restricted *polútropos*.[10] A Hermes role for Odysseus in the beggar phase of his *nostos* complements the Apollo role we discussed in Chapter 6. The two gods typify two stages in the male initiation process, from struggling youngster to successful initiand (see further below).[11]

In this important way the traits of the disenfranchised younger or illegitimate family member come to typify Odysseus king of Ithaca and Cephalonia himself, even though he is an only, not a younger son. But he is like a younger brother to heroes with much larger and more centrally located

---

[6] Levaniouk 2000; 2011: 36–50, 56–81.
[7] On bastardy in the Homeric world in an anthropological perspective, see Gottschall 2008: 70–3.
[8] Levaniouk 2011: 62–5, 93–108.   [9] Cf. *Od.* 19.184, πρότερος καὶ ἀρείων.
[10] *Od.* 1.1; 10.330; *HH Herm.* 13, 439.   [11] See also Levaniouk 2011: 64.

estates, being unable, unlike them, to fall back on his lineage. Odysseus is the quintessential self-made man, smart, gain-seeking, and resourceful.[12]

The world of hungry adventurers, then, is not an inferior alternative to the heroic code; it is an integral part of it. The role of unfulfilled wanderer typifies Odysseus not merely as a traveler eager for *nostos* and in need of disguise, but as the hero he is. By the same token the life of dispossessed or profit-seeking heroic wanderers comes to be typified with the concept of the *gastēr* and its related associations. In his tale to Eumaios, after stressing his martial prowess and resourcefulness in battle and ambush, he goes on to say that quiet residential life did not appeal to him (*Od.* 14.222–8):

τοῖος ἔα ἐν πολέμῳ· ἔργον δέ μοι οὐ φίλον ἔσκεν
οὐδ' οἰκωφελίη, ἥ τε τρέφει ἀγλαὰ τέκνα,
ἀλλά μοι αἰεὶ νῆες ἐπήρετμοι φίλαι ἦσαν
καὶ πόλεμοι καὶ ἄκοντες ἐΰξεστοι καὶ ὀϊστοί,
λυγρά, τά τ' ἄλλοισίν γε καταρριγηλὰ πέλονται.
αὐτὰρ ἐμοὶ τὰ φίλ' ἔσκε, τά που θεὸς ἐν φρεσὶ θῆκεν·
ἄλλος γάρ τ' ἄλλοισιν ἀνὴρ ἐπιτέρπεται ἔργοις.

Such I was in war; but work <in the fields> never appealed to me,
nor did responsible housekeeping, which always nourishes splendid children.
No, ships with oars were always dear to me,
as well as wars and javelins well polished and arrows,
grievous ones, which to other people are cause for shudder.
But they were dear to me, which I think some god put in my mind;
different types of men rejoice in different types of activity.

This is exactly the lifestyle that Odysseus will later, speaking again to Eumaios, attribute to the urgings of *gastēr*, when he says the cravings of his belly force him to beg among the Suitors (*Od.* 17.286–9):

γαστέρα δ' οὔ πως ἔστιν ἀποκρύψαι μεμαυῖαν,
οὐλομένην, ἣ πολλὰ κάκ' ἀνθρώποισι δίδωσι,
τῆς ἕνεκεν καὶ νῆες ἐΰζυγοι ὁπλίζονται
πόντον ἐπ' ἀτρύγετον, κακὰ δυσμενέεσσι φέρουσαι.

---

[12] Note that with two grandfathers attested in the tradition, Odysseus' genealogy is less established than that of other heroes. See Benardete 2005: 30–1; on Odysseus as "economical," profit-oriented man, see Redfield 1983. The palace of Menelaos, presumably the richest man in the Achaean world, makes on Telemachos through formulaic language the same impression as the fabulous palace of the Phaeacian King Alkinoos on Odysseus himself (ὥς τε γὰρ ἠελίου αἴγλη πέλεν ἠὲ σελήνης | δῶμα καθ' ὑψερεφὲς Μενελάου κυδαλίμοιο/μεγαλήτορος Ἀλκινόοιο, *Od.* 4.45–6; 7.84–5). Menelaus is also able to relocate Odysseus' entire kingdom and establish it in one of the towns he owns (*Od.* 4.174–7).

> There is no way to hide the *gastēr*, full of *menos* as it is,
> accursed thing, which gives many evils to humans,
> she on account of whom well-benched ships are prepared
> for the barren sea, carrying evils to enemies.

Odysseus' wording provides yet another twist in the complex relations between *epos* and *aoidē*. Odysseus invokes the syntax of the first two lines of the *Iliad*, with γαστέρα being placed, like μῆνιν, at the beginning of the line, both words being modified by the participle οὐλομένην, 'accursed', at the beginning of the next line, followed by a relative clause specifying the evils resulting from the central concept. This not only testifies to the pervasive bardic associations of the poem's central character, but also modifies and reanalyzes Iliadic heroism. The kind of expeditions that *gastēr* impels people to undertake, the allusion implies, include even the Trojan War itself, the epic tradition's most reliable and prestigious source of *kleos* and heroic excellence.[13] This is confirmed by the fact that immediately after Odysseus has stated his preferred way of life to Eumaios in the first of the two extracts he goes on to tell how he participated in the Trojan expedition (*Od.* 14.235–42). In other words, heroes can be hard to tell from pirates, pirates from merchants, and merchants from beggars; it is the greedy and needy *gastēr* that is the prime mover of them all.[14]

Gastēr and *thumos*

Characterizing heroism along with other kinds of human activity in terms of *gastēr* opens up, as Pucci has explored, room for parody and irony.[15] *Gastēr*, as Pucci shows, enters into a meaningful system of "synonymy" in interplay with *thumos*, another term denoting both an anatomical reality and an impulse.[16] *Thumos* is conventionally what drives the epic hero in his quest for glory, particularly in such formulaic expressions as θυμὸς ἀγήνωρ, 'man-leading *thumos*', or μεγαλήτορα θυμόν, 'great-hearted *thumos*', the latter, we may note, being used for Odysseus' state of mind when he fatally taunts the Cyclops (9.500).

The hidden heroism of the beggar is played out in a scene in which both terms are contrasted in one and the same context.[17] In Book Eighteen the

---

[13] Pucci 1987: 176. For an anthropological and biological approach to the Trojan War and similar expeditions, see Gottschall 2008.
[14] See *Od.* 3.72–4 = *Od.* 9.253–5 = *HH App.* 543–5. At *Od.* 17.425 the noun for "pirates" is modified with an epithet that eminently applies to Odysseus (ληϊστῆρσι πολυπλάγκτοισιν).
[15] Pucci 1987: 157–87.
[16] On *thumos* as "fiery breath," and hence associated with the *phrenes* 'lungs', see Clarke 1999: 75–92, building on the earlier work of Onians 1951.
[17] Pucci 1987: 161–2; see also Thalmann 1998: 102–4.

local beggar Irus enters the stage, a man who "excelled" (in mock heroic fashion) "with his wanton, raving belly" (μετὰ δ' ἔπρεπε γαστέρι μάργῃ, *Od.* 18.2): he challenges his newly arrived competitor, the hero in disguise, and the leading Suitor Antinoos quickly sees possibilities for crude entertainment.[18] A fight is arranged between the two beggars. The prize will be one of the *gasteres*, 'paunches', filled with fat and blood, that the Suitors have prepared for their meal. Odysseus answers as follows to the proposal (*Od.* 18.52–4):

ὦ φίλοι, οὔ πως ἔστι νεωτέρῳ ἀνδρὶ μάχεσθαι
ἄνδρα γέροντα δύῃ ἀρημένον· **ἀλλά με γαστὴρ
ὀτρύνει** κακοεργός, ἵνα πληγῇσι δαμείω.

My friends, there is no way to fight with a younger man
for an old man worn out by misery; but the *gastēr*
spurs me on, the evil-doer, in order that I be subdued by blows.

Odysseus goes on to express fear lest someone among the spectators will want to hit him, and so tip the balance in the fight. To which Telemachos, who at this point has, of course, already recognized his father, replies as follows (*Od.* 18.61–3):

ξεῖν', εἴ σ' ὀτρύνει κραδίη καὶ θυμὸς ἀγήνωρ
τοῦτον ἀλέξασθαι, τῶν δ' ἄλλων μή τιν' Ἀχαιῶν
δείδιθ', ἐπεὶ πλεόνεσσι μαχήσεται ὅς κέ σε θείνῃ.

Stranger, if your heart and manly *thumos* spurs you on
to defend yourself against this man, do not fear any other of the
   Achaeans,
since he will fight with many, the man who will hit you.

Telemachos' conditional clause is unnecessary in its context from an informational point of view. But it does not function in any *direct* communication. With the conditional Telemachos thematizes the beggar's motivation for entering the fight with Irus and "corrects" it, changing the γαστὴρ of his father's speech into κραδίη καὶ θυμὸς ἀγήνωρ; the change is a matter of personal coded speech between father and son, and confirms for the hearer that physical need and necessity is an integral part of heroism. In the special code that Telemachos and Odysseus use among themselves, the *gastēr* interacts with *thumos agēnōr*; for the Suitors, on the other hand, the two

---

[18] Odysseus in this way becomes an *akletos* to the Suitors' "symposium," an uninvited guest, who contributes to the entertainment of the symposiasts. See Fehr 1990, whose discussion is valuable for calling attention to the *akletos* "performing himself" (pp. 186–7), a detail germane to Odysseus' self-conscious performance as beggar.

are merely formulaic synonyms.[19] But the change also acts out the idea of *gastēr* as an outward appearance, the verbal means by which a disguise is enacted, hiding within it a very different substance. In this way the hero's *gastēr* comes to be aligned with the *gastēr* that serves as prize for the fight of the beggars. This is a theme that the poem will return to, as we shall see.

The semantics of *gastēr* in relation to *thumos* can also go beyond the confines of the *Odyssey* and involve the *Iliad*, the epic of conventional heroic values *par excellence*. The very first mention of *gastēr* in the *Odyssey* occurs in a simile that pointedly alludes to an equivalent simile in the *Iliad*.[20] The simile illustrates the scene in which Odysseus, naked and hungry, comes out of his lair-like sleeping place to approach Nausicaa and her maidservants (*Od.* 6.130–4):

βῆ δ' ἴμεν ὥς τε λέων ὀρεσίτροφος, ἀλκὶ πεποιθώς,
ὅς τ' εἶσ' ὑόμενος καὶ ἀήμενος, ἐν δέ οἱ ὄσσε
δαίεται· αὐτὰρ ὁ βουσὶ μετέρχεται ἢ ὀίεσσιν
ἠὲ μετ' ἀγροτέρας ἐλάφους· **κέλεται δέ ἑ γαστὴρ**
μήλων πειρήσοντα καὶ ἐς πυκινὸν δόμον ἐλθεῖν.

He went similar to a lion, mountain-bred and confident in his might,
who goes his way in rain and wind, and in <his face> his eyes
are flashing; he goes among a herd of cattle or of sheep,
or among the deer of the fields. His *gastēr* commands him
to enter into the well-built stable in order to have a taste of the sheep.

The equivalent simile in the *Iliad* is an image occasioned by the fighting frenzy of the Lycian hero Sarpedon at the beginning of the battle around the Greek camp (*Il.* 12.299–301):

βῆ ῥ' ἴμεν ὥς τε λέων ὀρεσίτροφος, ὅς τ' ἐπιδευὴς
δηρὸν ἔῃ κρειῶν, **κέλεται δέ ἑ θυμὸς ἀγήνωρ**
μήλων πειρήσοντα καὶ ἐς πυκινὸν δόμον ἐλθεῖν.

He went similar to a lion, mountain-bred, who for a long time
has been in need of meat. His manly *thumos* commands him
to enter into the well-built stable in order to have a taste of the sheep.

Lions are typically ravenous and are often called *aithōnes* in the *Iliad*, the name that Odysseus gives himself in his Cretan Lie to Penelope.[21] The

---

[19] Note that of the four occurrences of κραδίη καὶ θυμὸς ἀγήνωρ in the *Iliad*, three occur in Book Ten (10.220, 244, 319), twice equally with ὀτρύνει. This may suggest a special link with the ambush episode of the Doloneia, in which Odysseus plays a crucial role. See also n. 36, below.
[20] Pucci 1987: 157–61.
[21] The sense "tawny" (because of their reddish fur) is rejected by Levaniouk 2011: 37, but cannot be ruled out in a number of cases.

lions in both similes are equally hungry, but the Odyssean lion is urged on by his *gastēr*, the food-processing organ, whereas the impulse of the Iliadic lion is his *thumos agēnōr*, the manly heroic spirit. Yet, ironically, the mountain-bred *gastēr*-lion, identified with the naked and needy Odysseus as he emerges from the undergrowth to approach the Phaeacian girls, is described in straightforwardly heroic terms (ἀλκὶ πεποιθώς, 'confident in his might'; ἐν δέ οἱ ὄσσε δαίεται, 'and in his face his eyes are flashing'), whereas the equally mountain-bred *thumos*-lion is described in terms of dire physical need (ὅς τ' ἐπιδευὴς δηρὸν ἔῃ κρειῶν, 'who for a long time has been in need of meat'). And this animal is identified with the Lycian champion Sarpedon at the moment when he sets out on his famous discourse on the heroic code I discussed in Chapter 3.[22] The idea of food as culture, symbolic capital, in that disquisition contrasts with the lion's savage natural needs.

The two similes, then, are interlocking. The *gastēr*-driven lion is heroic, the *thumos*-driven lion needy. Pucci notes that the image of the Odyssean lion adds natural realism to the symbol of the heroic king by exposing the physical savagery of the animal, thus serving as parody of the heroic code.[23] Yet the two lions are more interrelated than would appear at first sight and the *Iliad* qualifies the heroic code no less than does the *Odyssey*.

Gastēr and *menos*

But the heroic code as it revolves around food is qualified in the *Iliad* by more than one lion simile. The system of food-after-fighting as distributed symbolic capital on a par with booty (discussed in Chapter 3) faces two diametrically opposed challenges. The one is from Achilles, who spurns food – whether as heroic capital or as biological sustenance – in his extreme mourning over Patroklos. The other is from Odysseus, who is accused by Agamemnon (*Il* 4.343–8) of not earning his share in the heroic *dais* with proportionate martial accomplishments, and who tends to conceive of food in a utilitarian, unheroic way.[24] The two sides collide head on in Book Nineteen.[25] After the reconciliation with Agamemnon, Achilles rejects any proposal to celebrate the reconciliation formally and wants to

---

[22] On this passage, see also Pucci 1998: 49–68, who notes (pp. 51–2) the αὐτίκα at *Il*. 12.309, which stresses the identity of the lion and Sarpedon.
[23] Pucci 1987: 159: "With this use of *gastēr* ..., which reduces the lion's high-minded Iliadic aspect to more prosaic but also more natural dimensions, the *Odyssey* bemusedly frames the heroic code."
[24] On Odysseus in the *Iliad*, see Clay 1999.
[25] Again extensively discussed by Pucci 1987: 165–72.

start the battle right away, without the delay necessitated by a communal meal (19.146–53). Odysseus objects that going into the battle without food is bad policy and urges Achilles to allow the people to have a meal (19.160–72). When Achilles refuses a second time, Odysseus addresses the latter's mourning directly by bringing in the *gastēr* (*Il.* 19.225–32):

> **γαστέρι** δ' οὔ πως ἔστι νέκυν πενθῆσαι' Ἀχαιούς
> λίην γὰρ πολλοὶ καὶ ἐπήτριμοι ἤματα πάντα
> πίπτουσιν· πότε κέν τις ἀναπνεύσειε πόνοιο;
> ἀλλὰ χρὴ τὸν μὲν καταθάπτειν ὅς κε θάνῃσι
> νηλέα θυμὸν ἔχοντας ἐπ' ἤματι δακρύσαντας·
> ὅσσοι δ' ἂν πολέμοιο περὶ στυγεροῖο λίπωνται
> **μεμνῆσθαι πόσιος καὶ ἐδητύος**, ὄφρ' ἔτι μᾶλλον
> ἀνδράσι δυσμενέεσσι μαχώμεθα νωλεμὲς αἰεί.

> With <denying the needs of> the *gastēr* there is no way for the
>   Achaeans to mourn a corpse.
> Too many, in dense numbers, each day
> fall: when can one get relief from this heavy toil?
> No, we must bury him, whoever dies
> without pity in our spirit, mourning for <no longer than> a day.
> And as for those of us who are left alive from this hateful war,
> we must remain mindful of drink and eating, so that even more
> we can fight the men of the enemy, unceasingly again and again.

Odysseus crudely reduces the dead hero and his mourners to their physical realities: a collective of eaters and a corpse, one out of the many that are collected after each day's battle. The *gastēr* and its continuous physical needs are bluntly stressed, and the heroic code is reduced to what is for us an athlete's diet. Odysseus' vision reverses the heroic order of fighting before food and strips food of all its heroic symbolics.[26]

Odysseus, then, is the *gastēr* man not only in the beggarly façade he shows to the Suitors, while behind the façade being eager to reconnect with epic heroism; he also acts according to the needs of *gastēr* when he is in the midst of epic action, advising others to do so too and offering a challenge to mainstream heroism. In his advice to Achilles and the army to take food before the fighting he goes against the heroic code, thus foreshadowing the *Odyssey*'s emphasis on the reality of food and the problems inherent in heroic feasting.[27] Odysseus also counters standard heroic psychology, which takes *thumos* for granted and treats it as a sufficient

---

[26] This is not to say that Achilles does not depart from the heroic code; his extreme eagerness to fight turns battle into the hunt of wild animals. See Grethlein 2005.
[27] Bakker 2006: 12–13.

Remembering the gastēr

condition for heroic impulses and heroic success. A man, Odysseus says (*Il.* 19.162–6), can have all the *thumos* in the world and still be weak in his knees for lack of food. For food, and nothing else, is the basis of a warrior's *menos*, the epic word for energy, vigor (*Il.* 19.160–1):

ἀλλὰ πάσασθαι ἄνωχθι θοῆς ἐπὶ νηυσὶν Ἀχαιοὺς
σίτου καὶ οἴνοιο, τὸ γὰρ **μένος** ἐστι **καὶ ἀλκή**.

But order the Achaeans to taste by the swift ships
of bread and wine, for that is <u>*menos* and strength</u>.

In heroic epic, *menos* comes into the *thumos* (e.g., μένος δέ οἱ ἔμβαλε θυμῷ, 'and he threw *menos* in his *thumos*', *Il.* 16.529) or the two are presented as one complex concept (e.g., ὄτρυνε μένος καὶ θυμὸν ἑκάστου, 'he spurred on the *menos* and *thumos* of each'). Odysseus locates *menos* and the quintessentially heroic concept of *alkē*, 'valor, might', in something as mundane as bread, thus reminding Achilles and the other Achaeans that heroism has a simple practical and biological basis.

In this connection we are reminded of Odysseus' words to Eumaios at the moment when he is to join the Suitors, cited earlier in this chapter (*Od* 17.286):

γαστέρα δ' οὔ πως ἔστιν ἀποκρύψαι μεμαυῖαν

There is no way to hide the <u>*gastēr*, full of *menos*</u> as it is,

Odysseus presents *gastēr* as being in a state of *menos* itself through the participle μεμαυῖαν, which is frequently used for heroes in a state of battle frenzy, typically complemented by an infinitive denoting violent action (e.g., διαρραῖσαι/διαπραθέειν μεμαῶτες, 'being eager to destroy/sack'). This attribution of violent agency to the food-processing organ breaks down the last barrier between *gastēr* and *thumos*, setting up both as engines of heroic action.

Remembering the *gastēr*

The link between *gastēr* and *menos* can be further developed when we observe that *memona*, the quintessential *menos*-verb, for all the violence of the disposition it denotes, is from the standpoint of historical-comparative linguistics identical with Latin *memini*, 'I remember', a verb denoting, it seems, mental, not physical activity.[28] And in one important passage the human

---

[28] This section on memory in Homer draws on Bakker 2008a.

gastēr is explicitly linked with "memory," in the form of the aorist verb *mnēsasthai*, whose root *mnē-* is an ablaut variant of *men-/mon-* (*Od*.7.215–21):

ἀλλ' ἐμὲ μὲν δορπῆσαι ἐάσατε κηδόμενόν περ·
οὐ γάρ τι στυγερῇ ἐπὶ **γαστέρι** κύντερον ἄλλο
ἔπλετο, **ἥ τ' ἐκέλευσεν ἕο μνήσασθαι ἀνάγκῃ**
καὶ μάλα τειρόμενον καὶ ἐνὶ **φρεσὶ** πένθος ἔχοντα,
ὡς καὶ ἐγὼ πένθος μὲν ἔχω **φρεσίν**, ἡ δὲ μάλ' αἰεὶ
ἐσθέμεναι κέλεται καὶ πινέμεν, ἐκ δέ με πάντων
ληθάνει, ὅσσ' ἔπαθον, καὶ ἐνιπλησθῆναι ἀνώγει.

But let me now have my meal, afflicted as I am;
for there is nothing else that is more shameful than the hateful
gastēr, she who orders one to "remember" her by sheer necessity,
no matter how worn out one is or how much sorrow one has in one's
phrenes, just as I too have sorrow in my *phrenes*, but she urges me
always to eat and drink, and makes me forget all that I suffered, and
urges that she be filled.

This is what Odysseus says in the *megaron* of Alkinoos, king of the Phaeacians, in response to the king's suspicion that the stranger might be a god. Odysseus replies in the negative, for is not being "reminded" of the *gastēr* and its needs what it means to be human? But what does it mean to be reminded of *gastēr*, or even to "remember" in Homer? Questions of memory are never trivial in epic, the song of memory, and especially not in the *Odyssey* with its interest in metapoetic narrativity. And in addition the passage talks about forgetting, an equally charged concept in the poem.

It is not immediately obvious that verbs for "remembering" – for us a mental, cognitive faculty – are semantically related to *menos* and *memona*, which denote vigorous physical dispositions. Yet the affinity that *mnēsasthai* has with terms associated with heroic battle, such as *alkē*, is no less strong than that of *menos* with battle-related concepts, as appears from such common formulas as:

ἀνέρες ἐστε, φίλοι, μνήσασθε δὲ θούριδος ἀλκῆς
be men, my friends, and "remember" furious strength

ἀλλὰ μνησώμεθα χάρμης
but let us "remember" battle

μνήσαντο δὲ χάρμης
they "remembered" battle

The "remembering" in these situations is not retrieval from memory, but the reaching of a certain vigorous disposition. The act of remembering is performative: "remembering" battle is to deliver battle, "remembering" strength is to be strong.[29]

At the same time, this remembering is acting on the impulse of something: the genitive object of the verb conveys that the "remembering" is not total: remembering *alkē* is to have access to a finite quantity of "strength," not to all of it. *Alkē*, in other words, becomes a *source* from which one draws *menos*. To "remember," especially when this action is denoted with the performative aorist *mnē-sasthai*, is to absorb the *menos* of something so as to *embody* it. Outside the Iliadic battle (where a great deal of "remembering" takes place) typical cases of the transfer of *menos* in the act of remembering include sons "remembering" (the *menos* of) their father, as in the case of Telemachos (*Od.* 1.320–3):

> τῷ δ' ἐνὶ θυμῷ
> θῆκε **μένος** καὶ θάρσος, **ὑπέμνησέν** τέ ἑ πατρὸς
> μᾶλλον ἔτ' ἢ τὸ πάροιθεν. ὁ δὲ φρεσὶν ᾗσι νοήσας
> θάμβησεν κατὰ θυμόν· ὀΐσατο γὰρ θεὸν εἶναι.

> And to him in his *thumos* she [Athena] placed *menos* and courage,
> and reminded him of his father <so that he was full of him> even
> more than before; and in his *phrenes* he saw and understood,
> and was amazed in his *thumos*: for he understood that this was
> a god.

The "reminding" (ὑπέμνησεν) that takes place is not an activation of the memory of his father (whom he has never known), but an infusion of paternal *menos*, administered by Athena. The shot is not just physical, like adrenalin, but also what we would call mental or intellectual: Telemachos is now seeing (*noēsas*) that it was Athena who talked to him. The injection of *menos* has sharpened his *noos*.

Another typical case is the "remembering" of food, which, as Odysseus emphasized, is an important source of *menos*. In his speech to Achilles in the *Iliad* Odysseus urges, as we saw, that he should be "mindful of drink and food" (μεμνῆσθαι πόσιος καὶ ἐδητύος); and we saw in Chapter 5 what Odysseus says to his Companions on Circe's island when he returns to the camp with the giant stag he has caught (*Od.* 10.176–7):

> ἀλλ' ἄγετ', ὄφρ' ἐν νηΐ θοῇ βρῶσίς τε πόσις τε,
> **μνησόμεθα** βρώμης μηδὲ τρυχώμεθα λιμῷ.

> Well, as long as in the swift ship there is food and drink,
> let us "remember" (take our *menos* from/draw on the *menos* of) food
>   and not be wasted by hunger.

---

[29] Bakker 2005: 139–45.

And the formulaic exhortation to sit down to eat, metrically equivalent to the battle-cry (μνησώμεθα χάρμης, 'let us "remember" <the joy of> battle') is μνησώμεθα δόρπου/δαιτός, 'let us "remember" the meal/feast' (*Od.* 20.246; *Il.* 24.601). In such cases the "remembering" of food is not only performatively the act of eating, but also, literally, the embodiment of the *menos* that inheres in food.

No exhortation is needed for *gastēr* itself, of course. In enforcing its own "remembrance," it does a number of things. Not only does it cry out for the *menos* that inheres in the food it needs; it also – and this is where *gastēr* becomes an epic agent – fills its bearer with *menos*. The man whose *gastēr* cries out, whose primary impulse is his empty stomach, is not only a needy beggar, but can also be a man – even a hero – ready for serious action. The *gastēr*'s remembrance (with *gastēr* being both subject and object of the act of remembering) also creates remembrance's notional opposite. As Odysseus' words indicate, he forgets his sufferings, past and present, and becomes focused exclusively on his present need for action. The enactment of forgetfulness by means of remembering, here effected by *gastēr*, is reminiscent of Hector's emerging from the coma he was in after being hit by Ajax's stone. The agent here is not an empty stomach, but a divine injection of *menos*, in Zeus' words to Iris after he has woken up from his sleep with Hera (*Il.* 15.59–61):

> Ἕκτορα δ' ὀτρύνῃσι μάχην ἐς Φοῖβος Ἀπόλλων
> αὖτις δ' ἐμπνεύσῃσι **μένος, λελάθῃ** δ' ὀδυνάων
> αἵ νῦν μιν τείρουσι **κατὰ φρένας**.
>
> and so that he exhorts Hector into the battle, Phoibos Apollo,
> and blows again *menos* into him and makes him forget the shooting
>   pains
> that are now afflicting him in his *phrenes*.

Forgetfulness resulting from the *menos* that comes with "remembering" is also a – in fact, the quintessential – poetic experience. In this regard, we are reminded of two memorable passages in the opening Hymn of the Hesiodic *Theogony* (Hes. *Theog.* 53–5; 99–103):

> τὰς ἐν Πιερίῃ Κρονίδῃ τέκε πατρὶ μιγεῖσα
> **Μνημοσύνη**, γουνοῖσιν Ἐλευθῆρος μεδέουσα,
> **λησμοσύνην** τε κακῶν ἄμπαυρά τε μερμηράων.
>
> These in Pieria she bore to Kronos' son after lying with the Father,
> Mnemosyne, who rules the high grounds of Eleuther,
> <to be> forgetfulness of evils and relief from sorrows.
>
> αὐτὰρ ἀοιδὸς
> Μουσάων θεράπων κλεῖα προτέρων ἀνθρώπων

Remembering the gastēr

ὑμνήσει μάκαράς τε θεοὺς οἳ Ὄλυμπον ἔχουσιν,
αἶψ' ὅ γε δυσφροσυνέων **ἐπιλήθεται** οὐδέ τι κηδέων
μέμνηται· ταχέως δὲ παρέτραπε δῶρα θεάων.

But the Singer, servant of the Muses, the fame of earlier men
he shall hymn and the blessed gods who hold Olympus,
and forthwith one <u>forgets</u> one's misery and <u>is not aware</u> of one's cares:
the gifts of the gods have turned these things away.

The inspired poet and his rapt audience have in common with heroes that the *menos* they derive from the song, which contains the heroic deeds of the past, ousts the sorrows they have in the present. The poet remembers because he draws on the divine *menos* of the Muses – and let us not forget that the Muses have a name derived from the *men*-root in addition to being the daughters of Mnemosyne, the essential abstraction of the idea.[30] Through the divine intervention of the Muses, the poet will draw on the inspired *menos* of the great men of the past.

Furthermore, the forgetting of sorrows resonates with the poem's "third proem" (see Chapter 1), in which the hero, asleep in the Phaeacians' ship, was said to be λελασμένος ὅσ' ἐπεπόνθει, 'forgetful of all that he had suffered' (13.92). The moment of the hero's *lēthē* is the moment when the poet's memory, as *aoidē*, the song driven by the Muses, takes over from *epos*, the tale of personal memory and suffering.

We see in a number of ways, then, that *gastēr*, at one level a matter of the needy beggar and his belly, takes part in networks of association that align it with heroism, even poetry itself.[31] Again Odysseus' characterizations of the human *gastēr*, in particular his own, provide a vision of heroism and human agency that is typical for this poem that is interested in exploring the ambiguities in such central epic concepts as *kleos*, poetry, and truth.

The *gastēr* typifies Odysseus' Iliadic identity and his Odyssean disguise, and so comes to denote both hero and beggar, both self and other. In this regard we may wonder whether in the crucial phrase with which Odysseus refers to the *gastēr*'s remembering (ἥ τ' ἐκέλευσεν **ἕο** μνήσασθαι ἀνάγκῃ, 7.217) the reflexive personal pronoun ἕο is not deliberately ambiguous: "<the *gastēr*>, which orders a man to remember *himself*" no less than "remember *it<self>*." This fusion is the natural consequence of the conception of remembrance in epic proposed above: the difference

---
[30] Bakker 2008a: 75.
[31] We may go one step further if we assume, with Katz and Volk (2000), that Hesiod's *gastēr*, as mentioned in the abusive address of the Muses in the *Dichterweihe* (Hes. *Theog.* 26: ποιμένες ἄγραυλοι, κάκ' ἐλέγχεα, **γαστέρες οἶον**), is associated with poetic inspiration.

between the *gastēr* and its bearer falls away, since the one remembering comes to embody that from which he draws his *menos*.

The unity of man (*anēr*) and *gastēr* is acted out in a remarkable simile which marks the end of Odysseus' *gastēr* stage and continues a theme started in the fight between Odysseus and Irus (see above); the simile illustrates the state of restless sleeplessness in which Odysseus on the night before the massacre ponders, deep inside him, on the destruction of the Suitors (*Od.* 20.25–8):

ὡς δ' ὅτε **γαστέρ' ἀνὴρ** πολέος πυρὸς αἰθομένοιο,
ἐμπλείην κνίσης τε καὶ αἵματος, ἔνθα καὶ ἔνθα
αἰόλλῃ, μάλα δ' ὦκα λιλαίεται ὀπτηθῆναι,
ὣς ἄρ' ὅ γ' ἔνθα καὶ ἔνθα ἑλίσσετο μερμηρίζων.

Just as when <u>a man</u> in the blaze of a big fire tosses a <u>*gastēr*</u>
filled with fat and blood, around and around,
and he is [it is] eager for it to be grilled quickly
– just so then he writhed around and around as he was pondering.

The simile begins syntactically as if the man, *anēr*, is the point of comparison, but when the image is developed further, it becomes clear that Odysseus is compared no less to the paunch on the grill. In fact, he is both; the man is eager to finish the cooking and enjoy the inside of the *gastēr*, just as Odysseus is burning with desire to drop his disguise and reap the fruits of his internal scheming. The *gastēr*, that unappealing outward appearance – think again of Prometheus presenting the *gastēr* to Zeus – is eager to be cooked, so that its delectable inside can be enjoyed. The subject of *lilaietai*, 'is eager', is ambiguous, applying both to the *anēr* and to his *gastēr*. And the outside paunch, which contains the delectable food – which is full of *menos*, we may add – is writhing on the blazing fire (described with the significant *aith*-root), just as Odysseus is tossing in his bed.

Odysseus and Achilles

After the last instantiation of the *gastēr* theme, as the narrative approaches the fulfillment of the beggar's burning desire, indications of the goal begin to appear, oblique and indirect at first, overt and direct when the massacre gets underway. The queen communicates her dilemma to the beggar: should she stay in the house and guard its possessions, or should she follow the man who is the "best of the Achaeans" (Ἀχαιῶν ὅς τις ἄριστος, *Od.* 19.528)? An anonymous Suitor refers to the beggar in a speech to Telemachos as "a mere burden of the field" (αὔτως ἄχθος ἀρούρης, 20.379), recalling the self-reference of Achilles, the best of the Achaeans, at *Il.* 19.104. And the Suitor Eurymachos recalls Achilles' exhortation to the final massacre (*Il.* 19.148) in uttering ἀλλὰ μνησώμεθα χάρμης, 'but let us "remember" the battle' (*Od.* 22.73), ironically exhorting to battle the side that will be massacred. The last two allusions are not just to the *Iliad*, but to points in the *Iliad* at approximately the same place in the poem. The *Odyssey*'s final battle, the climax of Odysseus' return, is looking at the *Iliad*'s final battle, the climax of Achilles' return. Both heroes appeared in disguise at first, to shed it with destructive force.

Odysseus' homecoming is not only a return in geographical space to a desired location, his home and the center of his world, but also a return to the networks of epic out of the anonymity he was forced to undergo. He not only sheds his disguise as beggar, but also his Iliadic persona with its propensity to *gastēr*. Odysseus will turn out to be more heroic than he was before his Wanderings and will be competing directly with the *Iliad*'s "best of the Achaeans." A third template for Odysseus in the completion of his return is being added to the ones we have already reviewed, those of the Cyclops and of Helios. The mercurial trickster turns out to be a stern avenger vying with Achilles, and the disinherited wanderer comes to claim his inheritance, protected by Apollo and ready to (re)join the ranks of the established players in the heroic world. But unlike the old Achilles, this new Achilles returns to epic, not in order to die, but in order to live.

The allusions become more elaborate and explicit when the climax approaches. Odysseus wins the bow contest, kills Antinoos with his first arrow, leaving the Suitors in Cyclopean ignorance (see Chapter 4) until he reveals himself as Odysseus. At this moment, Eurymachos, the other ringleader of the Suitors, tries to make a deal: he pledges that everything that has been eaten in Odysseus' *megaron* will be repaid, each Suitor bringing in a restitution "worth twenty oxen" (ἐεικοσάβοιον, 22.57), and on top of that bronze and gold. If the Suitors had actually produced twenty head of cattle each, Odysseus would have received almost four times the number of animals he had possessed before he set out on his voyage, as the various pieces of numerical information scattered through the poem (each reviewed in previous chapters) allow us to calculate.[32] But Odysseus categorically rejects such a lucrative settlement (*Od.* 22.61–4):

Εὐρύμαχ᾽, οὐδ᾽ εἴ μοι πατρώϊα πάντ᾽ ἀποδοῖτε,
ὅσσα τε νῦν ὔμμ᾽ ἐστὶ καὶ εἴ ποθεν ἄλλ᾽ ἐπιθεῖτε,

---

[32] There are 108 Suitors (*Od.* 16.247–53), or 107 if we do not count the dead Antinoos. This gives 2,140 head of cattle. If fifty animals make up a herd, as argued in Chapter 6, this gives us forty-three herds. Odysseus' original wealth was twelve herds (*Od.* 14.100).

οὐδέ κεν ὥς ἔτι χεῖρας ἐμὰς λήξαιμι φόνοιο
πρὶν πᾶσαν μνηστῆρας ὑπερβασίην ἀποτῖσαι.

Eurymachos, not if you Suitors gave me all your ancestral wealth in return,
<u>all that is now yours and even if you somehow added more wealth to it,</u>
not even so would I stop my hands from the slaughter,
not until the Suitors have paid for all their transgression.

This response is distinctly Achillean in its uncompromising refusal even to make a settlement that would have yielded him great profit. Odysseus is here certainly not acting on the impulse of or in the interest of *gastēr*. As Seth Schein has seen, the response recalls Achilles' own words in his response in the *Iliad* – to no one other than Odysseus himself, who has offered him the materially lucrative terms on which Agamemnon offers to settle their dispute (*Il.* 9.379–80):[33]

οὐδ' εἴ μοι δεκάκις τε καὶ εἰκοσάκις τόσα δοίη
ὅσα τέ οἱ νῦν ἔστι, καὶ εἴ ποθεν ἄλλα γένοιτο.

Not if he gave me ten times, even twenty times as much,
<u>all that is now his, and even if more wealth would somehow come to him.</u>

And at almost the exact same point in the *Iliad* as is Odysseus' response to Eurymachos is Achilles' rejection of the ransom which the dying Hector says his parents will pay for his body (*Il.* 22.349–52):

οὐδ' εἴ κεν δεκάκις τε καὶ εἰκοσινήριτ' ἄποινα
στήσωσ' ἐνθάδ' ἄγοντες, ὑπόσχωνται δὲ καὶ ἄλλα,
οὐδ' εἴ κέν σ' αὐτὸν χρυσῷ ἐρύσασθαι ἀνώγοι
Δαρδανίδης Πρίαμος·

Not if they were to set up a ransom tenfold, twenty times as large,
bringing it here, not if they were to pledge even more,
nor even if he were to order to draw up your own weight in gold,
Priam son of Dardanos;

In invoking the words and mindset of Achilles at these two crucial junctures Odysseus revokes his earlier persona of *gastēr*-man, the crafty, practical man of *mētis* who would have accepted the deal offered and become very wealthy. The needy, gain-seeking impulses of *mētis* have given way to the implacable, destructive forces of heroic wrath. The term *mēnis* is not actually used in the narrative of the massacre in the *megaron*, but Odysseus' revenge is Apollonian in its ruthless

---

[33] Schein 1999: 352–4.

punishment of the transgression of boundaries and Achillean in the havoc it wreaks on his fellow Ithacan Achaeans.[34]

The massacre comes in two stages. First, there is far-shooting like that of Apollo, resembling the hunt more than heroic warfare. When the Suitors get access to arms, a real battle ensues, replete with Iliadic battle language.[35] This is not just formulaic language for battle narrative; the formulas are used in the second degree, not being simply the expression of their "essential idea," but referring specifically to heroic battle in the *Iliad* (on this aspect of formulaic language, see the Epilogue). Such referencing becomes particularly striking, to the point of quotation (but again see the Epilogue), when the fight becomes a battle at close quarters. When Odysseus has killed Agelaos (22.292–3), who in the absence of Antinoos and Eurymachos had become the Suitors' leader, the four fighters wreak havoc among the Suitors and are compared (22.302–6) to raptors among frightened birds (*Od.* 22.307–9):[36]

ὣς ἄρα τοὶ μνηστῆρας ἐπεσσύμενοι κατὰ δῶμα
τύπτον ἐπιστροφάδην· τῶν δὲ στόνος ὄρνυτ' ἀεικὴς
κράτων τυπτομένων, δάπεδον δ' ἅπαν αἵματι θῦε.

Thus pursuing the Suitors all over the house,
they were striking them left and right, and from them groaning rose, unseemly,
as they were struck on their heads, and all of the floor was seething with their blood.

The scene and its verbal articulation unmistakably evoke the carnage Achilles creates when pursuing large numbers of frightened Trojans into the river Xanthus (*Il.* 21.20–1):

τύπτεν ἐπιστροφάδην· τῶν δὲ στόνος ὄρνυτ' ἀεικὴς
ἄορι θεινομένων, ἐρυθαίνετο δ' αἵματι ὕδωρ.

He was striking them left and right, and from them groaning rose, unseemly,
as they were savaged by his sword, and it turned red with their blood, the water.

---

[34] On the destructive aspects of Odysseus' return, see Chapter 7.
[35] For example, *Od.* 22.79–81; 92–4; 123–5; 172, etc.
[36] Pucci 1987: 131–2 n. 5 observes that the ἐπιστροφάδην formula is also used for Diomedes during his joint expedition with Odysseus in the *Iliad* (*Il.* 10.483–4), where Odysseus has a secondary role, pulling away the corpses as Diomedes slaughters the Thracians. The scene in Odysseus' own *megaron* may therefore also be a statement on the part of the *Odyssey* in competing traditions regarding the respective roles of Diomedes and Odysseus in their joint expeditions. Note, further, that through δάπεδον δ' ἅπαν αἵματι θῦε Odysseus' violently successful return comes to be contrasted with Agamemnon's equally violent and unsuccessful one (*Od.* 11.420).

154   *Remembering the* gastēr

Achilles' victims are likened (*Il.* 21.22–4) to frightened fish pursued by a large dolphin – a not irrelevant detail when compared with the eventual fate of the Suitors, who end up, in a simile discussed earlier in Chapter 6, like dead fish piled up on a beach. The parallelism between the Iliadic and Odyssean scenes is further enhanced by the choice of the verb *ptōsō*, 'cower', which is used both for Achilles' Trojan victims (*Il.* 21.14, 26) and for the frightened birds in the simile in the *Odyssey* (22.304).

In the midst of this carnage someone comes forward out of the crowd of opponents being slaughtered and pleads for his life: Leodes to Odysseus and Lycaon to Achilles. Both suppliants utter the same line although they are addressing different heroes, due to the pervasive interchangeability of the names of Odysseus and Achilles in all cases and in all metrical positions (*Od.* 22.312 and *Il.* 21.74):

γουνοῦμαί σ' Ὀδυσεῦ· σὺ δέ μ' αἴδεο καὶ μ' ἐλέησον
γουνοῦμαί σ' Ἀχιλεῦ· σὺ δέ μ' αἴδεο καὶ μ' ἐλέησον.

I beseech you, Odysseus/Achilles, and you, show consideration and have mercy on me.

Achilles' famous response to Lycaon, in which he abnegates all *aidōs*, 'respect' that he used to give innocent Trojans before Patroklos' death, comes to frame Odysseus' refusal to pardon even the weakest and least violent of the Suitors, who served among them as *thoskoos*, 'diviner'.[37] He was the first to try the bow (*Od.* 21.144–66) and is now the last to be slain, in exactly the same way as Lycaon, with a sword thrust in the neck.[38]

There is no need, in light of Pucci's extensive discussion,[39] to go into further details of the parallelism between the two scenes. Suffice it here to stress that Achilles' paradigmatically heroic actions in the *Iliad* are performed in total disregard for the *gastēr* and its needs. Odysseus, too, just like Achilles, is killing, not for gain, nor even for fame, but simply out of murderous rage. The killing sprees of both heroes occur at about the same stage in the monumental compositions devoted to each, a fact that puts

---

[37] Louden 1999: 35–49 notes a number of similarities between Leodes and Elpenor (martial ineptitude, wine consumption, connection with prophecy and the dead). If this paradigmatic link is valid, then Odysseus' savage murder of the unarmed Leodes becomes even more significant, since Odysseus goes out of his way to provide Elpenor with a burial, and can even be seen (as suggested in Chapter 5) as escorting Elpenor to the dead. Note in this connection that the ghost of Elpenor makes a supplication to Odysseus just as does Leodes (γουνάζομαι, *Od.* 11.66).

[38] Pucci 1987: 136 observes that the *Odyssey* "goes out of its way to provide [Odysseus] with a sword," since the hero, who has been fighting with spears, has to pick up the sword of the dead Agelaos whose body is lying nearby (*Od.* 22.326–9).

[39] Pucci 1987: 127–38.

their respective *nostoi* in the starkest contrast: Achilles returns to the battle in order to die, Odysseus delivers the battle of his life in order to start a new life. The lion that Odysseus becomes in a simile marking the end of the fighting could not be more different from the lion Odysseus is at Scheria at the beginning of his interstitial beggar period (*Od.* 22.401–6):

εὗρεν ἔπειτ' Ὀδυσῆα μετὰ κταμένοισι νέκυσσιν,
αἵματι καὶ λύθρῳ πεπαλαγμένον ὥς τε λέοντα,
ὅς ῥά τε βεβρωκὼς βοὸς ἔρχεται ἀγραύλοιο·
πᾶν δ' ἄρα οἱ στῆθός τε παρήϊά τ' ἀμφοτέρωθεν
αἱματόεντα πέλει, δεινὸς δ' εἰς ὦπα ἰδέσθαι·
ὣς Ὀδυσεὺς πεπάλακτο πόδας καὶ χεῖρας ὕπερθεν.

Thereupon she [Eurycleia] found Odysseus among the dead corpses,
spattered and defiled with blood and gore, as a lion
who has feasted on a bull from the field and walks away from the
    slaughter.
All his breast and his cheeks on either side
are covered with blood; he is fearsome to look in the face:
thus Odysseus was spattered and defiled, his legs and his arms above.

This lion is neither needy nor hungry; he does not care about his *gastēr*, as did the lion that came out of the bush to meet with Nausicaa and her maidservants. This lion returns from a killing spree, his life no longer at stake, and lust for blood has eclipsed all his need for food.

Odysseus' display of violence, at the end of a narrative in which he was barred from heroic recognition for most of the time, is modeled on Achilles in his return to battle. But he outperforms his Iliadic rival. Through the simile Odysseus not only does to the Suitors what the Cyclops did to his Companions in the cave; the simile also materializes Achilles' suppressed desire to cut up the body of his enemy and eat it raw (*Il.* 22.346–7). The extreme violence with which Odysseus retakes his house is not only a harsh necessity imposed on him by Poseidon (see Chapter 7), who forces him to become just as savage as his son; it also places Odysseus in the rarefied sphere where Achilles obtains immortal *kleos* without playing by the rules of the heroic code and without being part of the community of his peers and fellow Achaeans.

Yet both heroes make another turn before their poems come to a close. - Achilles, the fasting hero, returns to food and its pleasurable and biologically necessary sustenance. It is not the *dais*, the ritualized heroic division-meal framed by privilege and obligation that he returns to, but the *dorpon*, the meal one enjoys when one is hungry and has to "remember" the *gastēr*. "Let us now remember the meal" (νῦν δὲ μνησώμεθα δόρπου, *Il.* 24.601), he says to Priam, "there will be time later for mourning and lamentation" (*Il.* 24.618–20), taking the side of Odysseus in the earlier confrontation of the two heroes over Achilles' own mourning. Just as Odysseus is modeled on Achilles in his poem, so Achilles comes to act like Odysseus in *his*.

Odysseus, for his part, ends the scene in his *megaron* with a significant act of mercy, even though the execution of Leodes is not his last violent act in the poem (he will go on to fight the relatives of the Suitors, see Chapter 7). After Leodes yet another suppliant steps forward, Phemios son of Terpis, the local *aoidos*. He makes the same supplication that Leodes had made a few moments before, but continues in a significant way (*Od.* 22.344–6):

> γουνοῦμαί σ', Ὀδυσεῦ· σὺ δέ μ' αἴδεο καί μ' ἐλέησον.
> αὐτῷ τοι μετόπισθ' ἄχος ἔσσεται, εἴ κεν ἀοιδὸν
> πέφνῃς, ὅς τε θεοῖσι καὶ ἀνθρώποισιν ἀείδω.

> I beseech you, Odysseus/Achilles, and you, show consideration and
>   have mercy on me.
> For you there will be grief hereafter, if you kill
> an *aoidos*, I who sing for gods and men.

The language used for the deliberation preceding his act of supplication (whether to escape from the *megaron* and flee to the altar of Zeus or to grasp the hero's knees, *Od.* 22.333–9) recalls Odysseus' own deliberation before confronting Nausicaa (*Od.* 6.141–7). The two suppliants have in fact some important things in common. Odysseus is the hero who strings his bow just as a professional *aoidos* strings his lyre; the *dais* of death that follows portrays Odysseus as notional singer, whose "song" breaks down all barriers between word and action, *epos* and *ergon*. This singer is the hero, performing his exploits in and through the song.

Odysseus once attended an epic performance, in Alkinoos' hall, that was unique in having an audience member who was a witness to the events of the tale and who was thus in an ideal position to testify to the song's veracity and accuracy. He offered the singer of that tale, the blind singer Demodokos, a choice piece of meat that turned the latter into a hero. What is more appropriate than the fact that this unique recipient of the epic tale is now a hero performing his deeds with an epic poet to witness them? Being as ferocious as Achilles is not enough for this hero, who elevated *epos* to the height of *aoidē* and whose deeds are never independent of the act of turning them into language. This hero cannot just demonstrate his valor and get his *kleos*; he needs to spare the life of the poet, the witness to his deeds. Phemios the poet, whose songs were constrained by the meals he was forced to enliven now becomes the lifeline to the future of the meal that his master had turned into song.

Epilogue: on "interformularity"

"Grammars code best what speakers do most."
(Dubois 1985: 363)

The argument in the preceding chapters has relied at various moments on the poetic and semantic significance of repetition and allusion. Chapter 8 provides perhaps the clearest example, the repetition of Lycaon's supplication to Achilles in the form of Leodes' supplication to Odysseus, across the boundary posed by the poem. Another example, from Chapter 1, was the invocation of the Iliadic Muse invocation at precisely the moments when Odysseus in his recounting of what he saw in the Underworld touches on subject matter that is particularly poetic (catalogic *Ehoiai* poetry and the Trojan War). But in the middle chapters we observed significant repetitions as well, internal ones marking the linkage of scenes at Ithaca with episodes from Odysseus' Wanderings.

Seeing literary significance in repetitions across the boundary of work or poet is unproblematic to students of Hellenistic or Augustan poetry. Poets are expected to make conscious allusions to the work of other poets as well as to their own, and the appreciation of such intertextuality is an important part of the art of reading. To Homerists, however, conscious repetition, even when seemingly self-evident and poetically meaningful, poses a challenge. The oral-formulaic approach to the Homeric poems may today have lost some of the status it had in the 1960s and 1970s, at least in the English-speaking world, as the premier paradigm in the study of Homer; but the formulaic nature of Homeric poetry has been digested, not rejected. Scholars may no longer be writing books and articles about formulas in Homer, but they can still hesitate to assign direct literary agency and conscious allusion to Homer. It is therefore not surprising that attempts at studying "intertextuality" in Homer and early Greek epic have come from the side of Neoanalysis, the study of the "transfer" of motifs from poem to poem and from tradition to tradition.[1] In what follows I will attempt to account for the significance of repetition in Homer against the background of the study of speech and spoken language, integrating "intertextuality" and "orality."

Can deliberate repetition be formulaic? Can formulas be quotes? There used to be a time when such questions were seen as internal contradictions. In a strict dichotomy between "orality" and "literacy," formulaic language was placed firmly on the oral side of the divide, and intentional design on the literate side.[2] In more recent times positions have softened, but not due to any systematic rethinking of the original concept of "formula" that informed the "oral poetry" approach to Homer. In my attempt to arrive at an answer to the questions, I will consider Leodes' entreaty and Odysseus' *recusatio* formula as the end point of a scale, a continuum of increasing specificity of formulaic expressions, based on the memorability of the contexts in which they are uttered. The end point of this scale is where "intertextuality" in principle becomes an appropriate term, but in order to emphasize the fact that this intertextuality takes place within and is enabled by the formulaic system, I will speak (creating an analogous neology) of a scale of increasing *interformularity*. But before going into the details of this scale, let us first briefly review some of the tenets in the original theory of oral-formulaic composition.

In the conception of Milman Parry and Albert Lord formulas are ready-made phrases that are (i) *traditional*, in the sense that they are not the personal creation of the poet of the *Iliad* or *Odyssey*; and (ii) *oral*, in the sense that they enable the singer to compose his verses rapidly in performance, without having to make the conscious stylistic choices that characterize written, literary poetry. In this conception repetition is not significant in itself, since it is simply the consequence of a system of versification that is to a certain extent automated.[3] Yet the use of a

---

[1] Most recently Burgess 2012, who opposes the "oralist perspective" to the "neoanalyst argument" (p. 173). See also Tsagalis 2008, a reading of Homer as a "text" showing inevitable traces of previous writings. Similar questions can be asked in the study of the repetition of higher-level units, such as entire story patterns or "motifs." On the interaction between oral poetry theory and neoanalysis, see Kullmann 1984; Burgess 2006. Pucci 1987 works neither in the oralist nor in the neoanalyst tradition, but can be useful to both. A conception of epic poetry conducive to the argument presented here is Nagy's (e.g., 1996: 29–63) evolutionary model of Homeric poetry, which posits a gradual textual fixation of the Homeric tradition, providing a climate favorable to conscious quotation. More traditional and "literary" observations are offered in Rutherford 1993 and Usener 1990.

[2] For example, Parry 1971: 269–70, 377.

[3] In the development of Parry's work and thought, "traditional" (the key concept of his 1928 Paris thesis, *L'épithète traditionnelle dans Homère. Essai sur un problème de style homérique*, translated as Parry 1971: 1–190) preceded "oral," which did not come to play the central role in his work until after his fieldwork in the Serbo-Croatian oral traditions (see his "Studies in the Epic Technique of Oral Verse-Making": Parry 1971: 266–364).

"formula," that is, a phrase that has been created in order to be uttered repeatedly and routinely, must ultimately depend on the similarity between two contexts, or, to make an important precision, on a poet's *judgment* as to the (degree of) similarity between two contexts. The utterance of a formula is more than saying something without having to think about it.

The Parry–Lord conception does not take sufficiently into account the semantic and pragmatic aspects of Homeric formulas; it treats the production and distribution of phrases as a more or less random process. This misses the point that not all formulas are distributed equally, for all kinds of reasons, semantic, thematic, and narratological. Some are distributed throughout the Homeric poems, and no doubt beyond, belonging to no epic poem or tradition in particular. Other phrases, however, are more restricted, occurring in one poem only or only in certain contexts. And in some cases, such as Lycaon's supplication to Achilles, we have a memorable phrase marking a memorable scene recurring only in one other memorable scene in another poem. Context has here become indissolubly connected with work or poem

The degree to which formulaic phrases are restricted determines their place on the interformularity scale. The more restricted an expression, the more specific the context in which it is uttered, and the higher the point at which it can be placed on the scale. (On the other hand, a high frequency of a context to which a given phrase is restricted will lower its position on the scale, since frequency diminishes specificity.) It is also important to observe that the continuum of increasing specificity is quintessentially cognitive: it is based on the judgment of the performer/poet and the audience as to the degree of similarity between two contexts: the more specific a formula and/or the more restricted its distribution, the greater the possible awareness of its recurrence and of its potential for signaling meaningful repetition. In this way the scale of interformularity does not code what is for the modern reader or scholar – the scholar of Virgil or Apollonius of Rhodes – the *likelihood of allusion or quotation*, but what is for the epic poet and his audience *specificity of the similarity of scenes to each other*.

This idea brings the Homeric formula in line with language use in general as a conscious utterance of phrases in relation to their context; it also brings out important differences with the well-known definition of "formula" in the Parry–Lord tradition: "a group of words which is regularly employed under the same metrical conditions to express a given essential idea."[4] There are two problems with this definition. The first is that the context understood to be typical for the formula is not narrative, semantic, or poetic, but strictly metrical: a formula's context is understood as the position in the verse available for the regular expression of the "essential idea." This element of the definition, however, widely commented on and at the core of an extensive debate on the nature of the Homeric formula, is based on a mechanistic idea of "context," which turns formulaic language into an autonomous process, driven by the recurrent movement of the verse.

The second, related, problem is less obvious and possibly more controversial. Parry's definition separates language from utterance context. The "essential idea" is thought to exist before its expression, which, in turn, is separate from the narrative context in which a poet uses it. In other words, language in general in this conception is *autonomous*. The idea of language as an autonomous system underlies in some form or another most of linguistics, which studies language as a code, a self-contained system of signification or communication, separate from the messages it is meant to convey, and equally separate from the interactive contexts in which those messages are sent.[5]

It makes sense, however, both for the study of Homeric formulas and for the study of language in general, to think of utterances as indissolubly connected with the situations in which they are performed. Language is autonomous and discrete only for its academic students; real speakers in real situations, speakers who are not trained in linguistic or grammatical analysis, are more likely to see what they say as appropriate or desirable *behavior* in a given situation.[6] If the situation is a recurring one, then language can become "formulaic." And if language is a matter of behavior, of *doing*, then the thing done, the formula, is not only a reaction to a recurrent context; doing the thing, performing the phrase, is also creating the context.

Within the domain of the Homeric formula (though without reference to the wider issues of the language involved) an important suggestion in

---

[4] Parry 1971: 272; the earlier variant at p. 13; Lord 1960: 4, 30.
[5] This pertains to the long-standing debate between "functionalism" and "formalism" in linguistics; see Hymes 1974; Leech 1983: 46–78; critique of theoretical (formal) linguistics in Baker and Hacker 1984. Parry's work is indebted to the structuralist program of Ferdinand de Saussure and can hence be aligned with formalist linguistics: Bakker 1997: 15; 2008b: 82–4; for the historical (Paris) context, see de Vet 2005.
[6] "Behavior" in connection with language is a term from anthropological linguistics; overview in Schiffrin 1994: 138–41.

this regard, with respect to metrical context, was offered by Gregory Nagy. In addition to seeing formula as conditioned by meter (à la Parry), Nagy proposes to see meter, conversely, as conditioned by formula. For Nagy, meter emerges out of the tradition's favorite and most frequently uttered phrases as a process of streamlining and regularization.[7] The difference between the two ways of viewing is that between synchrony and diachrony: the idea of formula conditioned by meter takes the existence of meter for granted, whereas the idea of meter conditioned by formula views meter as emergent, a structure in the process of being shaped in continuously repeated performance.

The same principle can be applied to grammar in general. A relevant linguistic framework here is the study of language as *grammaticalization*, which sees language, ordinary, natural language, as a diachronic process driven by communicative need and pressure.[8] Frequently occurring situations lead to routinized language behavior, speech that is regular and "grammatical." So just as we can speak, diachronically, of emergence of meter out of formula, we can speak of the emergence of grammar out of frequently occurring discursive situations. Language will become more regular and predictable when the context in which it is the appropriate or required course of action recurs frequently: in a reciprocal process context will turn language into grammar, and language, conversely, will turn context into ritual.

Nor is this an involuntary and "natural" process. The conscious judgment of speakers plays an important role. What they say may be based on their judgment as to the degree of similarity of the present situation to previous, remembered situations. In uttering the appropriate phrase they can actively make the present situation resemble those earlier ones. So speech is metaphorical in the sense that it may involve the use of "old" expressions for "new" situations. Or, put differently, speakers are to a certain extent always quoters.

Returning now to Homer, let us substitute "formula" for "grammar." Meter creates formula (Parry) and formula creates meter (Nagy), but formula also creates situation. That is, a formula uttered to create a given situation can be uttered again in order to create a new situation that is similar to the previous one (situations are rarely completely identical). The best example of this in Homer, and one particularly relevant to the present book with its emphasis on the interplay between *epos* and *aoidē*, is the introduction of a hero as speaker and performer, the transition from

---

[7] Nagy 1976.   [8] For example, Heine, Claudi, and Hünnemeyer 1991; Hopper and Traugott 1993.

narrative to the *mimesis* of a character in the context of the performance. This is the single most frequent and salient, indeed, the prime occasion for the use of the noun–epithet formula:

This is, of course, the system of combination and substitution that lies at the core of Milman Parry's analysis of Homeric language as a traditional formulaic system. One might say, with Parry, that the occurrence of πολύμητις Ὀδυσσεύς after προσέφη is formulaic in the sense that once the line has progressed to the verb at the hephthemimeral caesura there is no choice but to continue with the "traditional" noun–epithet formula for the required character. Or, put differently, there is no choice but to add the appropriate (and metrically conditioned) epithet to that character's name.[9] The fact that there is in each case only one such phrase (Parry's well-known notion of thrift) has been an important impulse to oral-formulaic research.[10]

The consequence of this, however, is not explored by Parry. The noun–epithet formula is bound to the phrase ending in προσέφη. Its distribution is therefore limited to the contexts created by that phrase, and the noun–epithet formula cannot have the sole function Parry ascribes to it in his later work, that of facilitating as formula the oral composition of the poem. This is strikingly exemplified by the noun–epithet formula πολύμητις Ὀδυσσεύς. As was seen earlier by Norman Austin, out of its sixty-six occurrences in the *Odyssey* no fewer than sixty-two are preceded by the speech-introducing formula τὸν δ' ἀπαμειβόμενος προσέφη or its variants.[11] The question of the distribution of πολύμητις Ὀδυσσεύς, then, becomes the question of the distribution of what I once called its

---

[9] Parry 1971: 14: "This fidelity to the formula is even more evident in the case of πολύτλας δῖος Ὀδυσσεύς, which the poet uses 5 times in the *Iliad* and 33 times in the *Odyssey*, without ever thinking of using other words to express the same idea, without ever so much as considering the possibility of utilizing the portion of the line taken up by the epithetic words for the expression of some original idea."

[10] Parry 1971: 17 ("an extended system of great simplicity"); 276 ("The thrift of a system lies in the degree in which it is free of phrases which, having the same metrical value and expressing the same idea, could replace one another.").

[11] Austin 1975: 28–9. The number comes to sixty-three if *Od.* 20.183, where Odysseus does *not* speak is added (ὣς φάτο· τὸν δ' οὔ τι προσέφη πολύμητις Ὀδυσσεύς). The exceptions are *Od.* 2.173; 21.404; and 22.1.

"staging-formula," the phrase that prepares the way for the "epiphany" of the god or hero whose formula it precedes in the verse.[12] The noun–epithet formula is used under certain metrical conditions, but more significantly it is uttered in – and constitutive of – the situation created by the preceding formula. Odysseus is staged as the man full of *mētis* precisely and almost exclusively when he takes the floor in order to speak.

The formulaic line consisting of the speech-introducing staging formula followed by a noun–epithet formula, then, is not a device that in and of itself facilitates oral composition. But that does not make it any less grounded in speech and performance. The coalescence of the two formulas is a case analogous to what I called grammaticalization earlier, a regularized adaptive response to a recurrent need. The noun–epithet formula and its staging are the most regular and "grammaticalized" expressions in the Homeric grammar of poetry. The resulting highly formulaic lines are not so much ready-made ways of saying "and Odysseus answered him" as the performance of a recognizable verbal ritual that is the tradition's coding of a frequently recurring poetic need. Epic grammar codes best what epic poets do most.

We are talking here about the low end of the scale of interformularity. The verbal ritual with which speech is introduced is a way of signaling that a number of events are judged to be *similar to each other*. This is true to the dynamics of speech, where speakers will say the same thing they said in a situation to which they feel the present situation bears a resemblance. No single instance of the speech-introducing formula has primacy in the sense that it is "first," a prototype "quoted" by other, secondary, instances, although poets may have a special recollection of certain cases.

The idea of a speech act that constitutes a situation which is judged to be similar to previous situations opens up, even for ordinary speech, the possibility of conscious, even self-reflexive, repetition. Speakers may unreflectively – and most grammar is created unreflectively – judge a new situation to be sufficiently similar to previous ones they remember and utter the phrase that served them well at those earlier occasions. But they may also be aware of their choice, (self)-reflexively repeating an utterance that they thought was memorable or giving the present situation a special twist by linking it to a previous occasion. And the motivation for such conscious behavior is, of course, greatest when speakers can assume that they share the memory of that earlier occasion with their listeners.

Acknowledging this possibility is also moving up the scale of interformularity. The speech-introducing noun–epithet formulas and their staging

---

[12] Bakker 1997: 162–5. For the syntax of noun–epithet formulas, see Bakker 1997: 89–115.

formulas occur, of course, throughout any given epic and the entire tradition, running across compositions and performances. But formulaic repetition may also be more restricted, being specific to a particular composition or an episode within it. The "unlimited meat" formula we encountered in Chapters 4 and 5 is a good example:

ὣς τότε μὲν πρόπαν ἦμαρ ἐς ἠέλιον καταδύντα
ἤμεθα δαινύμενοι κρέα τ' ἄσπετα καὶ μέθυ ἡδύ.
(*Od.* 9.161–2, 556–7; 10.184–5, 467–8; 10.476–7; 12.29–30)

In this way, at that time, all day long until the setting of the sun
we sat there feasting on unlimited meats and sweet wine.

The Parryan way of dealing with these lines would be to say that this is a formulaic sequence expressing the essential idea "and then we had a lavish feast." But the first-person plural restricts the use of the sequence to *epos*, an important limitation, and within *epos* the lines are further restricted to a Wanderings context, the narrative function we defined in Chapter 2 as Odysseus' interaction with a future donor. Within that type of narrative the lines are associated with the theme of pre-cultural plenitude as opposed to Ithacan limitations. Odysseus and his men are living in the *real* paradisiacal conditions that the Suitors in Odysseus' palace are trying to attain, and in this way they highlight the difference between the Otherworld and the real world in the *Odyssey*. Formulaic repetition, then, in a well-defined section of the narrative has important thematic consequences for the poem as a whole.

The lines are an encoding of important parallels between the Cyclops and Circe episodes that are not otherwise explicitly signaled by Odysseus' narrative. By the principle outlined above, they are not merely uttered in similar contexts; they actively *create* similarity between contexts, establishing a link between the innumerable wild goats in the Cyclops adventure and the endlessly abundant meat on Aeaea. But they are also used for a third situation, the meal that Odysseus and his men make of the Cyclops' sheep, a situation that is decidedly *dissimilar*: as we saw in Chapter 4, the meats of which this meal consists are not limitless and the animals are stolen property. The *Odyssey* is thus able, through formal repetition, to portray the meal as incongruous. There is no primacy in the sense that any one particular instance of the consumption of "unlimited meats" is quoted by the others; rather, the use of the formula for the consumption of the Cyclops' sheep "quotes" the totality of the generic situation created by the κρέα ἄσπετα formula. Here, formulaic similarity has brought out semantic dissimilarity.

Epilogue: on "interformularity"

A case of interformularity that can be placed at approximately the same place on the scale is constituted by Alkinoos' invitation to Odysseus, presented earlier in Chapter 1, to tell the story of his Wanderings (*Od.* 8.572–6):

ἀλλ' ἄγε μοι τόδε εἰπὲ καὶ ἀτρεκέως κατάλεξον,
ὅππη ἀπεπλάγχθης τε καὶ ἅς τινας ἵκεο χώρας
ἀνθρώπων, αὐτούς τε πόλιάς τ' ἐΰ ναιεταούσας,
ἠμὲν ὅσοι χαλεποί **τε καὶ ἄγριοι οὐδὲ δίκαιοι,**
οἵ τε φιλόξεινοι καί σφιν νόος ἐστὶ θεουδής.

> But now tell me this and give me the report, unswerving, on
> what ways you were blown off course, and what lands you reached,
> of humans, they themselves and their cities well-built,
> <on the one hand> all those who are hard to deal with, <u>and savages, unjust,</u>
> and <on the other hand> <u>those who are friendly to strangers, with a mind that fears the gods.</u>

This instance of the formulaic theme of the wanderer's encounters with the humans on his path is not necessarily the quotable "first"; but in the poem it is a neutral articulation of an idea that is pulled in two different directions. On the one hand, there is the hero's utterance of it in his own narrative, the encounter with the Cyclops, when the neutral encounter becomes a matter of active exploration (*Od.* 9.174–6):

ἐλθὼν τῶνδ' ἀνδρῶν πειρήσομαι, οἵ τινές εἰσιν,
ἤ ῥ' οἵ γ' ὑβρισταί τε καὶ ἄγριοι οὐδὲ δίκαιοι,
ἦε φιλόξεινοι, καί σφιν νόος ἐστὶ θεουδής.

> Having come <here> I'll put these people to the test, <to see> who they are,
> <u>whether they are brutes, savages, and unjust</u>
> <u>or friendly to strangers, with a mind that fears the gods.</u>

The verbal repetition evokes the basic idea, the encounter with strangers, but the formulaic sequence ἤ ῥ' ὑβρισταί etc. is here not a question, but the complement of the verb πειρήσομαι, 'I will try out'. in the previous line, a verb denoting active exploration of someone who is (or thinks he is) in control of the situation: he is going to put these people, whoever they are, to the test. On the other hand, there is the hero's utterance of the same theme when *aoidē*, not his own but the poet's narrative, is underway (*Od.* 6.119–21 = 13.200–2):

ὤ μοι ἐγώ, τέων αὖτε βροτῶν ἐς γαῖαν ἱκάνω;
ἤ ῥ' οἵ γ' ὑβρισταί τε καὶ ἄγριοι οὐδὲ δίκαιοι,
ἦε φιλόξεινοι καί σφιν νόος ἐστὶ θεουδής;

> Oh, my – of what mortals am I now again reaching the land?
> Are they brutes, savages, and unjust,
> Or <would they be> friendly to strangers, with a mind that fears the gods?

This is what Odysseus exclaims upon arriving at Scheria of the Phaeacians and later again at his own Ithaca. What are confident words in Odysseus' own narrative are here, ironically, anguished words in the poet's. The complement of the active questing verb πειρήσομαι is now an uncertain and insecure double question. The two instances of Odysseus' anguished exclamation are suggestive allomorphs of the two other instances of the theme. In other words, there is "rewriting" (in the sense of ironic adaptation) of this Wanderings theme in the poem: inclusion takes place with an eye toward bringing out the various possibilities inherent in a given theme.

A move further up the scale involves cases of the formulaic alignment of the crimes of the Suitors with the adventures of the Companions in the Otherworld.[13] The similarity between Eurylochos telling about the disappearance of his companions in the house of Circe, on the one hand, and the Suitors laughing hysterically over blood-defiled pieces of meat, on the other is not immediately obvious, but is signaled with the formulaic repetition we earlier observed in Chapter 5 (respectively, *Od.* 10.247–8 and *Od.* 20.348–9):

> ἐν δέ οἱ ὄσσε/ ὄσσε δ' ἄρα σφέων
> δακρυόφιν πίμπλαντο, γόον δ' ὠΐετο θυμός
>
> and his/their eyes
> were filled with tears, and his/their *thumos* foresaw lamentation

We might think of the striking use of an existing term with established meaning for a novel concept, so as to produce a strong metaphoric effect. In the present case, however, there is no clear way to assign primacy to either instance of the expression, although the "lamentation" seems more immediately appropriate to the situation of the Suitors. The two instances "extend" each other, bound together by the unusual role assigned to *thumos*: instead of spurring on the body to vigorous action it foresees the body's demise and death.

---

[13] In addition to the examples to be discussed, there is ἐχολώσατο κηρόθι μᾶλλον (*Od.* 17.458, applying to Antinoos throwing a stool at Odysseus' head, a formula recalling the throwing of the Cyclops' first rock (9.480); see Chapter 4.

Epilogue: on "interformularity"   167

At approximately the same point on the scale is the formula linking the Suitors in Odysseus' *megaron*, unaware of their imminent death, with the Cyclops at the threshold of his cave, unaware of the escape of his victims (respectively, *Od.* 22.31–3 and *Od.* 9.442–3):

ἴσκεν ἕκαστος ἀνήρ, ἐπεὶ ἦ φάσαν οὐκ ἐθέλοντα
ἄνδρα κατακτεῖναι· **τὸ δὲ νήπιοι οὐκ ἐνόησαν**
ὡς δή σφιν καὶ πᾶσιν ὀλέθρου πείρατ' **ἐφῆπτο**.

Each man was guessing, since they thought that, yes, unintentionally
he had killed a man; <what> they, clueless, did not grasp <was>
   that at that point for all of them the ropes of their demise <u>had been
   fastened</u>.

τὸ δὲ νήπιος οὐκ ἐνόησεν
ὡς οἱ ὑπ' εἰροπόκων ὀίων στέρνοισι **δέδεντο**

   <What> he, clueless, did not grasp <was>
   that they under the chests of the wool-fleeced sheep <u>were bound</u>.

The formulaic linkage between the two situations marks them as "similar," but as we saw in Chapter 4 the similarity points up multiple reversals and ironies. The Suitors are like the Cyclops in their total lack of understanding of their situation, but they are at the same time in the position in which Odysseus once was, trapped in the cave. But Odysseus was able to escape, whereas they are not. The similarity thus sets up Odysseus as a successful Cyclops and the Suitors as the equivalent of an unsuccessful Odysseus, the link between the cave and Odysseus' *megaron* being established in the process. The contrast between the two linked situations is ironically signaled by the two passive pluperfect verbs for fastening and binding in the line following. Odysseus' and the Companions' binding under the sheep (δέδεντο) is the way to survival, whereas the Suitors' binding, by the ὀλέθρου πείρατα, 'cables of destruction', is the seal of death.

The formulas through which the Suitors are linked with the Companions and with the Cyclops are found in these scenes only; they do not occur elsewhere. We might want to say that the instance occurring later in the poem, applying to the Suitors, is an internal quote of the earlier instance, applying to the Companions and the Cyclops. But, first, it is a quote that takes place entirely within the mechanisms and conventions of the traditional formulaic system. And, second, it is not clear which of the two occurrences is the quoting and which is the quoted one. In a strict linear progression (and composition) of the poem the later occurrence would be a quote of the first one. But such primacy is not certain or even necessary. The importance of linear ordering diminishes when we take the poem's recomposition and reperformance into account.[14] The quotation could be reversed, or, more attractively, the quotation is mutual. The second instance can be a quote of the first in a given performance, but the first can quote the second through the memory of previous performances, and through knowledge of the work as a whole.

Instances of repetition where quotable primacy of one of the occurrences is probable or possibly even certain move us to the top of the scale of interformularity, where the repetition may extend across the boundary of the work. Context here is maximally specific and memorable and hence repetition most conscious. Examples include the supplication of Lycaon as "quoted" in *Odyssey* 22 and the invocation of the Muses before the *Catalogue of Ships* in the *Iliad* as "quoted" by Odysseus (Chapter 1) in his report of his journey to the dead (respectively, *Il.* 2.484 and *Od.* 11.328):

πληθὺν δ' οὐκ ἂν ἐγὼ μυθήσομαι οὐδ' ὀνομήνω

Their multitude, there is no way I could tell or name <them all>.

πάσας δ' οὐκ ἂν ἐγὼ μυθήσομαι οὐδ' ὀνομήνω

All of them, there is no way I could tell or name <them all>

We could speak of "intertextuality" here, but that term runs the risk of underemphasizing the fact that the intertextual allusion takes place entirely within the system of epic formulaic diction. The "quotation" of the *Iliad* is seen as "literary" – and therefore incompatible with oral composition and oral tradition – *only* in a rigid orality–literacy contrast that evidence from various sources has long disproved. If the modern reader or scholar can consider particular lines or scenes from the *Iliad* striking and memorable, so, and *a fortiori*, can the ancient epic singer or rhapsode.

But beyond literary quotation or allusion is the idea of similarity and its articulation, on which the interformularity scale is based. The repetition of the epic *recusatio* formula is not a textual effect, but a way of signaling, in and through formulaic language, a similarity between Odysseus and an epic *aoidos*, while at the same time leaving room for the differences between the two situations. The "quoted" line comes to stand metonymically for the entire situation picturing the epic poet and his fundamental challenge. In the same way the supplication of Lycaon summons the entire

---

[14] See also Nagy 1996: 65–111.

situation of Achilles' savage massacre to the present of Odysseus' domestic revenge. These repetitions have the desired effect only on listeners who have the required "hearing knowledge." This is true not only for poetry, but also for any skilled or ambitious speech, which requires matching levels of competence of the speakers and their listeners.

Oralists of previous generations would presumably have found such a fine-tuned sensitivity questionable and improbable, too much a matter of "literary" composition and appreciation. But if ordinary speech can be uttered with conscious awareness of the repetition involved, so can highly concentrated epic speech. And this becomes more plausible when we look at the matter from the point of view of Nagy's ideas on the gradual crystallization of the Homeric poems,[15] which amounts to an essential correction of the old concept of "composition in performance": the reality of Homeric composition and transmission seems to be better captured by the idea of *recomposition in performance*, which turns each new performance of the poem into a conscious quote of the previous one. Quoting, in other words, is what the Homeric tradition explicitly does in order to be itself.

The interformularity continuum, then, runs from the idea of a formulaic grammar coding best what epic speakers do most to a reperformance of what one epic speaker has done best. In this way the continuum comes to typify the *Iliad* and *Odyssey* themselves, those formulaic poems that encode what is common and recurrent, but that are reperformed themselves, because they are unique and best.

---

[15] For example, Nagy 1996; 2004.

Bibliography

PRIMARY SOURCES

CEG = P. A. Hansen, *Carmina Epigraphica Graeca Saeculorum VIII–V a.Chr.N.* (Texte und Kommentare 12). Berlin: de Gruyter.
Inscriptiones Creticae, vol. III, *Tituli Cretae orientalis*, 1942, ed. M. Guarducci, Rome.
Inscriptiones Graecae, vol. XIV, *Inscriptiones Siciliae et Italiae, additis Galliae, Hispaniae, Britanniae, Germaniae inscriptionibus*, 1890, ed. E. G. Kaibel, Berlin.
SEG = *Supplementum Epigraphicum Graecum*. Leiden: Brill, available online at: www.brill.com/publications/online-resources/supplementum-epigraphicum-graecum-online, 1923–.
Syll.^{3} = W. Dittenberger, *Sylloge Inscriptionum Graecarum*, 3rd edn. (1915–24).

SECONDARY SOURCES

Aarne, A. and S. Thompson (1981) *The Types of the Folktale: A Classification and Bibliography*, 2nd edn. Helsinki: Academia Scientiarum Fennica.
Ahl, F. and H. M. Roisman (1996) *The Odyssey Re-Formed*. Ithaca, NY: Cornell University Press.
Alexander, C. (1991) "A note on the stag: *Odyssey* 10.156–72," *Classical Quarterly* 41 (2): 520–4.
Århem, K. (1996) "The cosmic food web: human–nature relatedness in the northwest Amazon," in *Nature and Society: Anthropological Perspectives*, eds. P. Descola and G. Pálsson. London: Routledge, 162–72.
Asatrian, G. (2002) "The lord of cattle in Gilan," *Iran and the Caucasus* 6: 75–85.
Auffarth, Chr. (1991) *Der drohende Untergang. "Schöpfung" in Mythos und Ritual im Alten Orient und in Griechenland*. Berlin: de Gruyter.
Austin, N. (1975) *Archery at the Dark of the Moon: Poetic Problems in Homer's Odyssey*. Berkeley, CA: University of California Press.

Baker, G. P. and P. M. S. Hacker (1984) *Language, Sense and Nonsense: A Critical Investigation of Modern Theories of Language*. Oxford: Blackwell.
Bakhtin, M. (1981) *The Dialogic Imagination*, eds. C. Emerson and M. Holquist. Austin: University of Texas Press.
  (1986) *Speech Genres and Other Late Essays*, eds. C. Emerson and M. Holquist. Austin: University of Texas Press.
Bakker, E. J. (1988a) *Linguistics and Formulas in Homer: Scalarity and the Description of the Particle Per*. Amsterdam: Benjamins.
  (1988b) "Restrictive conditionals," in *In the Footsteps of Raphael Kühner*, eds. A. Rijksbaron, H. A. Mulder, and G. C. Wakker. Amsterdam: Gieben, 5–26.
  (1993) "Discourse and performance: involvement, visualization, and 'presence' in Homeric poetry." *Classical Antiquity* 12: 1–29.
  (1997) *Poetry in Speech: Orality and Homeric Discourse*. Ithaca, NY: Cornell University Press.
  (2002a) "*Khrónos, kléos*, and ideology from Herodotus to Homer," in *EPEA PTEROENTA: Beiträge zur Homerforschung. Festschrift für Wolfgang Kullmann zum 75. Geburtstag*, eds. M. Reichel and A. Rengakos. Stuttgart: Franz Steiner, 11–30.
  (2002b) "Polyphemos," *Colby Classical Quarterly* 38: 135–50.
  (2005) *Pointing at the Past: From Formula to Performance in Homeric Poetics*. Washington, DC and Cambridge, MA: Center for Hellenic Studies/Harvard University Press.
  (2006) "Homeric epic between feasting and fasting," in *La poésie épique grecque. Métamorphoses d'un genre littéraire*, eds. F. Montanari and A. Rengakos. Entretiens sur l'antiquité classique 52. Geneva: Fondation Hardt, 1–39.
  (2008a) "Epic remembering," in *Orality, Literacy, Memory in the Ancient Greek and Roman World*, ed. A. Mackay. Leiden: Brill, 65–77.
  (2008b) "Homerphilologie zwischen Prämodernität und Postmodernität," in *Der geteilte Gegenstand. Beiträge zu Geschichte, Gegenwart und Zukunft der Philologie(n)*, ed. U. Schaefer. Frankfurt am Main: Peter Lang, 79–89.
  (2009) "Homer, Odysseus, and the narratology of performance," in *Narratology and Interpretation: The Content of Narrative Form in Ancient Literature*, eds. J. Grethlein and A. Rengakos. Berlin: de Gruyter, 117–36.
  (2010) "Remembering the *gastēr*," in *Allusion, Authority, and Truth*, eds. Ph. Mitsis and Chr. Tsagalis. Berlin: de Gruyter, 37–50.
Ballabriga, A. (1998) *Les fictions d'Homère. L'invention mythologique et cosmographique dans l'Odyssée*. Paris: Presses Universitaires de France.
Baudy, G. J. (1983) "Hierarchie oder die Verteilung des Fleisches," in *Neue Ansätze in der Religionswissenschaft*, eds. B. Gladigow and H. G. Kippenberg. Munich: Kösel, 131–74.
Baumann, H. (1938) "Afrikanische Wild- und Buschgeister," *Zeitschrift für Ethnologie* 70: 208–39.
Bendall, L. M. (2004) "Fit for a king? Hierarchy, exclusion, aspiration and desire in the social structure of Mycenaean banqueting," in *Food, Cuisine and*

Society in Prehistoric Greece, eds. P. Halstead and J. C. Barrett. Oxford: Oxbow Books, 105–35.
Bergren, A. L. T. (1983) "Odyssean temporality: many (re)turns," in *Approaches to Homer*, eds. C. A. Rubino and C. W. Shelmerdine. Austin: University of Texas Press, 38–73.
Bernadete, S. (2005) *Achilles and Hector: The Homeric Hero*. South Bend, IN: St. Augustine's Press.
Bettini, M. and C. Franco (2010) *Il mito di Circe. Immagini e racconti dalla Grecia a oggi*. Turin: Einaudi.
Bondi, A. (1982) "Nutrition and animal productivity," in *CRC Handbook of Agricultural Productivity*, ed. M. Recheigle. Boca Raton, FL: CRC Press, 195–212.
Bonifazi, A. (2009) "Inquiring into *nostos* and its cognates," *American Journal of Philology* 130: 481–510.
Borthwick, E. (1988) "Odysseus and the return of the swallow," *Greece and Rome* 35: 14–22.
Bremmer, J. N. (2002) "Odysseus versus the Cyclops," in *Myths and Symbols*, vol. I, ed. S. des Bouvrie. Athens: Norwegian Institute, 135–52.
Brendel, O. (1934) *Die Schafzucht im alten Griechenland*. Würzburg: Triltsch Verlag.
Burgess, J. S. (2006) "Neoanalysis, orality, and intertextuality: an examination of Homeric motif transference," *Oral Tradition* 21: 148–89.
  (2012) "Intertextuality without text in early Greek epic," in *Relative Chronology in Early Greek Epic Poetry*, eds. Ø. Andersen and D. T. T. Haug. Cambridge University Press, 168–83.
Burkert, W. (1975) "Apellai und Apollon," *Rheinisches Museum* 118: 1–21.
  (1979) *Structure and History in Greek Mythology and Ritual*. Berkeley: University of California Press.
  (1983) *Homo Necans: The Anthropology of Ancient Greek Sacrificial Ritual and Myth*, trans. P. Bing. Berkeley: University of California Press.
  (1996) *Creation of the Sacred: Tracks of Biology in Early Religions*. Cambridge, MA: Harvard University Press.
Carpenter, R. (1956) *Folktale, Fiction, and Saga in the Homeric Epics*. Berkeley, CA: University of California Press.
Chandezon, Chr. (2003) *L'élevage en Grèce ancienne (fin Ve–fin Ier s.a.C). L'apport des sources épigraphiques*. Bordeaux: Ausonius.
Charachidzé, G. (1986) *Prométhée ou le Caucase*. Paris: Flammarion.
Clarke, H. C. (1967) *The Art of the Odyssey*. Englewood Cliffs, NJ: Prentice Hall.
Clarke, M. (1999) *Flesh and Spirit in the Songs of Homer: A Study of Words and Myths*. Oxford University Press.
Clay, J. S. (1983) *The Wrath of Athena: Gods and Men in the Odyssey*. Princeton University Press.
  (1999) "A ram among the sheep: some notes on Odysseus in the *Iliad*," in Kazazis and Rengakos (eds.), *Euphrosyne*, 363–7.
Cook, E. F. (1995) *The Odyssey in Athens: Myths of Cultural Origins*. Ithaca, NY: Cornell University Press.

(1999) "'Active' and 'passive' heroics in the *Odyssey*," *Classical World* 93: 149–67.
Crane, G. (1988) *Calypso: Background and Conventions of the Odyssey*. Frankfurt: Athenäum.
Csapo, E. (2005) *Theories of Mythology*. Malden, MA: Blackwell.
Danek, G. (1998) *Epos und Zitat. Studien zu den Quellen der Odyssee*. Vienna: Österreichische Akademie der Wissenschaften.
Depew, M. (1997) "Reading Greek prayers," *Classical Antiquity* 16: 229–58.
Detienne, M. (1998) *Apollon le couteau à la main. Une approche expérimentale du polythéisme grec*. Paris: Gallimard.
Dimock, G. E., Jr. (1956) "The name of Odysseus," *Hudson Review* 9: 52–70.
Doughtery, C. (1993) *The Poetics of Colonization: From City to Text*. New York: Oxford University Press.
Dowden, K. (1992) *The Uses of Greek Mythology*. London: Routledge.
Dubois, J. W. (1985) "Competing motivations," in *Iconicity in Syntax*, ed. J. Haiman. Amsterdam: Benjamins, 343–65.
Duerr, H. P. (1984) *Sedna: oder die Liebe zum Leben*. Frankfurt: Suhrkamp.
Duerr, J. (2010) "Fear of the lord," in *Hunting: In Search of the Wild Life*, ed. N. Kowalsky. Malden, MA: Wiley-Blackwell, 134–48.
Dumont, P. (2003) "Le nom d'Eumée dans l'*Odyssée*," *Revue des études grecques* 116: 377–85.
Dundes, A. (1997) "Binary opposition in myth: the Propp/Lévi-Strauss debate in retrospect," *Western Folklore* 56: 39–50.
Edmunds, L. (2005) "Epic and myth," in *A Companion to Ancient Epic*, ed. J. M. Foley. Oxford: Blackwell, 31–44.
Eliade, M. (1949) *Traité d'histoire des religions*. Paris: Payot.
Fehr, B. (1990) "Entertainers at the *symposion*: the *akletoi* in the Archaic period," in *Sympotica: A Symposium on the Symposion*, ed. O. Murray. Oxford University Press, 185–95.
Fell, J. L. (1977) "Vladimir Propp in Hollywood," *Film Quarterly* 30: 19–28.
Fenik, B. (1974) *Studies in the Odyssey*. Hermes Einzelschriften 30. Wiesbaden: Steiner.
Focke, F. (1943) *Die Odyssee*. Stuttgart: Kohlhammer.
Foley, J. M. (1990) *Traditional Oral Epic: The Odyssey, Beowulf, and the Serbo-Croatian Return Song*. Berkeley: University of California Press.
 (2004) "Epic as genre," in *The Cambridge Companion to Homer*, ed. R. Fowler, Cambridge University Press, 171–87.
Ford, A. (1992) *Homer: The Poetry of the Past*. Ithaca, NY: Cornell University Press.
 (1997) "Epic as genre," in Morris and Powell (eds.), *A New Companion to Homer*, 396–414.
Frame, D. (1978) *The Myth of Return in Early Greek Epic*. New Haven, CT: Yale University Press.
Friedrich, R. (1987) "Thrinakia and Zeus' ways to men in the *Odyssey*," *Greek, Roman and Byzantine Studies* 28: 375–400.

(1991) "The hybris of Odysseus," *Journal of Hellenic Studies* 111: 16–28.
Gagné, R. (2009) "'Spilling the sea out of its cup': Solon's *Elegy to the Muses*," *Quaderni Urbinati di Cultura Classica* (N.S.) 91: 23–49.
Georgoudi, S. (1990) *Des chevaux et des bœufs dans le monde grec. Réalités et représentations animalières à partir des livres XVI et XVII des Géoponiques*. Paris and Athens: De Boccard/Daedalus.
Germain, G. (1954) *Genèse de l'Odyssée. Le fantastique et le sacré*. Paris: Presses Universitaires de France.
Glenn, J. (1971) "The Polyphemus folktale and Homer's *Kyklopeia*," *Transactions of the American Philological Association* 102: 133–85.
Gottschall, J. (2008) *The Rape of Troy: Evolution, Violence, and the World of Homer*. Cambridge University Press.
Grethlein, J. (2005) "Eine Anthropologie des Essens: Der Essensstreit in der 'Ilias' und die Erntemetapher in Il. 19, 221–224," *Hermes* 133: 257–79.
Griffin, J. (1980) *Homer on Life and Death*. Oxford: Clarendon Press.
Griffiths, A. (1999) "Euenios the negligent nightwatchman (Herodotus 9.92–6)," in *From Myth to Reason? Studies in the Development of Greek Thought*, ed. R. Buxton. Oxford University Press, 169–82.
Grimm, C. W. (1857) "Die Sage von Polyphem," *Abh. der königl. Akademie der Wissensch. zu Berlin*, 1–30.
Grottanelli, C. (1989) "La distribution de la viande dans la *Cyropédie*," *Metis* 4: 185–209.
Halstead, P. (1981) "Counting sheep in Neolithic and Bronze Age Greece," in *Pattern of the Past: Studies in Honour of David Clarke*, eds. I. Hodder, G. Isaac, and N. Hammond. Cambridge University Press, 307–30.
Hamayon, R. (1990) *La chasse à l'âme. Esquisse d'une théorie du chamanisme sibérien*. Paris: Société d'ethnologie.
Hamilton, T. (2006) "Beef bull fertility," Ontario Ministry of Agriculture, Food, and Rural Affairs, available at: www.omafra.gov.on.ca/english/livestock/beef/facts/06–015.htm#cow.
Hansen, W. (1997) "Homer and the folktale," in Morris and Powell (eds.), *A New Companion to Homer*, 442–62.
Harris, M. (1985) *Good to Eat: Riddles of Food and Culture*. London: Allen & Unwin.
Harrod, H. L. (2000) *The Animals Came Dancing: Native American Sacred Ecology and Animal Kinship*. Tucson: University of Arizona Press.
Hayden, B. (2001) "Fabulous feasts: a prolegomenon to the importance of feasting," in *Feasts: Archaeological and Ethnographic Perspectives on Food, Politics, and Power*, eds. M. Dietler and B. Hayden. Washington, DC: Smithsonian Institution Press, 23–64.
Heine, B., U. Claudi, and F. Hünnemeyer (1991) *Grammaticalization: A Conceptual Framework*. University of Chicago Press.
Helmig, Chr. (2008) "Plutarch of Chaeronea and Porphyry on transmigration – who is the author of Stobaeus I 445.14–448.3 (W.-H.)?," *Classical Quarterly* 58: 250–55.

Heubeck, A. (1950) "Der Odyssee-Dichter und die Ilias," dissertation, Erlangen.
Higbie, C. (1995) *Heroic Names, Homeric Identities*. New York: Garland.
Hitch, S. (2009) *King of Sacrifice: Ritual and Royal Authority in the Iliad*. Washington, DC and Cambridge, MA: Center for Hellenic Studies/ Harvard University Press.
Hodkinson, S. (1988) "Animal husbandry in the Greek polis," in *Pastoral Economies in Classical Antiquity*, ed. C. R. Whittaker. Cambridge Philological Society, Suppl. 14, 33–74.
Homolle, T. (1891) "Observations épigraphiques," *Bulletin de correspondence hellénique* 15: 625–9.
Hopper, P. and E. C. Traugott (1993) *Grammaticalization*. Cambridge University Press.
Howe, T. (2008) *Pastoral Politics: Animals, Agriculture and Society in Ancient Greece*. Claremont, CA: Regina Books.
Hughes, J. D. (1994) *Pan's Travail: Environmental Problems of the Ancient Greeks and Romans*. Baltimore, MD: Johns Hopkins University Press.
Hymes, D. (1974) "Why linguistics needs the sociologist," in *Foundations in Sociolinguistics: An Ethnographic Approach*. Philadelphia: University of Pennsylvania Press, 69–82.
Isager, S. (1992) "Sacred animals in Classical and Hellenistic Greece," in *Economics of Cult in the Ancient Greek World*, eds. T. Linders and B. Alroth. Boreas 21: Uppsala, 15–19.
Isager, S. and J. E. Skydsgaard (1992) *Ancient Agriculture: An Introduction*. London: Routledge.
Jackson, J. E. (1983) *The Fish People: Linguistic Exogamy and Tukanoan Identity in Northwest Amazonia*. Cambridge University Press.
Jaeger, W. (1926) "Solons Eunomie," *Sitzungsberichte der Preussischen Akademie der Wissenschaften zu Berlin*, 69–85.
Jong, I. J. F. de (1987) *Narrators and Focalizers: The Presentation of the Story in the Iliad*. Amsterdam: Grüner.
  (2001) *A Narratological Commentary on the Odyssey*. Cambridge University Press.
Jörgensen, O. (1904) "Das Auftreten der Götter in den Büchern ι–μ der Odyssee," *Hermes* 39: 357–82.
Kahane, A. (1992) "The first word of the *Odyssey*," *Transactions of the American Philological Association* 122: 115–31.
Katz, J. and K. Volk (2000) "Mere bellies? A new look at *Theogony* 26–8," *Journal of Hellenic Studies* 120: 122–9.
Kazazis, J. N. and A. Rengakos (eds.) (1999) *Euphrosyne: Studies in Ancient Epic and its Legacy in Honor of Dimitris N. Maronitis*. Stuttgart: Steiner.
Kirk, G. S. (1970) *Myth: Its Meanings and Functions in Ancient and Other Cultures*. Cambridge and Berkeley: Cambridge University Press/University of California Press.
Kitts, M. (2011) "Ritual scenes in the *Iliad*: rote, hallowed, or encrypted as ancient art?" *Oral Tradition* 26: 221–46.

Koller, H. (1972) "Epos," *Glotta* 50: 16–24.
  (1973) "Λυκάβας," *Glotta* 51: 29–34.
Kroll, H. J. (1984) "Zum Ackerbau gegen Ende der mykenischen Epoche in der Argolis," *Archäologischer Anzeiger* 1984: 211–22.
Kullmann, W. (1984) "Oral poetry theory and Neoanalysis in Homeric research," *Greek, Roman and Byzantine Studies* 25: 307–24.
Lamberton, R. (1986) *Homer the Theologian: Neoplatonist Allegorical Reading and the Growth of the Epic Tradition*. Berkeley: University of California Press.
Larson, J. (2001) *Nymphs: Myth, Cult, Lore*. New York: Oxford University Press.
Leech, G. N. (1983) *Principles of Pragmatics*. London: Longman.
Levaniouk, O. (2000) "Aithōn, *aithon*, and Odysseus," *Harvard Studies in Classical Philology* 100: 25–51.
  (2011) *Eve of the Festival: Making Myth in Odyssey 19*. Washington, DC and Cambridge, MA: Center for Hellenic Studies/Harvard University Press.
Lévi-Strauss, C. (1955) "The Structural Study of Myth," *Journal of American Folklore* 78: 428–44.
Lord, A. B. (1960) *The Singer of Tales*. Cambridge, MA: Harvard University Press.
  (1972) "The effect of the Turkish conquest on Balkan epic tradition," in *Aspects of the Balkans: Continuity and Change*, eds. H. Birnbaum and S. Vryonis, Jr. The Hague: Mouton, 298–318.
  (1991) *Epic Singers and Oral Tradition*. Ithaca, NY: Cornell University Press.
Louden, B. (1995) "Categories of Homeric wordplay," *Transactions of the American Philological Association* 125: 27–46.
  (1999) *The Odyssey: Structure, Narration, and Meaning*. Baltimore, MD: Johns Hopkins University Press.
Malkin, I. (1998) *The Returns of Odysseus: Colonization and Ethnicity*. Berkeley: University of California Press.
Marinatos, N. (2000) *The Goddess and the Warrior: The Naked Goddess and Mistress of Animals in Early Greek Religion*. London: Routledge.
Marks, J. (2008) *Zeus in the Odyssey*. Washington, DC and Cambridge, MA: Center for Hellenic Studies/Harvard University Press.
Martin, R. P. (1989) *The Language of Heroes: Speech and Performance in the Iliad*. Ithaca, NY: Cornell University Press.
  (2001) "Rhapsodizing Orpheus," *Kernos* 14: 23–33.
  (2005) "Epic as genre," in *A Companion to Ancient Epic*, ed. J. M. Foley. Oxford: Blackwell, 9–19.
McCabe, D. F. (1984) *Miletos Inscriptions: Texts and List*. Princeton, NJ: Institute for Advanced Study.
McInerney, J. (1999) *The Folds of Parnassos: Land and Ethnicity in Ancient Phokis*. Austin: University of Texas Press.
  (2010). *The Cattle of the Sun: Cows and Culture in the World of the Ancient Greeks*. Princeton University Press.
Menrad, J. (1910) *Der Urmythos der Odyssee und seine dichterische Erneuerung. Des Sonnengottes Erdenfahrt*. Munich: Lindau.
Meuli, K. (1935) "Scythica," *Hermes* 70: 121–76.

(1946) "Griechische Opfergebräuche," in *Phyllobolia. Festschrift Peter von der Mühll*. Basel: Schwabe, 185–288.
Mikalson, J. D. (1975) *The Sacred and Civil Calendar of the Athenian Year*. Princeton University Press.
Minchin, E. (2007) *Homeric Voices: Discourse, Memory, Gender*. Oxford University Press.
Mondi, R. (1983) "The Homeric Cyclopes: folktale, tradition, and theme," *Transactions of the American Philological Association* 113: 17–38.
Morris, I. and B. Powell (1997) (eds.), *A New Companion to Homer*. Leiden: Brill.
Most, G. W. (1989) "The structure and function of Odysseus' *Apologoi*," *Transactions of the American Philological Association* 119: 15–30.
Nagler, M. N. (1990) "Odysseus: the proem and the problem," *Classical Antiquity* 9: 335–56.
  (1996) "Dread goddess revisited," in *Reading the Odyssey: Selected Interpretive Essays*, ed. S. Schein. Princeton University Press, 141–61.
Nagy, G. (1976) "Formula and meter," in *Oral Literature and the Formula*, eds. B. Stolz and R. S. Shannon. Ann Arbor, MI: Center for Coordination of Ancient and Modern Studies.
  (1979) *The Best of the Achaeans: Concepts of the Hero in Archaic Greek Poetry*. Baltimore, MD: Johns Hopkins University Press.
  (1990) *Pindar's Homer: The Lyric Possession of an Epic Past*. Baltimore, MD: Johns Hopkins University Press.
  (1996) *Homeric Questions*. Austin: University of Texas Press.
  (2004) *Homer's Text and Language*. Urbana: University of Illinois Press.
Nakassis, D. (2004) "Gemination at the horizons: east and west in the mythical geography of archaic Greek epic," *Transactions of the American Philological Association* 134: 215–33.
Nieto Hernández, P. (2000) "Back in the cave of the Cyclops," *American Journal of Philology* 121: 345–66.
Niles, J. D. (1978) "Patterning in the Wanderings of Odysseus," *Ramus* 7: 46–60.
Nordenskiöld, E. (1924) *Forschungen und Abenteuer in Südamerika*. Stuttgart: Strecker & Schröder.
Onians, R. B. (1951) *The Origins of European Thought about the Body, the Mind, the Soul, the World, Time and Fate*. Cambridge University Press.
O'Sullivan, J. (1990) "Nature and culture in the *Odyssey*," *Symbolae Osloenses* 55: 7–17.
Pache, C. O. (2011) *A Moment's Ornament: The Poetics of Nympholepsy in Ancient Greece*. New York: Oxford University Press.
Page, D. L. (1955) *The Homeric Odyssey*. Oxford: Clarendon Press.
Palaima, T. G. (2004) "Sacrificial feasting in the Linear-B documents," *Hesperia* 73: 217–46.
Parry, M. (1971) *The Making of Homeric Verse: The Collected Writings of Milman Parry*, ed. A. Parry. Oxford University Press.
Paulson, I. and N. Auer (1964) "The animal guardian: a critical and synthetic review," *History of Religions* 3: 202–19.

Perry, G. and D. Patterson (2007) "Determining reproductive fertility in herd bulls," University of Missouri Extension, available at: http://extension.missouri.edu/publications/DisplayPub.aspx?P=G2011.
Perysinakis, I. N. (1991) "Penelope's EEΔNA again," *Classical Quarterly* 41(2): 297–302.
Petropoulos, J. C. B. (2011) *Kleos in a Minor Key: The Homeric Education of a Little Prince*. Washington, DC and Cambridge, MA: Center for Hellenic Studies/Harvard University Press.
Propp, V. (1968) *Morphology of the Folktale*, trans. Laurence Scott, 2nd edn. Bloomington: Indiana University Press.
Powell, B. B. (1977) *Composition by Theme in the Odyssey*. Meisenheim am Glan: Hain Verlag.
Pucci, P. (1987) *Odysseus Polytropos: Intertextual Readings in the Odyssey and the Iliad*. Ithaca, NY: Cornell University Press.
  (1998) *The Song of the Sirens: Essays on Homer*. Lanham, MD: Rowman & Littlefield.
Redfield, J. M. (1983) "The economic man," in *Approaches to Homer*, eds. C. A. Rubino and C. W. Shelmerdine. Austin: University of Texas Press, 218–47.
Reichel-Dolmatoff, G. (1971) *Amazonian Cosmos: The Sexual and Religious Symbolism of the Tukano Indians*. University of Chicago Press.
  (1976) "Cosmology as ecological analysis: a view from the rain forest," *Man* (N.S.) 11: 307–18.
Reinhardt, K. (1996) "The adventures in the *Odyssey*," in *Reading the Odyssey: Selected Interpretive Essays*, ed. S. L. Schein. Princeton University Press, 63–132 [= Reinhardt (1948) "Die Abenteuer der Odyssee," in *Von Werken und Formen*. Bad Godesberg, 52–162].
Ringsted, J. (1800) *The cattle-keeper; or Complete directory for country gentlemen, sportsmen, farmers, graziers, farriers, game and cow keepers, horse dealers, carriers, &c.* 13th edn. London.
Roessel, D. (1989) "The stag on Circe's island: an exegesis of a Homeric digression," *Transactions of the American Philological Association* 119: 31–6.
Röhrig, L. (1959) "Europäische Wildgeistersagen," *Rheinisches Jahrbuch für Volkskunde* 10: 79–162.
  (1961) "Die Sagen vom Herrn der Tiere," in *Internationaler Kongress der Volkserzählungsforscher in Kiel und Kopenhagen 1959*. Berlin: de Gruyter, 341–9.
Rose, P. W. (1992) *Sons of the Gods, Children of Earth: Ideology and Literary Form in Ancient Greece*. Ithaca, NY: Cornell University Press.
Rosivach, V. J. (1994). *The System of Public Sacrifice in Fourth-Century Athens*. Atlanta, GA: Scholars Press.
Rundin, J. (1996) "A politics of eating: feasting in early Greek society," *American Journal of Philology* 117: 179–215.
Russo, J. (1993) "*Odyssey* 19, 440–443, the boar in the bush: formulaic repetition and narrative innovation," in *Tradizione e innovazione nella cultura greca da Omero all'età ellenistica: scritti in onore di Bruno Gentili*, ed. E. Pretagostini. Rome: Gruppo editoriale internazionale, 51–9.

Rutherford, I. C. (2012) "The *Catalogue of Women* within the Greek epic tradition: allusion, intertextuality and traditional referentiality," in *Relative Chronology in Early Greek Poetry*, eds. Ø. Andersen and D. T. T. Haug. Cambridge University Press, 152–67.
Rutherford, R. B. (1993) "From the *Iliad* to the *Odyssey*," *Bulletin of the Institute of Classical Studies* 38: 37–54. (Reprinted (2001) in *Oxford Readings in Homer's* Iliad, ed. D. Cairns. Oxford University Press, 117–46.)
Saïd, S. (1979) "Les crimes des prétendants, la maison d'Ulysse et les festins de l'*Odyssée*," in *Études de littérature ancienne*, eds. S. Saïd, F. Desbordes, J. Bouffartigue, and A. Moreau. Paris: Presses de l'École normale supérieure, 9–49.
  (2011) *Homer and the Odyssey*. Oxford University Press.
Schadewaldt, W. (1960) "Der Helios-Zorn in der Odyssee," in *Studi in onore di L. Castiglioni*. Florence, 961–76.
Schein, S. L. (1999) "Homeric intertextuality: two examples," in Kazazis and Rengakos (eds.), *Euphrosyne*, 349–56.
Schiffrin, D. (1994) *Approaches to Discourse*. Oxford: Blackwell.
Schmidt, J-U. (2003) "Die Blendung des Kyklopen und der Zorn des Poseidon. Zum Problem der Rechtfertigung der Irrfahrten des Odysseus und ihrer Bedeutung für das Anlegen des Odysseedichters," *Wiener Studien* 116: 5–42.
Schmitt-Pantel, P. (1992) *La cité au banquet. Histoire des repas publiques dans les cités grecques*. Rome: École française de Rome.
Schmitz, W. (2004) *Nachbarschaft und Dorfgemeinschaft im archaischen und klassischen Griechenland*. Berlin: Akademie Verlag.
Schmoll, E. A. (1987) "Odysseus and the stag: the parander," *Helios* 14: 22–8.
Schoenian, S. (2006) "Reproduction in the ram," *Sheep 201: A Beginner's Guide to Raising Sheep*, available at: www.sheep101.info/201/ramrepro.html.
Schwyzer, E. (1922) "Deutungsversuche griechischer, besonders homerischer Wörter," *Glotta* 12: 8–29.
Scodel, R. (1994) "Odysseus and the stag," *Classical Quarterly* 44: 530–4.
Scott, J. A. (1917) "Odysseus as a sun-god," *Classical Philology* 12: 244–52.
Seaford, R. (1994) *Reciprocity and Ritual: Homer and Tragedy in the Developing City-State*. Oxford: Clarendon Press.
Segal, C. (1994) *Singers, Heroes, and Gods in the Odyssey*. Ithaca, NY: Cornell University Press.
Semple, E. C. (1922) "The influence of geographic conditions upon ancient Mediterranean stock-raising," *Annals of the Association of American Geographers* 12: 3–38.
Shaw, B. D. (1982/3) "'Eaters of flesh, drinkers of milk': the ancient Mediterranean ideology of the pastoral nomad." *Ancient Society* 13/14: 5–31.
Sherratt, S. (2004) "Feasting in Homeric epic," *Hesperia* 73: 301–37 (= Wright (ed.), 2004: 181–217).
Stengel, P. (1910) *Opferbräuche der Griechen*. Leipzig: Teubner.
Stevenson, H. N. C. (1937) "Feasting and meat division among the Zahau Chins of Burma," *Journal of the Royal Anthropological Institute* 67: 15–32.

Svenbro, J. (1976). "La parole et le marbre. Aux origines de la poétique grecque," Ph.D. dissertation, University of Lund.
Swindle, M. M. and A. C. Smith (2000) "Comparative anatomy and physiology of the pig," United States Department of Agriculture, available at: http://www.nal.usda.gov/awic/pubs/swine/swine.htm.
Tanner, A. (1979) *Bringing Home Animals: Religious Ideology and Mode of Production of the Mistassini Cree Hunters*. St. John's: Memorial University of Newfoundland.
Thalmann, W. G. (1998) *The Swineherd and the Bow: Representations of Class in the Odyssey*. Ithaca, NY: Cornell University Press.
Thieme, P. (1951) "Etymologische Vexierbilder," *Zeitschrift für vergleichende Sprachforschung* 69: 172–8.
Thornton, A. (1970) *People and Themes in Homer's Odyssey*. Dunedin: McIndoe.
Tsagalis, Chr. C. (2008) *The Oral Palimpsest: Exploring Intertextuality in the Homeric Epics*. Washington, DC and Cambridge, MA: Center for Hellenic Studies/Harvard University Press.
Tuite, K. (1998) "Achilles and the Caucasus," *Journal of Indo-European Studies* 26: 289–344.
  (2006) "The meaning of Dael: symbolic and spatial associations of the south Caucasian goddess of game animals," in *Language, Culture and the Individual: A Tribute to Paul Friedrich*, eds. C. O'Neil, M. Scoggin, and K. Tuite. Munich: Lincom Europa, 165–88.
Usener, K. (1990) *Beobachtungen zum Verhältnis der Odyssee zurIlias*. Scriptoralia 21. Tübingen: Gunter Narr.
Valeri, V. (1994) "Wild victims: hunting as sacrifice and sacrifice as hunting in Huaulu," *History of Religions* 34: 101–31.
  (2000) *The Forest of Taboos: Morality, Hunting, and Identity among the Huaulu of the Moluccas*. Madison, WI: University of Wisconsin Press.
Verdenius, W. J. (1969) "NOSTOS," *Mnemosyne* 22: 195.
Vernant, J-P. (1979) "Manger au pays du soleil," in *La cuisine du sacrifice en pays grec*, eds. M. Detienne and J-P. Vernant. Paris: Gallimard, 239–49.
  (1990) *Myth and Society in Ancient Greece*, trans. J. Lloyd. New York: Zone Books.
  (1991) "A general theory of sacrifice and the slaying of the victim in the Greek Thusia," in *Mortals and Immortals: Collected Essays*, ed. F. Zeitlin. Princeton University Press, 290–302.
Versnel, H. S. (1993) *Inconsistencies in Greek and Roman Religion, vol. II: Transition and Reversal in Myth and Ritual*. Leiden: Brill.
  (2011) *Coping with the Gods: Wayward Readings in Greek Theology*. Leiden: Brill.
Vet. T. de (2005) "Parry in Paris: structuralism, historical linguistics, and the oral theory," *Classical Antiquity* 24: 257–84.
Vidal-Naquet, P. (1986) *The Black Hunter: Forms of Thought and Forms of Society in the Greek World*, trans. A. Szegedy-Maszak. Baltimore, MD: Johns Hopkins University Press.
West, M. L. (1997) *The East Face of Helicon: West Asiatic Elements in Greek Poetry and Myth*. Oxford University Press.

(2005) "*Odyssey* and *Argonautica*," *Classical Quarterly* 55: 39–64.
(2007) "Phasis and Aia," *Museum Helveticum* 64: 193–8.
West, S. (1988) "Books I–IV," in *Homer's Odyssey, vol. I: Introduction and Books I–VIII*, eds. A. Heubeck, S. West, and J. B. Hainsworth. Oxford: Clarendon Press.
(2012) "Odyssean stratigraphy," in *Relative Chronology in Early Greek Epic Poetry*, eds. Ø. Anderson and D. T. T. Haug. Cambridge University Press, 122–37.
Whitman, C. (1958) *Homer and the Heroic Tradition*. Cambridge, MA: Harvard University Press.
Wight, D. T. (1986) "Vladimir Propp and 'Dubliners,'" *James Joyce Quarterly* 23: 415–33.
Wilamowitz-Moellendorff, U. von. (1927) *Die Heimkehr des Odysseus. Neue homerische Untersuchungen*. Berlin: Weidmann.
Wilson, D. F. (2002) *Ransom, Revenge, and Heroic Identity in the Iliad*. Cambridge University Press.
Wright, J. C. (ed.) (2004) *The Mycenaean Feast*. Princeton, NJ: American School of Classical Studies at Athens (= *Hesperia* 73: 121–337).
Yen, A. (1973) "On Vladimir Propp and Albert B. Lord: their theoretical differences," *Journal of American Folklore* 86: 161–6.
Zangger, E. (1992) "Prehistoric and historic soils in Greece: assessing the natural resources for agriculture," in *Agriculture in Ancient Greece*, ed. B. Wells. Stockholm: Swedish Institute in Athens, 9–19.
Zeissig, K. (1934) "Die Rinderzucht im alten Griechenland," dissertation, Giessen.

Index locorum

(figures in bold refer to pages where passages are cited as extracts)

Apollonius of Rhodes, *Argonautica*
  1.419: 91n
Archilochus
  6: 53
  122: 98n
Aristotle, *Historia animalium*
  522b: 49n
Aristotle, *Politics*
  1256b29–40: 60n

Callimachus
  Hymn 2.59: 91n

[Demosthenes]
  47.52: 105

Empedocles
  B16 DK: 63
  B136 DK: 74
Euboulos
  fr 120: 36
Euripides, *Iphigeneia at Aulis*
  965–6: 18n
  1261: 18n

Galen, *On the Properties of Foodstuffs*
  6.663 Kühn: **87**

Heraclitus, *Homeric Questions*
  75: 98n
Herodotus
  1.43.3: 121n
  4.8–9: 21n
  4.155.3: 50n
  4.157.2: 50n
  9.92–5: 58n, 101, 121n
Hesiod, *Theogony*
  53–5: 148–9
  99–103: **148–9**
  129–30: 61
  143–5: 69
  487: 135n
  539: 137
Hesiod, *Works and Days*
  26: 149n
  116: 92n
  225: 114n
  238–42: 114n
  270–2: 114, 131
  405: 48
  760–4: 121n
Homer, *Iliad*
  1.37–42: 120n
  1.424: 40n
  1.457–74: 41
  1.464–8: 39n
  1.601–2: 39n, 40n
  2.402–32: 41n
  2.431: 39n
  2.484: 2n, **168**
  2.486: 10
  2.488–92: **9**, 10
  3.277: 110n
  4.48–9: **40**
  4.338–48: 37n
  4.343–8: 143
  4.385–6: 41
  5.436–44: 100
  7.213: 57
  7.313–23: 39, 41n
  8.161–6: 37n
  8.228–44: 37
  8.558: 63
  9.70–5: 41, 48
  9.217: 41
  9.225: 41
  9.379–80: 47n, **152**
  9.412–13: **17**

Index locorum

9.535: 40
10.220: 142n
10.244: 142n
10.319: 142n
10.483–4: 153n
11.218: 2n
11.245: 64
11.300: 63
11.560: 45n
11.677–9: 65
11.704–5: **37**, 64
12.299–301: **142–3**
12.310–21: **36–7**
12.326: 37
14.508: 2n4
15.59–61: **148**
15.95: 40n
16.529: 145
16.702–9: 100
16.787: 45n
18.403: 63
19.148: 151
19.160–6: **145**
19.171: 39n
19.208: 39n
19.225–31: **144**
21.14–26: **153**, 154
21.74: **154**
22.346–7: 155
22.349–52: **152**
23.56: 39n
23.845–6: 49n
24.69–70: **40**
24.601: 148, 155
24.618–20: 155
24.802: 41
Homer, *Odyssey*
1.1–10: 2n, **4–5**, 6, 17n, **115**, 138n
1.20: 133
1.26: 40n
1.32–43: **115–16**
1.50: 24, 130
1.62: 132n
1.69: 124
1.74–80: 118, 130
1.94: 16n
1.104: 99
1.141: 46
1.150–5: x
1.152: x
1.160: 45n
1.248: 45
1.277: 44n
1.287: 16n, 17n, 45n
1.298–300: 137

1.320–3: **147**
1.325–7: x, 16n
1.347–8: 119
1.374–80: 45n, **46**
1.426: 93
2.10–11: 99
2.26–7: 56
2.71–8: 43
2.85–92: 43
2.130–7: 43–4
2.139–45: **46**
2.146–56: 47, 116
2.173: 162n
2.197: 44n
2.203–4: 46
2.218: 17n, 45n
2.408: 99
3.4–9: 41
3.58: 106
3.65–6: **38**
3.72–4: 140n
3.113–14: 9n
3.316: 45n
3.418–74: 42, 107n
3.421: 51
3.431: 51
4.3–4: 41
4.17–19: x
4.45–6: 139n
4.65–6: 39
4.84–9: **50–1**
4.174–7: 139n
4.240: 9n
4.242: 10n
4.411: 64, 104
4.451: 64, 104
4.502–11: 125n
4.601–8: 49n, 51
4.626: 45
4.634–5: 51n
4.669–72: 44
4.686: 45n
5.75: 66
5.101: 63
5.110–11: 6n
5.133–4: 6n
5.239: 32
5.243–61: 32
5.272: 96
5.303–5: 116n
5.343–5: **17–18**
5.346: 33
5.478–80: 28n, 87
5.488–90: 28
6.119–21: **28**, **165**

Homer, *Odyssey* (cont.)
6.126: 29n
6.130–4: **142–3**
6.141–7: 156
6.149–85: 33
6.229–35: 33
6.255–315: 29–30
6.303–15: 29
7.14–20: 30, 33
7.84–5: 139n
7.133: 66
7.215–21: **146**, 149
7.238: 30
7.241–97: 30, 33
7.253: 108n
8.62–82: x
8.76: 42
8.99: 47n
8.158–64: 30
8.265: 66
8.302: 110
8.471–520: x
8.474–83: 39
8.483: x
8.548–63: 5, 27
8.572–6: **5**, 27, 29n27, **165**
8.577–86: 27
9.1: 27
9.16–7: 6
9.37: **16**
9.39–46: **5–6**
9.41–2: 38n, 68
9.45–51: 43, 128
9.82: 108n
9.86: 129
9.98: 22
9.105–15: **56**, 57, 59, 60n, 73, 133
9.118–35: 60–1
9.125: 66, 67
9.140–1: 61
9.153–5: **61**, 76, 129
9.158: 62, 123
9.161–2: **63**, **68**, **164**
9.163–4: 63
9.166–7: 66
9.172–6: **28–9**, **165**
9.184–5: 92n
9.189: 54
9.199–200: 22
9.218–23: 57, **66**
9.224–30: 22, 59, 67, 123
9.238–9: 57, 92n
9.244: 57
9.246: 57
9.253–5: 140n

9.259–65: 136
9.270: 72
9.275–8: 57
9.290: 70
9.292: 72
9.296: 135
9.308: 57
9.314: 71
9.316: 54
9.347: 72
9.370: 55
9.374: 72
9.384–6: 67
9.391–3: 67
9.415: 132n
9.428: 54
9.442–3: **71–2**, **167**
9.450: 57
9.456–60: **70–1**
9.465: 67
9.475–9: **55**, **125**
9.480: 54, 166n
9.500: 140
9.502–5: **34**, 137
9.507–14: 76, 120
9.523–5: **125**
9.528–35: 32, **119–22**, 130
9.548–55: **38**, **68**, **122–3**
9.556–7: **63**, **68**, **164**
10.1–27: **23**, 25, 74
10.57: 129
10.80: 108n
10.87–90: 75
10.105–8: 29
10.111: 22
10.124: 75
10.137–9: 75
10.153–5: 77, 129
10.157: 77
10.160: 78
10.168: 78
10.174–7: **77**, 86, **147**
10.183–4: 63n, 77, **164**
10.190–2: **79**
10.211: 92
10.219: 78
10.231: 85
10.239–40: 79, 85
10.246–8: **94**, **166**
10.251–60: 21
10.274–399: 22
10.285: 21
10.330–2: 21n, 76, 138n
10.350–1: 85
10.371–9: 85–6

Index locorum

10.383–7: **86**
10.396: 87
10.410: 49n
10.431–7: 78, 107, **123–4**
10.452: 88
10.467–8: **63**, 89, **164**
10.471–4: 85, **88–9**
10.476–70: **63**, **88**, **164**
10.490–5: 89–90, 126n
10.524–37: 24, 90n
10.539–40: 90
10.552–60: 91
11.44–5: 90n
11.51–80: 91; 66: 154n
11.100–18: 13, 45n, **102**, 110n, 124, **126–7**
11.136–7: 131
11.185–6: 41
11.225–327: 8, 90
11.328–30: **9**, **168**
11.333–84: 8n
11.367–8: 1, **8**
11.420: 43, 153
11.517: 9n18
11.519: 10n
12.3–4: 75
12.8–15: 91
12.22: 90
12.29–30: **63**, **164**
12.35: 25
12.37–141: 90
12.62–5: 104
12.127–31: 102
12.131–9: 101, **102**
12.183: 11
12.228–30: 137
12.278: 107
12.297: 107, 116
12.312–16: 116
12.323: 110n
12.330–1: 135
12.332: 128, 135
12.340: **108**
12.345–82: 101, 106
12.377–83: **109–10**
12.389–90: 109, 123
12.397–400: **108**
12.417: 113
12.447: 108n
13.88–92: **7**, 149
13.200–2: 28, 31, **165–6**
13.221–5: 31
13.242: 51n
13.246: 51n
13.256–86: 31, 33, 137
13.341: 133

13.343: 124
13.377: 130
13.393–6: 45n, **70**
13.428: 45n
13.429–38: 31
14.5–6: 92
14.13–15: 104
14.16: 92n
14.21: 92
14.92–4: 45, **92**, 94n
14.96–8: **64–5**
14.99–104: 51, 65, 151n
14.161–2: **97**
14.192–359: 31, 33, 137–9
14.196–8: **11**
14.222–8: **139**
14.249–50: 108n
14.377: 45n
14.432–8: **40**
14.457: 96
15.13: 45n
15.32: 45n
15.398–402: x
15.404: 91
15.406: 51, 92
15.407–11: 92n
16.125: 45
16.246–53: 14, 72n, 151n
16.292–4: 42
16.315: 45
16.479: 39n
17.168: 45
17.205–11: 61
17.251–2: 100n
17.261–3: x
17.271: 47n
17.286–9: **139–40**, **145**
17.331: 46
17.425: 140n
17.458: 54, 166n
17.465: 54
17.494: 100
17.495: 54
17.518–21: **11**
17.549: 2n
17.556: 2n
17.561: 2n
18.2: 141
18.52–4: **141**
18.61–3: **141**
18.202: 100n
18.280: 45n
18.343–4: **112**
18.353: 112
18.402–4: 43

Homer, *Odyssey* (cont.)
19.11–13: 42
19.83–8: 100n
19.165–202: 31, 33, 112, 137–8
19.306–7: **97**
19.394–466: 100
19.407–9: 132n
19.425: 39n
19.429–38: 99
19.440–2: 28n, 87
19.518–19: 97
19.528: 150
19.530–4: 97
20.2–3: 54
20.18–21: **53–4**
20.25–8: **150**
20.98–101: 120n
20.100: 121n
20.105: 121n
20.145–6: 99
20.155–6: 98
20.183: 162n
20.184: 54
20.201–2: 119
20.209–12: 51n, **65**; 215–6: 65
20.246: 148
20.267–8: **99**
20.279–83: 93
20.287: 54
20.292–8: **54–5**
20.345–9: **93, 166**
20.352–7: **95**, 98, **109**, 116
20.379: 150
21.125–9: 100
21.144–66: 47n, 154
21.258–9: 100n
21.404: 162n
21.411: 97
21.428–30: x, 47, **110**
22.1: 162n
22.6: 131n
22.21: 94
22.32–3: **71–2, 167**
22.36: 45n
22.49–53: 44
22.55–9: 46, 106, 151
22.60–7: 47, 131, **151–2**
22.73: 151
22.79–81: 153n
922.4–4: 153n
22.117–18: 72
22.123–5: 153n
22.240: 97
22.269: 70, 72

22.292–309: **153**
22.299–301: 72, 97
22.304: 154
22.309: 43
22.312: **154**
22.318: 47n
22.326–9: 154n
22.333–9: 156
22.344–6: **156**
22.369: 45n
22.383–9: 75, **111**, 112
22.402–6: **72–3, 155**
22.407: 72
22.413–5: **55**, 113, **114**, 129
22.481–2: 113
22.494: 113
23.118–22: **130**
23.192–201: 32
23.301: 2n
23.306–7: 131
23.310–41: 33
23.356: 45n
23.357: 70, 131
24.185: 43
24.351–2: 119
24.426–9: **129–30**
24.459: 45n
24.528–40: 131
Homeric Hymn to Apollo
410–13: 101
469–72: 18n
543–5: 140n
Homeric Hymn to Hermes
13: 138n10
71–2: 101
74: 105
195–6: 105
439: 138n

Inscriptions
CEG 326: 106n
IG I³ 426.58–60: 49
IG VII.3171: 49n
IG XIV.645: **102**
Inscriptiones Creticae III.4: **102**
SEG 24.439: 105n
SEG 26.1305.4: 49n
Syll. 407: 105n
Isocrates
14.31: 60n

Mimnermus
20W: 98n

Pausanias
   5.7.3: 91–2n
   10.35.7: 101n
Pindar
   Pythian 9.56–8: 50n
   Paean 9.2–5: 98n
[Plato] *Alcibiades*
   122d: 49n
Plato, *Critias*
   111c: 50n
Plato, *Republic*
   404b–c: 36
Plutarch, *De facie in orbe lunae*
   931E: 98n
[Plutarch], *De vit. Hom.*
   126: **79–80**
Polybius
   4.18.10: 101n
Porphyry, *De abstinentia*
   1.25.8: 101n

Scholia to the *Odyssey*
   7.216: 135
   12.129: 104n
   20.155: 98n
Solon
   4.70–10W: 42
Sophocles, *Oedipus the King*
   42–3: 121n
   723: 121n
Stesichorus
   271 PMG: 98n
Stobaeus
   1.445.14–448.3: 79

Theocritus
   25.129: 101n
Theognis
   53–6: 60n

Varro, *Res Rustica*
   2.5.18: 105

Index

Achilles 14, 17, 41–2, 46, 151
  fasting 143, 155
  as Odysseus 156
Agamemnon 41, 43, 45–6, 137, 143, 152
Aigisthos 115–16, 118–19
Aiolos 23, 25–6, 31, 35, 74, 107
Aithon 112, 138, 142
Alkinoos x, 1, 5, 8, 27, 31, 66, 146, 156, 165
allegorical interpretation of Homer 79–80, 86, 96, 98, 112
allusion 157
analysts, analyst tradition 8, 90, 117
Antinoos 43–4, 46, 54, 71–2, 94, 100, 141, 151
aoidē, 'epic song', narrator speech 2–5, 7, 11, 15, 27, 29, 32, 51, 108, 112, 114, 137, 149, 156, 165.
  See also *epos*
Apellai 99
Apollo xi, 98, 100, 105, 131, 138
  festival of 98–100. See also New Moon
Ares and Aphrodite, song of 110, 131
Arete 29–30
Aristotle 104
assembly 43, 56, 133
atasthalia, 'criminal recklessness' 4–5, 46n. 22, 47, 106–7, 114–15, 117, 119, 123–4, 128–9
Athena 29–32, 70, 72, 97, 106, 131, 133, 137, 147
Augustan poetry 157, 159
Austin, Norman 96, 162

banquet x, xi, 110. See also *dais*; feast
belly 116, 128, 135, 137, 139, 141. See also *gastēr*
bow contest 15, 31, 98, 100
Bronze Age xi, 1, 50, 50n. 38, 58, 107
Burkert, Walter 18, 57–9, 63, 67
Buryat (central Siberia) 83

Calypso 14, 23–4, 26–7, 66, 96, 109, 123, 130
cannibals, cannibalism 22, 26, 45, 57, 74, 87, 94
Catalogue of Women 8n. 17.1, 8–10, 89, 157
cattle 37, 48–50, 69
  herd size 104–6

Cattle of the Sun 4–5, 23, 25–6, 92, 115
  complementary to Circe 104
  number of 104–5
  paradigmatic relations with 53, 69, 101, 123
  as test 127
Caucasus 75, 84
Circe 11, 14, 19, 21–2, 24, 26, 31–2, 84, 101, 116
  as donor 24, 27, 103–4, 116
  location of 75–6, 84, 91
  Mistress of Animals 25, 76, 90
  paradigmatically related to the Cyclops 53, 76, 164
  paradigmatically related to Ithaca 91–4
  power over human life cycle 87, 89–91
  solar associations 75–6, 91, 103
  underworld connections 78–9, 87
  "witch" or "sorceress" 75, 78, 90
colonization 50, 60
Companions
  aligned with Suitors 35, 52, 67, 69, 93–4, 107, 109, 112–15, 117–18, 129
  destroy *nostos* 26
  guilt of 115–18, 128
  loss of 32, 122, 128
  and Poseidon 125–6, 128
  separated from Odysseus 69, 74–5, 77, 107, 124, 127–9
  undue feasting of 43, 106–8, 128–9
  and Zeus 116, 118, 126, 128
Cretan Lies 23, 31, 112, 137–8, 142
Cyclops, Cyclops episode 26, 53, 101, 104, 107
  and the Cattle of the Sun 124
  as donor 32–4, 121
  paradigmatically related to Ithaca 53–4, 67, 69–70, 101
  prayer to Poseidon 32, 53, 73, 102, 118–22, 125, 130
  as quest sequence 22, 53, 58–60, 67

Dæl (Georgian goddess) 83–4, 88, 91, 104
dais
  culminating moment of *nostos* 43

equitable 39–40, 62
moment of distribution 38–41, 46, 68
moment of storytelling 42
perversion of 42, 47–8, 52, 54, 57, 95, 106
ritual 41, 63, 93, 95, 106, 133, 155
scene of death x, xi, 47, 156
See also feast
dawn 75, 84
Delphi 50, 99, 101, 105
Demodokos x, 40, 42, 110, 131, 156
diachrony, diachronic 2, 3n. 7, 56, 117, 161
disguise 13, 15, 31, 136–7, 139, 142, 149, 150, 151.
See also gastēr
donor 19, 21–4, 27–35, 70, 76, 89, 93, 121, 137, 164. *See also* folktale; Propp

Elpenor 91
epic
    and fame 6, 132, 136, 151
    as genre 1–3, 20
    matrix narrative 2–3, 8
Epic Cycle 134
epithet 54–5, 63, 65, 90, 138, 162
epos
    Odysseus' tale 3, 8, 15–16, 23, 27, 52, 108, 110, 149, 156, 164
    as part of quest sequence (interaction with future donor) 23, 27, 32, 137, 164
    term for hexameter 3
    utterance within epic 2
    versus *aoidē* 3–5, 7, 10–12, 16, 19, 29, 34–5, 42, 52, 112, 114, 137, 140, 156, 161
See also aoidē; Odysseus
etymology 69
Eumaios x, 11, 31, 40, 51, 64–5, 91–3, 96, 105, 111, 113, 137
Eurylochos 78, 94, 106–7, 116, 123–4, 127–8, 166
Eurymachos 44, 46, 106, 111–12, 131, 151

Fame. *See kleos*
farming 48–9
feast x–xi, 36–7, 41. *See also dais*
Foley, John Miles 13
folktale 1–2, 14, 18–20, 78
    imported in the *Odyssey* 20, 35, 59
    See also Propp
forgetting 85, 148–9
formula, formulaic 9–10, 28–9, 34, 38–9, 45, 61, 63, 68, 85, 87–8, 92, 99, 102, 106, 108, 121, 140, 142, 148, 153, 158–61
    cognitive nature of 159
    and context 159–61, 164
    definition of 159–60
    difference between character's and narrator's speech 165–6

and meter 160–1
noun-epithet formula 99, 162–3
as routinized behavior 160
specificity of 159
staging formula 162–3
See also epithet; *krea aspeta*; repetition

Galen 87
gastēr 135
    and disguise 137, 142
    and heroic code 139–40, 144, 148–9
    and *menos* 143–5, 148
    and narrative structure of the *Odyssey* 136–7
    and social status 136
    versus *thumos* 136, 140–3
Gilgamesh Epic 18, 24, 76
Golden Age xi, 51, 56–7, 62, 66, 107, 133
    See also paradise
grammaticalization 161, 163

Helios 75–6, 98, 102, 106
    and Apollo 100–1
    Master of Animals 78, 81, 101, 103, 108
    sees and hears all 110–11
Hellenistic poetry 157, 159
Hermes 77
    allegorical interpretation of 79
    and Apollo 131, 138
    cattle thief 101, 105
    donor 19, 21, 31, 84, 138
    messenger 63, 66, 109, 119
    model for Odysseus 138
    trickster 138
Herodotus 101, 103, 121
heroic code/life/world 36–8, 42, 45, 48, 50, 52, 78, 133, 137, 139, 143–4, 155
Hesiod 1, 3, 8, 69, 132–3, 137, 148
hexameter 3, 8
Homecoming Husband (folktale motif) 1, 13–15
Homer. *See aoidē*; Odysseus, rivalry with Homer
hospitality 25–6, 29, 40, 42, 47, 54–5, 59, 67, 131
Huaulu (Moluccan tribe) 82
human–animal relationship 81–2, 86, 95
human responsibility 116, 124, 128–9
hunt(ing) 18, 58–64, 67, 72, 76, 78, 80–6, 133
    and initiation 99
    as sacrifice 81
    sexual symbolism of 80–5

Iliad
    allusion to (quote of) 9–10, 151–6, 168
    feasts in 41–2
    heroic poetry 1, 6, 134, 140, 142
    plot of 14

initiation 97, 99–100, 138
interformularity (scale of) 10, 158–9, 163–8
intertextuality 2, 8n. 16, 157–8, 168
Iron Age 1, 50, 66, 107, 133
Ithaca, geography of 51, 60

Jörgensen's Law 77, 122

kleos 17, 34, 37, 132, 136–40, 149, 155–6
  suspension of Odysseus' 136–7
krea aspeta 63–4, 68, 70, 77, 88, 164

Laertes 119
Laestrygonians 4, 22, 26, 29, 74–5, 112
language
  as autonomous system 160
  as (routinized) behavior 160–1
Leodes 154, 156–8
Levaniouk, Olga 138
linguistics 160
Lord, Albert xiii, 9, 14, 16, 34, 158
Lotus-Eaters 22, 26
lukabas 97–8, 101
lunar year 104
Lycaon, supplication of 154, 157, 159, 168

magical agent 21–4, 27–8, 30–1, 34.
  See also folktale; Propp
Master of Animals
  in hunting cultures 58–9, 62, 64, 81–3, 85, 88, 104
  paleolithic myth 58–9
  Sun as 78
meat
  and agriculture 48–50
  anxieties about consumption 86
  distribution of x, 37–9
  eating of as taboo 5–6, 52, 106, 128
  excessive consumption of by the Suitors 45, 52, 117
  and heroism 37, 45, 143
  luxury food 48–50, 52
  symbolic capital 37–9, 48, 77, 95, 143
  "unlimited" 52–3, 57, 61, 64–6, 68, 72, 77, 88, 92, 103–4, 108. *See also krea aspeta*
Melantho 111, 122
memory, remembering 10, 85, 88, 145–50, 155
menos 145, 146–50
metamorphosis 78, 87, 91, 93
metapoetic narrative 136, 146
metempsychosis 78–80, 86–7, 89–91, 93–4
  and hunting 81–2
mētis 53–4, 71, 138, 152, 163
moira 120, 122, 127–8
Muse(s) 6, 9–10, 149, 157, 168

Nagy, Gregory 161, 169
narratology, narratological 5, 159
narrator
  experiential 122
  omniscient 119, 121
  primary versus secondary 5–7, 77, 108
nature 59, 61, 80–1
Nausicaa 29, 31
Necyia ("Visit of the Dead") 7, 8n. 17.2, 25–6, 89–91, 103, 157
neoanalysis 157
Neoplatonism 79
New Moon (festival of the xi, 97–8
nostos. *See also* quest
  as journey 16
  of Odysseus as compromise 132, 134
  as return 4, 10–11, 17, 19–20, 24, 30, 53, 69, 88, 90, 107, 120, 128, 130
  return to epic 151
  as survival 11, 14, 17–19, 21, 28, 120
nymphs 61–2, 83, 85, 101, 113

Odysseus. *See also aoidē; epos*; narrator
  as Achilles 134, 136, 151, 155, 169
  aligned with Cyclops 69–73, 128, 130, 151, 155, 167
  ambiguity of 132
  as Apollo 100, 138, 151, 153
  breakdown of leadership 127–8
  as eyewitness 7, 10, 156
  as Helios 111, 113, 151
  as Hermes 138
  identity in the *Iliad* 143–5, 149, 151
  as "Master of Animals" 70, 113
  as narrator 6, 11, 16
  problematic Homecoming 129–31
  recklessness of 123–5
  rivalry with Homer 3, 5, 7–9, 168
  in tragedy 134
  as trickster 1, 67, 151
  unfulfilled wanderer 138–40, 152
  virtuous man 79–80, 128, 134
Odyssey
  diachronic development of 89–90
  favorable depiction of Odysseus 134
  feasting in 42–3
  generic status of 1
  layers of religion in 70, 132–3
  plot of 13–14, 19–20
  poetics of 1
  proem of 3–6, 117
  reperformance of 168–9
  as Return Song 13–14
  theology of 108, 117, 132
  Unitarian interpretation of 117
  versus *Iliad* 1–2, 48, 50–1, 136

Index

oral-formulaic theory 99, 157–9, 162
"orality versus literacy" 158, 168–9
oral tradition/poetry 10, 34, 117, 132, 158, 168
Oresteia 117

paradise 18, 51–2, 60, 63, 65, 68–9, 76, 85, 95, 107, 164. *See also* Golden Age
parody 140, 143
Parry, Milman xiii, 9, 34, 158–62, 164
pastoral(ism) 49–52, 57, 59–60, 66–7, 80, 103, 133
performance x, 34, 158
Penelope 11, 14, 43–4, 137
  aligned with Circe 14, 35, 93
  as donor 31
  as object of quest 32
Phemios x, 16, 119, 156
Plot. *See* folktale; Propp; *Odyssey*; quest
Plutarch 79
polar cultural opposition 56, 58–60
Polyphemos 32, 57, 101, 120
  name of 121
  See also Cyclops episode
pork 85–7
Porphyry 79
Poseidon 106
  primitive nature of 132
  wrath of 28, 32, 67, 96, 113, 118, 122, 124–5, 128, 130–1, 155
prayer 120
Prometheus 137, 150
prophecy 121. *See also* Theoklymenos; Tiresias
Propp, Vladimir 14–15, 19, 21–3, 30, 76
Proteus 104
Pucci, Pietro 136, 140, 143, 154

quest
  building block of the *Odyssey* 20–1, 24–5, 27–34, 76, 91, 103, 137
  as *nostos* 18, 27, 35
  as story pattern 18–20, 35, 44, 58, 69
quote, quotation 158, 163–5, 167–9

ransom (*apoina*) 46, 151–2
recognition 13, 15
repetition 9–10, 34, 71, 157–9, 163–4
retribution (*poinē*) 46–7, 69, 153
Return Song (return sequence) 13–15, 19, 30
rhapsode 8

sacred herd 50, 101–3, 115
sacrifice 40, 42, 47, 50–1, 57, 62–3, 81, 106, 119, 122–3, 133, 137
Saïd, Suzanne 45, 47
sanctuary 50
satyrs 61, 81

Schein, Seth 152
scholia 98, 104
Scylla 23, 26, 136
shaman, shamanism 18, 24, 69, 81–2
sheep 48–9
simile 28, 49, 63, 72, 97, 111–12, 142–3, 150, 153–5
singer
  at the banquet x, 110, 156
  and hero x, 8, 11, 27, 89, 114, 140, 156
Sirens 11, 23, 26
solar eclipse 95, 98, 109
solar year 92, 97
spring 97–8, 101
structuralism 14, 57
Suitors x, 4
  aligned with Cyclops 54–7, 71, 151, 167
  aligned with Odysseus 71, 167
  crimes of 42–7, 48, 64–5, 91, 94, 117, 133
  element in folktale pattern 14–15, 30
  part of Poseidon's wrath 130
  social conflict at Ithaca 43–4, 130
Sun God 64, 78, 81, 96, 98, 103–4. *See also* Helios
supplication 154, 156–7
synchrony, synchronic 56, 59, 117, 161

Telemachos 51, 57, 93, 119, 141, 147
  in assembly 43, 56
  initiation of 97, 99–100
  name of 100
  quest of 16, 38, 41–2
  targeted by Suitors 44, 46
theodicy 115, 118, 123–4
Theoklymenos 95, 98, 109, 116
Thrinacia 76. *See also* Cattle of the Sun
thumos 93–4, 140, 144, 166
Tiresias, prophecy of 24, 76, 89–90, 102–3, 116, 121, 126–7, 130–1
transmigration. *See* metempsychosis
Trojan War 11, 14, 17, 133, 140, 157
Tukano (Amazonian tribe) 64, 81–2, 85–6, 91, 103–4

Underworld 76–8, 89, 95, 109

vegetarianism 86

wanderings. *See epos*; Odysseus
winter 96, 112

year, completion of 84, 88, 93, 97

Zeus 55, 68–9, 74, 104, 113, 131
  different conceptions of 117–18, 123, 134
  justice of 115, 118, 126, 129, 131
  plan of 124–6, 128
  versus Poseidon 124, 126, 132–4